# RICHARD WRIGHT

# Modern Critical Views

*These and other titles in preparation*

*Modern Critical Views*

# RICHARD WRIGHT

*Edited and with an introduction by*
Harold Bloom
*Sterling Professor of the Humanities*
*Yale University*

CHELSEA HOUSE PUBLISHERS  ◇
New York  ◇  New Haven  ◇  Philadelphia

© 1987 by Chelsea House Publishers,
a division of Chelsea House Educational Communications, Inc.,
   95 Madison Avenue, New York, NY 10016


Introduction © 1987 by Harold Bloom

Printed and bound in the United States of America

∞ The paper used in this publication meets the minimum
requirements of the American National Standard for Permanence
of Paper for Printed Library Materials, Z39.48-1984.

Library of Congress Cataloging-in-Publication Data
Richard Wright.
   (Modern critical views)
   Bibliography: p.
   Includes index.
   1. Wright, Richard, 1908–1960—Criticism and
interpretation.   2. Afro–Americans in literature.
I. Bloom, Harold.   II. Series.
PS3545.R815Z814   1987      813'.52         87–10363
ISBN 0–87754–639–8 (alk. paper)

# Contents

# Editor's Note

This book gathers together the best criticism available upon the work of Richard Wright. The critical essays are reprinted here in the chronological order of their original publication. I am grateful to Henry Finder for his superb erudition and customary judgment in helping to edit this volume.

My introduction considers both *Native Son* and *Black Boy*, in an attempt to determine what their aesthetic achievement actually can be judged to be. Edward Margolies begins the chronological sequence of criticism with a discussion of Wright's *Lawd Today,* his first novel, but published posthumously.

In an overview of Wright's work, George E. Kent traces the articulation of "personal tension and double-consciousness." Wright's biographer, Michel Fabre, argues against assigning Wright to the tradition of naturalism of Dreiser and James T. Farrell. The complex ambivalence of Wright to black literary tradition is considered by Robert Stepto, who then relates *Black Boy* to the autobiographical writing of Du Bois, Johnson, and Frederick Douglass.

A. Robert Lee sees as a feature of much of Wright's fiction that the surface narrative masks a deeper story within. "The Man Who Lived Underground" is read by Houston A. Baker, Jr., as an example of black literary symbolism par excellence.

A sensitive analysis of *Native Son* by Michael G. Cooke shows how Bigger moves from the state of self-cancellation to a qualified kind of self-avowal. Froom an Africanist perspective, Kwame Anthony Appiah shrewdly assesses Wright's *Black Power* in the context of New World Pan-Africanism.

In this volume's final essay, Abdul JanMohamed explores Wright's book of short stories, *Uncle Tom's Children,* and shows how literal death functions as a desperate means of escape from "social" death.

# Introduction

W hat remains of Richard Wright's work if we apply to it only aesthetic standards of judgment? This is to assume that strictly aesthetic standards exist, and that we know what they are. Wright, in *Native Son,* essentially the son of Theodore Dreiser, could not rise always even to Dreiser's customarily bad level of writing. Here is Bigger Thomas, condemned to execution, at the start of his death vigil:

> In self-defense he shut out the night and day from his mind, for if he had thought of the sun's rising and setting, of the moon or the stars, of clouds or rain, he would have died a thousand deaths before they took him to the chair. To accustom his mind to death as much as possible, he made all the world beyond his cell a vast gray land where neither night nor day was, peopled by strange men and women whom he could not understand, but with those lives he longed to mingle once before he went.
>
> He did not eat now; he simply forced food down his throat without tasting it, to keep the gnawing pain of hunger away, to keep from feeling dizzy. And he did not sleep; at intervals he closed his eyes for a while, no matter what the hour, then opened them at some later time to resume his brooding. He wanted to be free of everything that stood between him and his end, him and the full and terrible realization that life was over without meaning, without anything being settled, without conflicting impulses being resolved.

If we isolate these paragraphs, then we do not know the color or background of the man awaiting execution. The intense sociological pathos of Wright's narrative vanishes, and we are left in the first paragraph with an inadequate rhetoric: "shut out the night and day," "died a thousand deaths," "a vast gray land," "strange men and women," "with those lives he longed

1

to mingle." Yet the second paragraph is even more unsatisfactory, as the exact word is nowhere: "gnawing pain of hunger," "resume his brooding," "full and terrible realization," "conflicting impulses being resolved." Wright's narrative requires from him at this point some mode of language that would individuate Bigger's dread, that would catch and fix the ordeal of a particular black man condemned by a white society. Unfortunately, Wright's diction does not allow us even to distinguish Bigger's horror from any other person's apprehension of judicial murder. Nor does Bigger's own perspective enter into Wright's rhetorical stance. The problem is not so much Wright's heritage from Dreiser's reductive naturalism as it is, plainly stated, a bad authorial ear.

It is rather too late to make so apparently irrelevant an observation, since Wright has become a canonical author, for wholesome societal purposes, with which I am happy to concur. Rereading *Native Son* or *Black Boy* cannot be other than an overdetermined activity, since Wright is a universally acknowledged starting point for black literature in contemporary America. Canonical critics of Wright speak of him as a pioneer, a man of rare courage, as a teacher and forerunner. None of this can or should be denied. I myself would praise him for will, force, and drive, human attributes that he carried just over the border of aesthetic achievement, without alas getting very far once he had crossed over. His importance transcends the concerns of a strictly literary criticism, and reminds the critic of the claims of history, society, political economy, and the longer records of oppression and injustice that history continues to scant.


## II

Bigger Thomas can be said to have become a myth without first having been a convincing representation of human character and personality. Wright listed five "Biggers" he had encountered in actuality, five violent youths called "bad Niggers" by the whites. The most impressive, Bigger No. 5, was a knife-wielding, prideful figure "who always rode the Jim Crow streetcars without paying and sat wherever he pleased." For this group of precursors of his own protagonist in *Native Son,* Wright gave us a moving valediction:

> The Bigger Thomases were the only Negroes I know of who consistently violated the Jim Crow laws of the South and got away with it, at least for a sweet brief spell. Eventually, the whites who restricted their lives made them pay a terrible price.

They were shot, hanged, maimed, lynched, and generally hounded until they were either dead or their spirits broken.

Wright concluded this same "Introduction" to *Native Son* with his own vision of the United States as of March 7, 1940:

> I feel that I'm lucky to be alive to write novels today, when the whole world is caught in the pangs of war and change. Early American writers, Henry James and Nathaniel Hawthorne, complained bitterly about the bleakness and flatness of the American scene. But I think that if they were alive, they'd feel at home in modern America. True, we have no great church in America; our national traditions are still of such a sort that we are not wont to brag of them; and we have no army that's above the level of mercenary fighters; we have no group acceptable to the whole of our country upholding certain humane values; we have no rich symbols, no colorful rituals. We have only a money-grubbing, industrial civilization. But we do have in the Negro the embodiment of a past tragic enough to appease the spiritual hunger of even a James; and we have in the oppression of the Negro a shadow athwart our national life dense and heavy enough to satisfy even the gloomy broodings of a Hawthorne. And if Poe were alive, he would not have to invent horror; horror would invent him.

The citation of James, Hawthorne, and Poe is gratuitous, and the perspective upon the United States in the months preceding the fall of France lacks authority and precision, even in its diction. But the dense and heavy shadow athwart our national life indubitably was there, always had been there, and for many is there still. That shadow is Richard Wright's mythology, and his embryonic strength. He was not found by Henry James, or by Hawthorne, or by Poe, and scarcely would have benefited by such a finding. A legitimate son of Theodore Dreiser, he nevertheless failed to write in *Native Son* a *Sister Carrie* or a new version of *An American Tragedy*. The reality of being a gifted young black in the United States of the thirties and forties proved too oppressive for the limited purposes of a narrative fiction. Rereading *Native Son* is an experience of renewing the dialectical awareness of history and society, but is not in itself an aesthetic experience.

And yet, I do not think that *Native Son*, and its reception, present us with a merely aesthetic dilemma. In the "afterword" to the current paperback reprint of *Native Son*, one of Wright's followers, John Reilly, defends Bigger Thomas by asserting that: "The description of Mary's murder makes

clear that the white world is the cause of the violent desires and reactions"
that led Bigger to smother poor Mary. I would think that what the description makes clear enough is that Bigger is indeed somewhat overdetermined,
but to ascribe the violence of his desires and reactions to any context what-
soever is to reduce him to the status of a replicant or of a psychopathic child.
The critical defenders of *Native Son* must choose. Either Bigger Thomas is
a responsible consciousness, and so profoundly culpable, or else only the
white world is responsible and culpable, which means however that Bigger
ceases to be of fictive interest and becomes an ideogram, rather than a
persuasive representation of a possible human being. Wright, coming trag-
ically early in what was only later to become his own tradition, was not able
to choose, and so left us with something between an ideological image, and
the mimesis of an actuality.

## III

I remember reading *Black Boy: A Record of Childhood and Youth*
when Wright's autobiographical book first apeared, in 1945. A boy of
fifteen, I was frightened and impressed by the book. Reading it again after
more than forty years, the old reactions do not return. Instead, I am compelled to ask the Nietzschean question: who is the interpreter, and what
power does he seek to gain over the text, whether it be his own text or the
text of his life? Wright, an anguished and angry interpreter, wrote a far
more political work in *Black Boy* than in *Native Son*. What passes for a
Marxist analysis of the relation between society and Bigger Thomas seems
to me always a kind of authorial afterthought in *Native Son*. In *Black Boy*,
this pseudo-Marxism usurps the narrator's function, and the will-to-power
over interpretation becomes the incessant undersong of the entire book.
Contrast the opening and closing paragraphs of *Black Boy*:

> One winter morning in the long-ago, four-year-old days of my
> life I found myself standing before a fireplace, warming my hands
> over a mound of glowing coals, listening to the wind whistle past
> the house outside. All morning my mother had been scolding me,
> telling me to keep still, warning me that I must make no noise.
> And I was angry, fretful, and impatient. In the next room Granny
> lay ill and under the day and night care of a doctor and I knew
> that I would be punished if I did not obey. I crossed restlessly to
> the window and pushed back the long fluffy white curtains—
> which I had been forbidden to touch—and looked yearningly out
> into the empty street. I was dreaming of running and playing and
> shouting, but the vivid image of Granny's old, white, wrinkled,

grim face, framed by a halo of tumbling black hair, lying upon a huge feather pillow, made me afraid.

With ever watchful eyes and bearing scars, visible and invisible, I headed North, full of a hazy notion that life could be lived with dignity, that the personalities of others should not be violated, that men should be able to confront other men without fear or shame, and that if men were lucky in their living on earth they might win some redeeming meaning for their having struggled and suffered here beneath the stars.

The young man going North, scarred and watchful, in search of redemption by meaning, has remarkably little connection with the four-year-old boy, impatient for the dream of running, playing, and shouting. Wright's purpose is to explain his fall from impulse into care, and his inevitable explanation will be social and historical. Yet much that he loses is to his version of the family romance, as he himself describes it, and some of what vanishes from him can be ascribed, retrospectively, to a purely personal failure; in him the child was not the father of the man.

What survives best in *Black Boy,* for me, is Wright's gentle account of his human rebirth, as a writer. At eighteen, reading Mencken, he learns audacity, the agonistic use of language, and an aggressive passion for study comes upon him. After reading the *Main Street* of Sinclair Lewis, he is found by the inevitable precursor in Theodore Dreiser:

"That's deep stuff you're reading, boy."
"I'm just killing time, sir."
"You'll addle your brains if you don't watch out."
I read Dreiser's *Jennie Gerhardt* and *Sister Carrie* and they revived in me a vivid sense of my mother's suffering; I was overwhelmed. I grew silent, wondering about the life around me. It would have been impossible for me to have told anyone what I derived from these novels, for it was nothing less than a sense of life itself. All my life had shaped me for the realism, the naturalism of the modern novel, and I could not read enough of them.

Steeped in new moods and ideas, I bought a ream of paper and tried to write; but nothing would come, or what did come was flat beyond telling. I discovered that more than desire and feeling were necessary to write and I dropped the idea. Yet I still wondered how it was possible to know people sufficiently to write about them? Could I ever learn about life and people? To me, with my vast ignorance, my Jim Crow station in life, it seemed a task impossible of achievement. I now knew what being a Negro meant. I could endure the hunger. I had learned to live with hate. But to feel that there were feelings denied me, that the very breath of life itself was beyond my reach, that more than anything else hurt, wounded me. I had a new hunger.

Dreiser's taut visions of suffering women renew in Wright his own memories of his mother's travails, and make him one of those authors for whom the purpose of the poem (to cite Wallace Stevens) is the mother's face. There is an Oedipal violence in Wright that sorts strangely with his attempt to persuade us, and himself, that all violence is socially overdetermined. *Black Boy,* even now, performs an ethical function for us by serving as a social testament, as Wright intended it to do. We can hope that, some day, the book will be available to us as a purely individual testament, and then, may read very differently.

EDWARD MARGOLIES

# *Foreshadowings:* Lawd Today

*Lawd Today,* Richard Wright's first novel (published posthumously in 1963), is in some ways more sophisticated than his second, the more sensational *Native Son,* which established his popularity, and to a large extent his reputation. It is ironic that this should be so in view of the fact that *Native Son* has subsequently come to be regarded as a brilliant but erratic work by an author who was perhaps ignorant of modern experimental techniques in prose fiction. For had *Lawd Today* been published when Wright completed it, such an impresion might never have gained acceptance. If the novel reveals anything about its author, it indicates that Wright had learned his Joyce, his Dos Passos, his James T. Farrell, his Gertrude Stein only too well. It is not that *Lawd Today* is a hodgepodge of the styles of the above authors—actually, Wright is usually in good control of his material—but that Wright here appears as much interested in craftsmanship, form and technique, as he is in making explicit social comment. Indeed, social comment derives from the way Wright structures the novel—twenty-four hours in the life of a Negro postal worker—and the theme does not confine itself to Negro oppression but says something about the very quality of life in urban America. Moreover, Wright uses here for the first time a Negro anti-hero: Jake Jackson is a loutish, heavy-handed, narrow, frustrated, and prejudiced petit bourgeois who, though unable to cope with his environment, refuses to reject it—and is incapable of dreaming of a life different from the kind he knows. Yet, for all his limitations, Wright invests him with a sense of life that simmers just below the surface of his dreary

From *The Art of Richard Wright.* © 1969 by Southern Illinois University Press.

existence. Here then lies the crux of Wright's success, for despite the huge indebtedness to other modern authors, the book is distinctly Wright's and the life and times he evokes are as immediate and as crushingly felt as his more popular radical fiction.

Wright was, of course, a Communist when he wrote the novel; he must have been a Party member for at least three years before *Lawd Today* was completed, but even a cursory glance at its contents will reveal what the Party would have found objectionable about its author. For one thing his principal character is a far cry from the ennobled, oppressed proletariat that Communists liked to depict at this time. Jake is not only disagreeable; his sense of oppression stems principally from what Farrell has called "spiritual poverty" rather than from overt racial and social causes. In other words Wright portrays a soul already corrupted rather than a Negro struggling manfully to maintain his integrity against a hostile, threatening environment. It is of course implicit in the whole of *Lawd Today* that Jake's sickness is environmentally induced, that the environment is itself sick, immature, and devious, but there is scarcely ever any explicit reference to capitalist exploitation. Indeed, Jake himself has faith in the system. Secondly, although the story takes place some time in 1935 or 1936 in the Chicago Negro ghetto, only the most casual mention is made of Communism or Communists (Jake is a virulent "anti-Red"), despite the fact that there existed a considerable body of Communist organizational activity on the South Side at that period. (Wright himself may have been a Party organizer.) Needless to say none of Wright's Negroes undergoes any lightning conversion to socialism; as a matter of fact, they are all racists in their own way. Finally, Wright, in the course of the novel quotes from three "bourgeois" writers (Van Wyck Brooks, Waldo Frank, and T.S. Eliot), each of whom was a particular anathema to the recognized Party aesthetician, Michael Gold. There are then obvious reasons why Wright chose not to publish the novel at the time he wrote it. His relationship to the Party intelligentsia, already sensitive, would have been considerably exacerbated. Yet Wright's decision to keep the manuscript, despite his knowledge that the Party would have disapproved, arouses the suspicion that, notwithstanding his dedication to the Party, somewhere in the back of his mind he foresaw the possibility of leaving the Party and using the story.

The novel is divided into three sections ("Commonplace," "Squirrel Cage," and "Rats' Alley"), each of which covers roughly eight hours in Jake Jackson's day. The first part, well over half the book, traces Jake's activities from the moment he awakens with a peculiarly disturbing dream in the morning until the time he goes to work in he afternoon. In the course of his day, Jake beats up his wife (whose demands on his income he feels are excessive), goes out into the neighborhood and loses at "policy numbers," loiters in front of a movie house regarding its rather flamboyant posters, gets a haircut, wanders aimlessly and restlessly about the city, plays cards for a while with his friends, resumes his wanderings, observes a Negro medicineman vending a "Cureall for All the Divers Ailments of the Human Body," and watches a Negro parade in which the participants wear uniforms of varying splendor representing the ranks, orders, and titles of a new, imaginary anticipated African empire. In sharp contrast to the transitory pomp and pride of this latter vision, Jake and his friends know that they must spend eight dreary, monotonous hours in the night shift of the Chicago main post office sorting letters. The second section of the novel, "Squirrel Cage," deals with this portion of Jake's day.

In "Squirrel Cage" Wright describes each of Jake's duties at the post office in assiduous detail—as if, in order to understand Jake one must understand his work. And this indeed becomes true as part of the dull, heavy, perfunctory nature of his chores is somehow mysteriously transferred to his personality and outlook. Part of Jake's day is given over to obtaining an advance loan on his salary. To do this he must first prove to the personnel authorities that he is a provident husband and worthwhile risk. Jake discovers in the process that he is in real danger of losing his job since his wife has again gone to the postal authorities (she has apparently visited them several times in the past) complaining of his vicious treatment. Jack fortunately had anticipated this kind of trouble and had earlier arranged that a bribe be paid to a corrupt postal official in order that he be allowed to keep his job. Jake finally manages to borrow a hundred dollars from the paymaster, but only after he promises to pay usurious interest rates. He and his friends plan to celebrate Jake's good fortune at the end of their work shift.

"Rats' Alley," the third part of *Lawd Today,* takes Jake and his comrades into a lurid night spot frequented by Negro gangsters, hoodlums, and protitutes. Jake lavishly offers to pay for all the food and entertainment his friends require. In the midst of what can only be described as a massive orgy of feasting, drinking, and dancing, Jake discovers his hundred dollars is gone. When he accuses his prostitute girl friend of helping a pickpocket steal his money, he is kicked and thrashed by the club patrons and thrown out into the subfreezing cold of the early February morning. Angered, humiliated, and frustrated by this final twist of bad luck, Jake somehow manages to stagger home under the weight of all the liquor he has been drinking.

When he sees his wife sleeping, he proceeds to beat her up unmercifully, and stops only when he falls to the floor asleep in a drunken stupor.

As a kind of choral accompaniment to all of Jake's activities throughout the day, a radio blares forth from time to time the principal events in Lincoln's life. It is Lincoln's birthday, February 12, and the "glorious" career of the Great Emancipator serves as ironic contrast to the sordid enslavement of the bondsmen's progeny. For Wright makes it clear that despite Jake's legal freedom, he is indeed a slave. As Jake figures it, the next sixteen years of his life is mortgaged away in debt simply to pay for his wife's medical expenses (Jake had once persuaded her to have an abortion and the consequences to her health seem irreparable). But Jake has other debts as well. He owes money to neighborhood shopkeepers, particularly grocers. He must pay in graft to keep his job—and he owes now at the end of the novel the hundred dollars more that he borrowed in advance on his salary. Each time Jake tries to improve his situation, he discovers himself more and more deeply in debt. But if Jake is the hapless victim of a ruthless money system, he is even more a slave to the values of the civilization that exploits him. For Jake too strives for what Wright has called elsewhere the American "lust for trash." He dreams of the millionaire life he would have if he could win at the policy game. He implicitly accepts graft as a political way of life—and expresses no resentment that he must pay a bribe to keep his job. Indeed, he rather admires the people to whom he must pay his money. Although he is heavily in debt, Jake regards with pride and a sense of achievement the ten new suits he has bought that are hanging in his closet. He is apparently captivated by Hollywood notions of sex, heroism, and adventure as he earnestly studies the posters for a lurid Hollywood film in front of a movie theater. He envies gangsters because "they have a plenty of fun. Always got a flock of gals hanging on their arms. Dress swell in sporty clothes. Drive them long, sleek automobiles. And got money to throw away." For Jake all women are "meat," to be conquered physically, but eschewed in any long term relationships. Jake also accepts uncritically all the current Negro middle-class shibboleths, pieties, and prejudices of America in the face of what he knows to be the truth. He believes millionaires have their troubles just the same as ordinary people do. He regards America as the freest, happiest nation on earth and views as Reds people who criticize his native land. Communists are "crazy"; they are unable to run their own country and want to run America. "Why don't they stay in their own country if they don't like the good old U. S. A.?" Jake agrees with his barber that the "colored folk ought to stick with the rich white folks" if they want to "get anywhere." Although Jake cannot tolerate his wife's long-suffering, bleeding-heart Christianity, he believes one has to take God seriously "be-cause you can't do nothing without 'Im." Finally, Jake shares in a charac-teristic touch of American xenophobia that "what's wrong with this country [are] too many Jews, Dagoes, Hunkies, and Mexicans. We colored people would be much better off if they had kept them rascals out."

But besides being enthralled by some of the shoddiest values of Amer-ican civilization, Jake is as much in bondage to subjective impulses, instincts and feelings which he only dimly understands. Perhaps the principal diffi-culty lies in his inability to acknowledge to himself the welter of contradic-tions he feels about himself as a Negro. The central revelation of Jake's nature is his dream which opens the novel. Jake dreams he is hurrying up a long flight of stairs. He is bending all his energy to reach the top, but try as he may, he does not appear to be making any progress; the steps seem endless. Unable to stop he hears the voice of his boss urging him on, insist-ing that he come at once, and Jake continues to run. The dream in a sense relates not only the futility of Jake's strivings—it is all he can do, apparently, to remain in the same place—but announces the theme of the book—the senselessness, the purposelessness, the absurdity of his life. Nonetheless, all of Jake's energies are directed towards denying the reality of his situation. In his way, of course, much of the time Jake is denying to himself that he is a Negro—since he knows in a profound sense that the goals he wants to achieve are denied him because he is a Negro. Jake will thus identify himself with white people in chauvinistically hating "foreigners" and "Reds." He will strive mightily before the mirror each morning to remove the kinks from his hair so that he will look less Negroid. He will try to overcompen-sate the shame of his blackness by buying expensive, ostentatious clothes he cannot afford. In denying his identity, he denies his experience as well. He seriously fancies he can resolve all his problems by winning at numbers and consults dreambooks for the lucky combination. He bitterly hates and re-sents his wife whom he regards as the source of all his difficulties when she is, after all, but another symptom of the malaise of being a Negro in Amer-ica. Sometimes Jake and his friends will attempt to lose sight of themselves over games of cards, liquor, or women. Or on other occasions they will surrender themselves under the guise of good-natured camaraderie to an orgy of self-hatred and race deprecation by telling "nigger" jokes.

But this does not by any means tell the whole story about Jake. There are moments of bitter lucidity, resentment, and self-pity as when Jake and his companions discover a white postal worker eavesdropping on a conver-sation they have been having about women: "Yeah, a white bastard's al-ways thinking we never talk about nothing but that." But there are moments too when Jake and his friends are capable of discovering vicarious revenge: "Lawd, it sure made me feel good all the way down in my guts when old Joe [Louis] socked Baer." What Wright does here is describe the slow dissolution of southern folk elements in the character of Jake and his friends as they face a new impersonal fragmentation of their lives in the city. Both Jake and his friends had migrated from the South to Chicago—to find better jobs, to look for freedom—but they have not yet quite forgotten their peasant orientation. They often speak of the South with bitterness. As they reminisce and compare their present condition to what they once experienced, they express a kind of folk humor or break into occasional "down home" rhyme:

> There ain't nothing worse'n a Southern white man
> but two southern white men.
> . . . and the only thing worse'n two Southern white
> men is two Southern rattle snakes!

> Don't like a liver
> Don't like hash
> Rather be a nigger
> Than poor white trash

But not all of their memories are so bitter. One of the attributes of Jake's southern nature is a kind of sensuous hedonism which undergoes an explosive transformation as a result of his city experiences. Just prior to the close of their work day, Jake and his friends remember the South in lush, physical terms. "You know we use' to break them honeysuckles off the stem and suck the sweetness out of 'em." The talk drifts to women and the men long to break out of their squirrel cage (which is what they call the post office) and find release from all the petty, meaningless activities of the past eight and a half hours. When the gong booms announcing the end of their shift, they are psychologically conditioned for the orgy that awaits them at the night club. All the accumulated frustrations that Jake has suffered throughout the day are now forgotten as he gives himself in joyous abandon to food, liquor, jazz, and women. It is as if all of Jake's secret memories, dreams, and desires have suddenly become accessible to him for only a short time—and he must bend all his energies to make them materialize. Jake expands with generosity and ebullient spirits, and wishes his friends to share in his good fortune. Even after he is thrown out of the club beaten, drunk, and cheated of his money, he is able to cry out in the February cold, "BUT WHEN I WAS FLYING I WAS A FLYING FOOL!" and "WHEN YOU GET TO WHERE YOU GOING TELL 'EM ABOUT ME!" It is only in these episodes where Jake loses himself in baccanalian revelry that he becomes somehow oddly attractive. Sunk below the dull, heavy, platitudinous exterior there boils a zest for life which can find expression only in frenzied moments like these. But even here the moment passes too rapidly and Jake descends to the depravity of wife-beating.

*Lawd Today* is thus as much an indictment of the northern and southern cultures that produced Jake as it is of Jake himself. Jake's naïveté, his credulousness, his superstitious nature are all made to appear southern traits that Jake carried North with him—but they are traits that northerners use to exploit him. Jake and his fellows are constantly being besieged by purveyors of dreambooks and quack health-cures for everything from arthritis to alcoholism and sexual impotence. Jake, in turn, has apparently adapted himself to the deviousness and deceit of which he has been made such a victim. In his own way Jake is a petty corrupter and cheat—conspiring with an abortionist to deceive his wife that a baby would be detrimental to her health, paying bribes to keep his job, scheming calculated lies in order to obtain illegal loans. Thus, wedded to Jake's naïve ignorance is a furtive duplicity—which allows him to survive.

In producing *Lawd Today* Wright had clearly worked from several prose models. The Studs Lonigan trilogy by Wright's fellow Chicagoan comes immediately to mind. Jake, like Studs, was incapable of transcending the limitations of his environment; both protagonists as a result suffer an impoverishment of the spirit, though both in different circumstances possess conceivably heroic possibilities. Their activities, strivings, ambitions are shown to be petty, meaningless, and futile—matching somehow the shallowness of their characters, the dreariness of their culture. Above all, both Wright and Farrell aim at achieving a phonographic reality of the speech patterns in their principal protagonists, their conversational colloquies, and their silent musings. Wright takes great pains to record Jake and his friends rendering stale jokes, and iterating platitudinous remarks about life, religion, and politics. Often the things they say do not correspond to what they really think or feel—but they are unaware of any inconsistency or hypocrisy on their part. Their conversations do, nonetheless, have the effect of conveying the dehumanization of their lives as they exchange perfunctory, hollow banalities.

Wright's desire to achieve as close a verisimilitude as possible to the conditions and quality of Jake's environment extends to reproducing verbatim the words on billboards, movie marquees, newspaper headlines, the words of popular songs, "throwaways," and advertising leaflets advising Negroes new "guaranteed" ways of discovering their lucky numbers, God, and various other desirable goals. Crudely written and vulgarly conceived this material would be almost laughable were it not for the fact that the reader knows it is intended to exploit the very anxieties and insecurities it promises to assuage. Perhaps Wright's tour de force—along the lines of total recall and reproduction—is a recreation of a bridge game Jake plays with his friends. Each card held by each player and each play he makes is carefully described. Finally, as in his early short stories, Wright attempts not only to reproduce accurately the words people speak, but the volume and sounds they make as well. Here for example are the opening remarks of a street corner medicine man as he prepares to vend his mystery elixir:

> "LAdees 'n' Gen'meeeeeeens: Ah 'm 's the SNAKE MAN! Ah WUZ BO'N 'bout FORTEEEEY YE ARS erGO on the banks of the FAMOUS NILE in the great COUNtreeeeeey of AFRIker, yo' COUNtreeeeeee 'n' mah COUNtreeeeeey—in tha' LAN' where, in the YEARS gone by, you' FATHER 'n' mah FATHER ruled SUPREME!

On occasion Wright moves away from the phonographic-photographic renderings of Dreiser and Farrell and experiments with a kind of poetic-journalese stream of consciousness that owes something perhaps to Dos Passos, such as when Jake scrutinizes the posters of a Hollywood adventure film:

> The first poster showed a bluehelmeted aviator in a bloodred monoplane darting shooting speeding zooming careening out of a bank of snow-white clouds in hot pursuit of two green monoplanes . . . and at the side of the hero sat a golden-haired blue-eyed girl operating a machinegun spewing fire and death and the girl's hair was blown straight back in the wind and her eyes were widened in fear and
>     the next poster showed the hero creeping into a darkened garage on feet of feathers upon a small rat-like creature who had a huge hammer.

In certain other respects Wright tried to probe even beyond consciousness and suggest the instinctive psychic forces that determine Jake's behavior. The theme of the novel is announced implicitly in Jake's stairclimbing dream. But besides Jake's dreams (and daydreams) Wright discloses glimpses of Jake's inner nature in circumscribed, repetitive phrases and expressions he catches in fragments and snatches of Jake's conversation. (Wright probably derived the idea from Gertrude Stein whose "Melanctha" was one of his favorite stories.)

Unlike many "proletarian" writers of the thirties, Wright was not afraid to use metaphor or imagery when he believed the occasion demanded. The unadorned statement of fact, the flat, prosaic rhythms of speech characterize a large proportion of the novel, but as we have seen, not all. Besides occasional forays into streams of consciousness and unconsciousness, Wright, from time to time, lyrically evokes character and mood—("outside an icy wind swept around the corner of the building, whining and moaning like an idiot in a deep black pit")—sometimes even, humor. In the beginning of the novel as Wright describes Jake at his toilet, Jake's head becomes a battlefield, the unruly strands of hair, "wire entanglements of an alien army" and Jake's comb, the patriotic army bent on destroying the invaders.

> The battle waxed furious. The comb suffered heavy losses, and fell back slowly. One by one teeth snapped until they littered bathmat and washbowl. Mangled and broken things they lay there, brave soldiers fallen in action, many of them clutched in the death grip of enemy hairs.

There are moments of course when Wright, the new novelist, loses control of his narrative. The action, for the most part, unfolds from the point of view of Jake, but Wright intrudes on two occasions, assuming the role of the omniscient author, in order to explain how the "numbers" racket works, and what the various technical procedures in the post office signify. Admittedly these are both rather specialized areas, but a more practiced writer would have known how to introduce them without jarring the focus of the reader. Wright, too, is sometimes clumsy at handling transitions: at times one feels that Wright wants to reveal Jake's views on religion, or race, or politics, and that these topics are rather forced out of Jake instead of flowing from the natural sequence of events or Jake's thoughts.

But these are minor details in what is otherwise an interesting, ambitious, and lively novel. Wright in the main succeeded in what he set out to do. He wanted to evoke the sights, the sounds, the smells of Jake's Chicago. He wanted to reveal its paucity of spirit, its shallowness of character, its false morality, its sanctimonious pride, and the energy and violence of life that exists below its dreary, placid exterior. All these are reflected in Jake's psychology and exemplified in one way or another in his activiites of the day. In this respect, of course, Wright must have been inspired by Joyce's *Ulysses*. There is danger in drawing too strong an analogy between the two books, but there are some related elements. Jake is obviously no Leopold Bloom, but the movements of the two anti-heroes are traced over a twenty-four hour period; moreover, both Joyce and Wright fix on a particular date

(June 16, 1904 and Februrary 12, 1936) in order to render the lives of their protagonists, and the specific tangible "feel" of their cities, more believable. Jake's twenty-four hour cycle does not assume the mythic proportions of Leopold's—but perhaps that is the point. Jake's life is meaningless on any terms. Indeed, at one other point, the two men are poles apart. Leopold's great sadness stems from the loss of his son, whereas one of the sources of Jake's misery is that he did not want his child and deceived his wife into aborting it. The wives of both men have drifted from their husbands, one dreaming solace in fantasies of other lovers and romance, the other dreaming peace in illusions of a Christian afterlife. Finally, both men seek relief in orgiastic revelry—Bloom in Night-town, and Jake at the Calumet night club—only to return to a continuing cycle of experience to which they are both bound.

Superficially, *Lawd Today* does not appear to have much in common with Wright's later fiction of flight, violence, and oppression. But a closer look will reveal that many of the themes for which Wright would become famous are present—if only in muted form. The Negro, as villain-hero, which so shocked the Negro community at the time of publication of *Native Son* was evidently first described by Wright several years earlier in his unpublished novel. Negro nationalism, and perhaps even Wright's dreams of Africa, are embodied in Jake's fantasies. *"Lawd if I had my way, I'd tear this building down!"*

> He saw millions of black soldiers marching in black armies; he saw a black battleship flying a black flag; he himself was standing on the deck of that black battleship surrounded by black generals; he heard a voice commanding: "FIRE!" Boooooooom! A black shell screamed through black smoke and he saw the white head of the Statue of Liberty topple, explode and tumble into the Atlantic Ocean.

Not unconnected with themes of Negro and African nationalism are problems relating to the huge twentieth century Negro migration from the rural South to the highly industrialized areas of the Midwest and Northeast. It was only under conditions peculiar to city life that nationalist activities and minority movements flourished. This is an idea Wright would develop at length in *Twelve Million Black Voices* and in his introduction to Clayton and Drake's *Black Metropolis*. In *Lawd Today*, Wright shows in part the rapid erosion of the Negro's folk ties and his gradual assumption of a new mode of life. Finally, the futility of Jake's strivings in the face of a hostile environment, his Sisyphus-like failure to reach the top of the stairs as illustrated in his dream, are translated easily into the absurdity of the existentialist hero. Wright must have made this latter observation himself after he broke with the Communist Party. He took the original manuscript of *Lawd Today* with him to Europe and rewrote it in several parts. The result was the existentialist *Outsider,* published in 1953—some seventeen years later.

GEORGE E. KENT

# Blackness and the Adventure
# of Western Culture

I shall try to focus upon three sources of Wright's power: his double-consciousness, his personal tension, and his dramatic articulation of black and white culture.

His double-consciousness and personal tension can be discussed at the same time, since one flows into and activates the other. His personal tension springs from a stubborn self, conscious of victimization but obsessed with its right to a full engagement of universal forces and to a reaping of the fruits due from the engagement. This right may be called the heritage of Man. And *double-consciousness*—W. E. B. Du Bois, in *The Souls of Black Folk*, described it as the black's sense of being something defined and imprisoned by the myths of whites and at war with his consciousness of American citizenship—his heir-apparency to the potentials announced by the so-called period of Enlightenment. The consciousness of American citizenship lights aspiration, but impels the artist to look worshipfully upon the general American culture, and to devalue his condition and that of his people, even when he is conscious of their beauty:

> The innate love of harmony and beauty that set the ruder souls of his people a-dancing and a-singing raised but confusion and doubt in the soul of the black artist; for the beauty revealed to him was the soul beauty of a race which his larger audience despised, and he could not articulate the message of another people.

From *Blackness and the Adventure of Western Culture*. © 1972 by George E. Kent. Third World Press, 1972.

Frantz Fanon, in *Black Skins, White Masks,* says simply that the black is overdetermined from without, and gives this dramatic picture: "I progress by crawling. And already I am being dissected under white eyes, the only real eyes." In literature, the war of two consciousnesses sometimes drives for an art that is "only incidentally" about Negroes, if it is about them at all; in which case the writer carefully reduces his particularism (the tensioned details of the black experience) and hustles to the "universal" (usually the culturally conditioned Western version). Other choices: to portray the exoticism that satisfies the symbolic needs of whites; to plead the humanity of blacks before a white audience; and, lately, to dig out and address a black audience, regarding its condition and its beauty. Within the concept of double-consciousness, it will be seen that Wright was both the cunning artificer and the victim.

But first, his personal tension, without which he may not have created at all, a tension, not really separable from the double-consciousness, that is one great source of his creative power. A slight handicap here, from the angle of scholarly documentation. The main source for information concerning Wright's early youth is still *Black Boy,* a great autobiography, but one whose claim to attention is the truth of the artist, and not that of the factual reporter. Both Ralph Ellison and Constance Webb, Wright's biographer, have identified incidents which Wright did not personally experience, incidents from folk tradition. I see no great to-do to be made over Wright's artistic license, since folk tradition is the means by which a group expresses its deepest truths. Thus the picture, if not all the pieces, is essentially true.

What *Black Boy* reveals is that more than any other major black writer, Wright, in his youth, was close to the black masses—and in the racially most repressive state in the union, Mississippi. Worse still, Wright received violent suppression without the easement provided by the moral bewilderment and escapism so available in black culture. Such institutionalized instruments of bewilderment as the otherworldly religion, the smiling side of the "good" white folks, sex, liquor, and the warmth of the folk culture, formed no sustaining portion of his psychic resources. Parents, whose complicity in oppression made for physical security in the South of the pre- and post-World War I periods, were ineffectual. Wright's father was a zero. His mother—a woman bearing up under tensions from the terrors of the daily world, abandonment by a shiftless husband, and painful and disabling sickness—was hard-pressed by Wright and her own tough-minded honesty. Under a persistent barrage of questions concerning black life, answers escaped her lips that merely confirmed the boy's sense of embattlement in a world of naked terror; first, for example, explaining that a white man did not whip a black boy because the black boy was his son, she then sharpened a distinction: "The 'white' man did not *whip* the 'black' boy. He *beat* the 'black' boy."

Constance Webb states Wright's conscious purpose: "To use himself as a symbol of all the brutality and cruelty wreaked upon the black man by the southern environment." By depressing his middle-class background, Miss Webb continues, he would create a childhood that would be representative of most Negroes. Both the power of the autobiography and its flaws develop from Wright's single-minded intention. Actually, for much of the work, his strategy is to posit a self-beyond-culture—that is, the self as biological fact, a very tough biological fact, indeed. A cosmic self, which reaches out naturally (though in twisted and violent patterns) for the beauty and nobleness of life. The self is battered by the white racist culture, and, for the most part, by a survival-oriented black culture, that counters the impulse to rebelliousness and individuality by puritanical repressiveness, escapism, and base submission. That is, black culture suppressed the individual, in order to protect the group from white assault. The dramatic rendering of these forces and the stubborn persistence of the outsider self comprise the major strategy of the book.

And out of that strategy comes an overwhelming impact. Tension, raw violence and impending violence, which evoke, psychologically, a nightmare world in the light of day. The autobiography's first great subject is the growth of consciousness, the stages of which are communicated by statements of the reactions of self to preceding events. In confronting a racist America the black boy's consciousness learns to hide its respones and to pursue its aspirations by secret means. It is damaged for life, but it has avoided becoming a natural product of the system: the stunted, degraded, shuffling black, almost convinced of its own inferiority and the god-like power of whites. In the latter part of the book, through reading rebellious books, the consciousness of that other self—the white-defined Negro-victim—loses ground to the consciousness of self as American: the heir to the energy releasing resources of the Enlightenment. A desperate hope is created.

Thus *Black Boy's* second great subject: the disinherited attempting to reclaim the heritage of Modern Man.

*Black Boy* is a great social document, but it could easily have been greater. Its simple naturalistic form, knocks the reader off balance, but then comes reflection. Its universe of terror is little relieved by those moments of joy that usually glide like silent ancestral spirits into the grimmest childhood. To account artistically for the simple survival of the narrator is difficult. Except for the "cultural transfusion" that the narrator receives near the end, Wright gives little artistic emphasis to cultural supports. The careful reader will pick up, here and there, scattered clues. For example, the extended family, with all its shortcomings, shows a desperate energy and loyalty. Reading was an early feeder of his imaginative life, and the role of his mother in supplying imaginative and emotional help was crucial. In *Black Boy*, the dramatic form does not, in itself, give her a decisive role, but the beatings, teasings, grim love, and sporadic periods of silent understanding, imply an unorthodox devotion. The narrator reveals something of the sort in stating the impact of her sickness upon him:

> Already there had crept into her speech a halting, lisping quality that, though I did not know it, was the shadow of her future. I was more conscious of my mother now than I had ever been and I was already able to feel what being completely without her would mean.

There were important facets of ordinary black life, which Wright did not understand because he saw them as an outsider or from the point of view of embattled adolescence. His father was simply the peasant-victim, with a life shaped by the rhythms of the season—a classification very likely to have been derived from his Marxian studies. In Memphis, Wright (or the narrator) meets Mrs. Moss, a spontaneously warm and generous black woman, with an equally warm and spontaneous daughter, Bess. Bess likes Richard and, in no time flat, wishes to marry him. The narrator is aware of her qualities, but ascribes their source to what he was later to understand as "the peasant mentality."

Yet this warm spontaneity, as much as the warped puritanism of his own environment, was a value bulwarked and preserved by the embattled black cultural tradition—not by nature or the rhythm of the seasons. Thus the utter bleakness of black life, its lack of tenderness, love, honor, genuine passion, etc., which Wright in a now famous passage in the second chapter of the autobiography noted as general characteristics, were partly reflections of his immediate home life and surroundings: "I had come from a home where feelings were never expressed, except in rage or religious dread, where each member of the household lived locked in his own dark world, and the light that shone out of this child's heart [Bess's] . . . blinded me.

Personal tension and the double-consciousness. In response to white definitions, Wright was able to say to whites that he formed an equation not known in their definitions. Regarding his people, he was able to say that they are much like you define them but you, and not nature, are responsible. If today, this no longer seems enough to say, or even to be free of a certain adolescent narcissism, we can at least concentrate upon what insights should have been available to Wright during his time. If Wright in *Black Boy* seems too much concerned with warfare upon white definitions, it is good to remember that our growing ability to ignore them exists because the single-minded assault of Wright and others shook up the confidence of a nation and impaired their efficiency.

What can be held against him is that he seemed to have had little awareness that black life, on its own terms, has also the measure of beauty and grandeur granted those who are often defeated but not destroyed. It would be good here to know more about his reading, especially works written by black men. How startling, for example, to learn from Constance Webb that at the age of thirty-two, in 1940, Wright had not read Booker T. Washington's *Up from Slavery*. In a footnote to chapter 13 of *Richard Wright,* Miss Webb states:

> Wright was almost ashamed to admit that he had never read *Up from Slavery*. He had escaped being educated in Negro institutions and never got around to reading those books which everyone was supposed to read. He did know that the greatest split among educated Negroes of a generation or so ago was over Washington's proposals.

Miss Webb is valiant, but the explanation is lame. That very boyhood which Wright was attempting to understand in *Black Boy* depends, for proper dimension, upon an intimate knowledge of Booker T. Washington and W. E. B. Du Bois and of the issues with which they grappled. Ironically, by 1903, Du Bois in "Of Our Spiritual Strivings," *The Souls of Black Folk,* had already defined the problems and the danger which Wright (born in 1908) would confront as a writer. Aside from such considerations, it would hardly seem that a person as obsessed with black problems as Wright was would require an education in Negro institutions to put him in touch with the major figures in his history.

The truth is probably that having caught a breath of life from the literature of revolt against the American small town and from Marxian dialectics Wright was over impressed with their efficiency as tools to explore the privacy and complexity of the black environment. Certainly, Ellison, in 1941, described a system that Wright used for mastering culture that was double-edged and required wariness. Ellison praised Wright for translating the American responses that he heard whites express into terms with which to express the life of Bigger Thomas in *Native Son*. Ellison credited Wright with thus building up within himself "tensions and disciplines . . . impossible within the relaxed, semi-peasant environs of American Negro life." Now such a system can immediately broaden and deepen perspective, but it also carries an obvious payload of distortion. In this regard, it is interesting to note that Ellison, who, in 1945, was obviously disturbed by Wright's famous description of black life as bleak and barren, now says that it is simply a paraphrase of Henry James's description in his *Hawthorne*, of "those items of high civilization which were absent from American life during Hawthorne's day, and which seemed so necessary in order for the novelist to function." One might add that the hard and sharp articulate terms of the black narrator's individualism and rationalism in *Black Boy* seem occasionally to be imports from Northern urban middle-class culture. Neither the folk black culture of the 1920s nor the general Southern culture allowed a childhood to escape the compulsion toward an almost superstitious display of forms of reverence for its elders—even when "reality" gave no justification for them. The rebellion against such a compulsion would, if natively expressed, have been less confident and articulate, more in the forms of silence, sullenness, and guilty outbursts.

In *Black Boy*, the young Richard Wright's impulse to individuality has already begun to engage the dominant forms of Western culture. It promises arms for the freedom of both the black artist and his people. On the other hand, the forms have, for him, their dead-end streets. Individualism in Western culture ranges from rugged activity to imprisonment in one's own subjectivity. While enabling one to escape the confines of a survival-oriented folk culture and to take arms against the West's racism, Western cultural forms threaten to subtly transform the emotional and psychic reflexes, so that while the black writer's status is one of alienation, his deepest consciousness is that of the exaggerated Westerner.

In successive autobiographical statements Wright's alienation was apparent. In "The Man Who Went to Chicago," the picture is one of alienated man trying to express impulses which the forms of Western culture are supposedly dedicated to promoting: the triumph of the human individual (as Fanon termed it), of curiosity, and of beauty. But in Chicago, the capitalistic culture was giving no public sanction to the possession of such qualities by black men, and "adjusted" blacks were themselves an obstacle, as they vied for status in their misery.

Within the Communist Party, as reflected in "I Tried to Be a Communist," Wright found the "triumph of the human individual" balked on ideological grounds. As to the racial thing, one leftist writer confessed, while recruiting Wright, for a Communist front group, that "We write articles about Negroes, but we never see any Negroes." When it came to getting Wright a room in the New York City of 1935, the Communists went through the same footshuffling affected by other white Americans, and, in order to attend the Communist-sponsored conference, Wright, himself, found a room in the Negro YMCA, miles from the site of the conference.

Wright, a very big man, was aware that the Communists had no understanding of the depths of the lives of black men. But Marxism was *the* dynamic philosophy for social change. Where else was he to go? Meanwhile, his life reflected, in an eighth grade dropout's mastery of world culture, the great Western ideal: the expression of the individual life as revolutionary will. The process jerked uptight his emotional and moral reflexes. When he confronted African culture in *Black Power* or met representatives of non-Western cultures, he was both the alienated black man and the exaggerated Westerner, and was at once sympathetic and guiltily sniffy. The fit of the two is uneasy. In *Black Power, Pagan Spain, The Color Curtain,* and *White Man, Listen!,* non-fictional works, the personality behind the print ranges from that of a bright, but somewhat snippish Western tourist to that of a Western schoolmarm, although his ideas are most frequently interesting and provocative.

But Wright remained embattled.

And in the 1950s, in the novel *The Outsider,* he was raising the question as to whether the Western game had not lost all vitality.

II

For Richard Wright the job of writing was most serious and his struggle was very great. In "Blue-Print for Negro Writing," he saw blacks as essentially a separate nation, and felt that the job of the black writer was to create the values by which his race would live and die. However, he argued that ultimately a nationalist perspective did not go far enough, and that having broadened his consciousness through an understanding of the nationalistic folklore of his people, the black writer must transcend nationalism and transform his own personality through the Marxist conception of reality.

Now Harold Cruse in *The Crisis of the Negro Intellectual* has ably pointed out that the American imported and unadapted Marxism was a dead-end street, since it had no conception of the black reality nor any real intention of acquiring one. As I have indicated, Wright was not unaware of the myopia of American Marxists. His positive gain was sufficient psychological distance from the American middle-class oriented cultural patterns to articulate perspectives and symbols of the black and white cultures. This gave him, at least, a version of the total American reality as it relates to blacks. Although Wright had qualified his Marxist stance by stating that Marxism was the bare-bones upon which the black writer must graft the flesh, he did ask that the writer mould Negro folklore "with the concepts that move and direct the forces of history today," that is, with Marxism. The negative effects of this Marxism, as well as the emphatic convictions that derived from psychology and the social sciences, were that the very lights they provided for gaining power over certain aspects of black humanity, by their very glare, blinded him to others.

Take that fine group of short stories that comprise *Uncle Tom's Children*. On a first reading, the reader is overwhelmed by the sheer power of naturalistic form, out of which several stories explode upon him. In "Big Boy Leaves Home," Big Boy and his gang are discovered by a Southern white woman bathing in the nude in a southern white man's creek. (The black man and the white woman are a Negro folklore theme.) Startled when they come toward her to get their clothes, she screams. Her nearby escort shoots and kills two of the boys, and Big Boy wrests the gun from him and kills him. With the help of the folk community and his family, Big Boy escapes, but his friend Bobo is brutally lynched by a mob. From his hiding place Big Boy witnesses the deed. He escapes the following morning in a truck bound for Chicago.

The story has been very justly admired. In the 1930s when the story first appeared the very type of lynching it described was horribly so much more than a mere literary reality. Black men, remembering the wariness with which they stepped around such women in real life and that lingering dread of being trapped with them in some unstructured situation where neither "racial etiquette" nor rational chat would absolve, could read and feel the stomach gone awry. Also that high, irreverence of boyhood smashed up against the system is so well pictured; the dialogue is so full of life, and the folk culture so carefully evoked—who could resist? Add to this powerful scenes, and narrative drive.

But then, a serious flaw. Wright's chief interest is in Big Boy—in his raw revolutionary will to survive and prevail. So that Wright forgets that youth does not experience the shooting down of two comrades and the horrible lynching of a third, without a sea change in its nature. But Big Boy remains simply preoccupied with physical well-being, and casually explains how it went with his comrade, Bobo: "They burnt im.... Will, ah wan some water; mah throats like fire."

"Down by the Riverside" continues the emphasis upon the will to survive, although Mann, the main character, is killed by soldiers under emergency flood conditions. Mann is determined to get his pregnant wife to a doctor and his family to the hills away from flood waters that already swirl at his cabin door. In a stolen boat, he is forced to kill a white man. Mann pits his will against nature and whites. It is a brilliant but losing battle and he knows well before the events that he will be captured and killed.

He expresses will by determining the moment when he will die. In this way, he briefly affirms for the universe that Mann existed:

> Yes, now he would die! He would die before he would let them kill him. Ah'll die fo they kill me! Ah'll *die*. . . . He ran straight to the right, through the trees, in the direction of the water. He heard a shot.

Although he is killed by the soldiers, they have been forced to accept the time that he offers.

With "Long Black Song," the third story, the focus is shifted. Silas, the character representing individual will, does not appear until the second half of the story. Wright instead focuses upon Silas's wife, a person conceived of as sunk-in-nature or as undifferentiated nature. The shift destroys the simple story line which Wright has followed. Blacks, uncommitted to struggle, in the earlier stories, were backstaged or absent.

Sarah, on the other hand, as a black person not emerged from nature, requires a creative energy to lift her from the category of stereotype which Wright was unable to give her. One has to see her as earth goddess or as the stereotype of loose sexuality. Since Silas's violent war with whites and his obvious needs and heroic struggle claim the sympathy of the reader, the symbols that have given Sarah a tenuous stature as earth goddess, above the wars of black and white men, crumble, and she appears as mere mindless stupidity and sensuality.

In her actions Sarah resists Western clock time. The sole clock in the house is out of repair. In an obviously symbolic action, her baby is unpacified when she holds him up to the sun (nature's time), but quietens when she allows him to beat upon the clock (Western time). She declares that they need no clock. "We just don't need no time, mistah." Wright gears her responses to images of the season and its rhythms.

Dreaming secretly of Tom, a man with a similar emotional structure, Sarah is seduced by a white salesman, whose music and personality evoke her maternal feelings and a sense of harmonious nature. Silas, her husband, upon discovering betrayal kills the salesman and other white men. Again the choice factor of the stern willed: Facing a lynch mob, Silas insists upon determining the mode of his death by remaining in his burning house which the mob has set on fire.

Silas breaks out in one powerful nationalistic chant against the way the cards are stacked against him as a black man in the universe. He has accepted the world of time, materialistic struggle, and manipulation of nature. He has worked for ten years to become the owner of his farm. Yet the tone and terms of his chant imply that the dread of day of reckoning had long been on his mind: "He began to talk to no one in particular; he simply stood over the dead white man and talked out of his life, out of a deep and final sense that now it was all over and nothing could make any difference."

> "The white folks ain never gimme a chance! They ain never give no black man a chance! There ain nothin in yo whole life yuh kin keep from 'em. They take yo lan. They take yo freedom! They take yo women! N' then they take yo life."

In addition, he is stabbed in the back by "Mah own blood," i.e., his wife. At bottom, Silas is concerned about the meaning of his life.

This nationalistic base is also a part of the two preceding stories. In "Big Boy Leaves Home" it is tacitly assumed. The folk elders' unspoken assumptions, the quickness with which they devise Big Boy's escape, and the white supremacy assumptions with which whites instantly and almost casually commit the most horrible violence, reflect nationalist stances. In "Down by the Riverside," a part of the same nationalistic assumptions are operative, and Mann expresses a lament for the failure of himself and others to live up to the nationalistic implications of their lives:

> "For a split second he was there among those blunt and hazy black faces looking silently and fearfully at the white folks take some poor black man away. Why don they help me? Yet he knew they would not and could not help him, even as he in times past had not helped other black men being taken by the white folks to their death.

In a vital creative formula, Wright has thus combined the idea of revolutionary will, embryonic nationalism, and Negro folklore moulded into a martial stance.

The pattern is continued in the last two stories, which differ from the first group by bringing the Communist movement into the picture and having the individual will relate to the group will. "Fire and Cloud" has the black minister Taylor to lead black and white workers in a march upon a Southern town, which has refused to relieve their hunger. At first Taylor's motivations are religious impulses and a concept of nature as communal. The tilling of the land brings organic satisfaction of great depth. But the whites have taken the land and confiscated nature. Taylor's will is strong. He endures vicious beatings by whites and learns that he must get with the people, if the problem is to be solved.

The last story "Bright and Morning Star" is superior to "Fire and Cloud," because it more carefully investigates the inner psychology of An Sue, a mother of communists, who gives up the image of Christ by which she has formerly shrunk from the world. Her nationalistic impulse is in her distrust for white comrades, a feeling which her son has enthusiastically transcended. An Sue, however, is all too prophetic. Booker, a poor white communist informer, tricks her into giving him the names of comrades, although her intuition sees him in the image of the oppressor, the "white mountain."

Now in order to see Johnny Boy, whom the mob has captured, and confirm her suspicions about Booker, she goes to the mob scene "lika nigga woman wid mah windin sheet t git mah dead son." In the sheet she conceals a gun. Defiantly refusing to make her captured son inform, she endures his being maimed; then as Booker begins to inform, she kills him. She and her son are then killed by the mob, although "She gave up as much of her life as she could before they took it from her."

The nationalist impulse thus overrides both escapist religion and communism. She is between two worlds without the benefit of the "grace" that either might confer. The impulse that sustains her defiance is more than nationalist; it is that of revolutionary will, the demand for the right to give final shape to the meaning of one's life. In a word, like all the heroic characters of *Uncle Tom's Children,* her choice is existential. The device of the winding sheet, with which she asserts her will, will be recognized as a well known Negro folklore story.

As Wright's fictional scene moved to the urban ghetto, he encountered a new challenge because the forces that attacked the lives of black people were so often abstract and impersonal, unlike the Southern mob, sheriff or plantation owner. Yet out of the urban area was to come the most prophetic images relevant to the ordinary black man in the ghetto.

Although *Lawd Today* was first published in 1963, a statement in the bibliographical section of Constance Webb's *Richard Wright* notes that it "was probably written sometime between 1935 and 1937." Constance Webb speaks of his working on a novel about post office workers during the summer of 1935. The book does have something of an exploratory air about it, and certainly does not immediately connect its wires to ideology or resound in defense of blacks. I think that critics have been offended by the brutality and lower depth quality, which its black characters project. Wright's flaming defense of blacks and indictment of whites had filled the vision of even mild-mannered black critics and given them the benefit of a genteel catharsis; therefore, it was very easy to miss the more negative attitudes that he held in regard to black life.

Yet, *Lawd Today* is very important in the study of Richard Wright for several reasons. It defines at least an essential part of black life, points up the importance of the inscriptions from other writings as aids to understanding his intentions, and enables us to see Wright examining a slice of black life practically on its own terms.

In addition to Wright's strictures on black life in *Black Boy*—cultural barrenness, lack of tenderness and genuine passion, etc., there had also appeared the statement that "I know that Negroes had never been allowed to catch the full spirit of Western Civilization, that they lived somehow in but not of it." *Lawd Today* addresses itself to this situation. The title *Lawd Today*, a folk exclamation on confronting the events of the day, is to express a people who have not been able to make their life their own, who must live "from day to day." And as Conrad Kent Rivers put it in his poem on Wright—"To Live from Day to Day is not to live at all."

To compound the problem: Wright was perfectly capable of seeing emptiness as characteristic of the life of the ordinary white worker. In "The Man Who Went to Chicago," his white female co-workers in a restaurant exposed "their tawdry dreams, their simple hopes, their home lives, their fear of feeling anything deeply." Although they were casually kind and impersonal, "They knew nothing of hate and fear, and strove instinctively to avoid all passion." Their lives were totally given to striving "for petty goals, the trivial material prizes of American life." To become more than children, they would have to include in their personalities "a knowledge of lives such as I lived and suffered containedly." Wright is on his way to describing a shallowly optimistic America, one that avoided the tragic encounter and the knowledge to be derived therefrom, one that excluded blacks from "the entire tide and direction of American culture," although they are "an organic part of the nation."

A similarity, yes, and yet a difference. Wright seems to see ordinary white life by its intrinsic relationship to Western technology, as pulled into some semblance of order—one that is sufficient for superficial living, elementary assertion of will and materialistic acquisitiveness. On the other hand, Saunders Redding comments perceptively on one of Wright's objections to black life: Wright knew "that survival for the Negro depended upon his not making choices, upon his ability to adapt to choices (the will of others) made for him. He hated this." In his introduction to the 1945 edition of St. Clair Drake and Horace R. Cayton's *Black Metropolis,* Wright more fully describes conditions which he feels deprive Modern Man of deep, organic satisfaction, and programs the stunted and frenzied lives of blacks.

As an expression of this extreme frustration, *Lawd Today* deserves a separate and more careful analysis than I can here give to it. Its universe provides its chief character, Jake Jackson, a Mississippi migrant, and his friends no true self-consciousness. It is a universe of violence, magic, quack medicine, numbers playing and dreambooks, roots and herbs, cheap movies, tuberculosis and venereal disease, hard liquor and sex, and corrupt politics. The relation between Jake Jackson and his wife Lil is that of warfare; the book begins with Jake's brutal beating of her, and it ends with Jake's drunken attempt to beat her again, an event that sees her, in self-defense, knocking him unconscious.

> "Lawd, I wish I was dead," she [Lil] sobbed softly.
> Outside an icy wind swept around the corner of the building, whining and moaning like an idiot in a deep black pit.

The brutal relations of Jake and Lil provide the one-day frame for the book. The only real value represented is the rough and ready fellowship between Jake and his friends—Al, whose pride stems from his membership in a national guard unit that breaks up strikes and leftist gatherings; Bob, who suffers throughout the story from a bad case of gonorrhea; and Slim, whose body is wracked with tuberculosis. Jake knows that something is missing from his life, but he can't pin it down. So he and his comrades turn to whatever will jolt their bodies into a brief illusion of triumphant living.

Wright uses several external devices in order to make his intentions apparent. For rather heavy-handed irony, he has the events take place on Lincoln's birthday. The radio delivers a steady barrage of talk about the war that freed the slaves while Jake and his friends, spiritually lost and enslaved in urban society, fumble through the events of the day. Part 1 bears the inscription taken from Van Wyck Brooks's *America's Coming of Age:* "a vast Sargasso Sea—a prodigious welter of unconscious life, swept by ground swells of half-conscious emotion." The inscription is obviously well chosen, and is to be applied to the lives of Jake and his friends. Part 2 is entitled "Squirrel Cage," a section in which the characters' actions are no more fruitful that that of caged animals. An inscription from Waldo Frank's *Our America* speaks of the lives of men and women as "some form of life that has hardened but not grown and over which the world has passed. . . ." Part

3 takes both its title, "Rat's Alley," and its inscription from T. S. Eliot's *Waste Land*: "But at my back in a cold blast I hear/The rattle of the bones, and chuckle spread from ear to ear." Thus the title headings and the inscriptions alert the reader to the themes of artificially stunted and sterile lives, half-conscious and inarticulate, and force a wider reference to their universe. Something very big and nasty is indeed biting the characters in *Lawd Today*, but it is part of the theme of the book that, though one character prays and most of the others beg, borrow, and "ball," they cannot name the water that would relieve their wasteland.

In concentrating upon simply presenting the lives and their surroundings, Wright displays gifts that are not the trademarks of his other novels. Sensational incidents do not threaten the principle of proportion, or make melodrama an end in itself. Of all things, Wright displays, in his opening portrait of Jake Jackson, a talent for biting satire! Humor, so limited in other works, is often wildly raucous. The gift for portraying extended scenes, apparent in other works and so important to the novelist, is still marvelously in evidence. So also is Wright's great talent for the recording of speech rhythms and color. In the character Al's narrative of a masochistic black woman, Wright even does credit to the tall story tradition.

But his most astonishing performance is section 4 of "Squirrel Cage," in which, for thirty pages, all speeches are anonymous and the postal workers render communally their inner life and feelings.

> They had worked in this manner for so many years that they took one another for granted; their common feelings were common knowledge. And when they talked it was more like thinking aloud than speaking for purposes of communication. Clusters of emotion, dim accretions of instinct and tradition rose to the surface of their consciousness like dead bodies floating and swollen upon a night sea.

Despite the negative simile about dead bodies, the speeches form a poem, a device which breaks the novel's tight realism and gives its rendering power a new dimension. It is strange that Wright did not develop the technique further, since his naturalism, in order to fully encompass his reach, required the supplement of his own intrusive commentary.

*Lawd Today* enlarges our perspective on *Native Son*, for it creates the universe of Bigger Thomas in terms more dense than the carefully chosen symbolic reference points of *Native Son*. The continuity of Wright's concerns stand out with great clarity and depth. Running through all Wright's works and thoroughly pervading his personality are his identification with and rejection of the West, and his identification with and rejection of the conditions of black life. *Lawd Today* is primarily concerned with the latter.

In *Native Son,* Wright's greatest work, he returned to the rebel outsider, the character with revolutionary will and the grit to make existential choices. Bigger Thomas, like the heroic characters of *Uncle Tom's Children* finally insists upon defining the meaning of his life: "What I killed for, I am," cries Bigger at the end of his violent and bloody life.

Wright early establishes the myth of the heritage of Man, Western Man, as a counterpoint to the disinherited condition of Bigger Thomas, a Southern black migrant with an eighth grade education. In the first section of the novel, Bigger expresses his frustration by violent and cowardly reactions, and by references to the rituals of power and freedom that he envies. What does he wish to happen, since he complains that nothing happens in his universe? " 'Anything,' Bigger said with a wide sweep of his dingy palm, a sweep that included all the possible activities of the world."

> Then their eyes [Bigger's and his gang's] were riveted; a slate colored pigeon swooped down to the middle of the steel car tracks and began strutting to and from with ruffled feathers, its fat neck bobbing with regal pride. A street car rumbled forward and the pigeon rose swiftly through the air on wings stretched so taut and sheer that Bigger could see the god of the sun through their translucent tips. He tilted his head and watched the slate-colored bird flap and wheel out of sight over the ridge of a high roof.
> "Now, if I could only do that," Bigger said.

Bigger, himself, instinctively realizes that a job and night school will not fundamentally alter his relationship to the universe. To the white and wealthy Mrs. Dalton's query concerning night school, his mind silently makes a vague response: "Night school was all right, but he had other plans. Well, he didn't know just what they were right now, but he was working them out." As to the job with the Daltons, it is but an extension of the system that holds him in contempt and stifles his being: the "relief" people will cut off his food and starve his family if he does not take it. Because of the resulting pressure from his family for physical comfort and survival, "he felt that they had tricked him into a cheap surrender." The job and night school would have programmed his life into conformity with what Wright called the "pet nigger system," but would not have gained respect for his manhood.

Bigger Thomas and Richard Wright were after the system—not merely its pieces.

A major source of the power of *Native Son* derives from Wright's ability to articulate the relevant rituals of black and white cultures—and Bigger's response to them. These rituals emphasize the presence in culture of rational drive, curiosity, revolutionary will, individualism, self-consciousness (preoccupations of Western culture)—or their absence.

Thus blindness (shared by white and black cultures), softness, shrinking from life, escapism, otherworldliness, abjectness, and surrender, are the meaning of the black cultural rituals from which Bigger recoils, and the counters with which blacks are allowed to purchase their meager allowance of shelter and bread. They contrast sharply with Bigger's (the outsider's) deep urges for freedom of gesture and spontaneous response to existence. Wright's indictment is that these negative qualities are systematically programmed into black culture by the all powerful white oppressor.

Having murdered the white girl Mary Dalton—thus defying the imprisoning white oppressor, Bigger Thomas feels a rush of energy that makes him equal to the oppressor. He now explains his revolt against black culture. Buddy, his brother, is "soft and vague; his eyes were defenseless and their glance went only to the surface of things." Buddy is "aimless, lost, with no sharp or hard edges, like a chubby puppy." There is in him "a certain stillness, an isolation, meaninglessness."

Bigger's sister Vera, "seemed to be shrinking from life with every gesture she made." His mother has religion in place of whiskey, and his girlfriend Bessie has whiskey in place of religion. In the last section of *Native Son,* his mother's epiphany is her crawling on her knees from one white Dalton to the other to beg for the life of Bigger. In "Flight," the second part of the novel, Bessie's epiphany is a prose-blues complaint concerning the trap of her life, and then, in a terrible sigh that surrenders to Bigger her entire will, she betrays her life completely. Finally, after Bigger is captured, a black minister epiphanizes the version of religious passivity that insured endurance of aimless and cramped life, as he unsuccessfully appeals to the captured Bigger. The gestures and rituals of the black minister are rendered with masterly brilliance.

In contrast, the symbols, rituals, and personalities of the white culture express directness, spontaneous freedom, at-homeness in the universe, will—and tyranny. While Bigger concentrates upon avoiding answering questions from the communist Jan Erlone and the liberal Mary Dalton in yes or no terms, he is confounded by their ability to act and speak simply and directly. In a very fine scene that evidences Wright's great novelistic talent, their very freedom and liberality dramatize his oppression and shame. Their gestures say that it is their universe. And the fact that Jan Erlone and Mary Dalton, in seconds, can, as individuals, suspend all racial restraints underlines the habitual racial rigidities ingrained in Bigger's life, which deprives him of spontaneous gesture. Oppressively, "To Bigger and his kind, white people were not really people; they were a sort of great natural force, like a stormy sky looming overhead, or like a deep swirling river stretching suddenly at one's feet in the dark." The white world is the "white blur," "white walls," "the snow,"—all of which place Bigger in the condition of the desperate rat with which *Native Son* begins.

The Jan Erlone–Dalton group of whites express the rituals mediated by a sufficient humanism to partially obscure their relationship to a brutal system. They inspire Bigger's hatred but also a measure of bewilderment. Even the elder Dalton can be nice because the system does the work. With one hand he functions in a company that restricts blacks to ghettos and squeezes from them high rents for rat infested, cramped apartments; with the other, and without conscious irony, he gives substantial sums to black uplift organizations. Although the Daltons' kindness cannot extend to sparing Bigger's life (since he has murdered their daughter—the flower of the system), he will prevent the ejection of Bigger's family from its rat dominated apartment.

The liberalism of the Communist Jan Erlone, his girl friend sympathizer Mary Dalton, and the rest of the Dalton family function as esthetic rituals that create an easy-going atmosphere for sullen submission and inhibition. In the militarized zone are the racial rituals of Detective Britten bouncing Bigger's head against the wall and spitting out definitions of blacks that deny their life. Then there are the agents of the mass media, the rhetoricians, the police, and the mob.

Bigger standing equally outside the shrinking black culture and the hard-driving white culture can only feel the existential choice demanded by his compulsion toward the heritage of man shoving upward from his guts, and sense that something very terrible must happen to him. Near the end he is tortured by the knowledge that his deepest hunger is for human communion, and by his lawyer's briefly raising it as a possibility. But the mirage is soon exposed and he must warm himself by the bleak embers of his hard-won and lonely existential knowledge: "what I killed for, I am!"

It is part of the greatness of *Native Son* that it survives a plethora of flaws. For example, despite Wright's indictment of white society, he shows in his major fiction little knowledge that, while black life is stifled by brutality, the private realities of white life find it increasingly impossible to free themselves from the imprisoning blandishments of a neurotic culture. His failure to image this fact, although we have seen that he had some understanding of it, makes it seem that Bigger's problems would have been solved by his entry into the white world. The great engagement of the universe that rages through the first and second parts of the novel sputters, at points, in the third part while Wright scores debater's points on jobs, housing, and equal opportunity. The famous courtroom speech that the attorney Max makes in behalf of Bigger hardly rises above such humanitarian matters. Thus a novel that resounds in revolutionary tones descends to merely reformist modulations that would make glad the heart of a New Deal liberal.

As the theme and situations of the novel increase in density of implication, Wright is too frequently touching the reader's elbow to explain reactions and make distinctions that are too complex for Bigger to verbalize. The style, therefore, fails at crucial points. Melodrama, as in the murder of Mary Dalton, is sometimes very functional. At other times, it is unfortunately its own excuse for being.

And so one may go on, but when he finishes he will find *Native Son* still afloat and waiting for the next reader to make it a reference point in the fabric of his being.

Wright's vision of black men and women rendered in the four books that I have discussed stormed its way into the fabric of American culture with such fury that its threads form a reference point in the thinking and imagination of those who have yet to read him. Quickly downgraded as more art-conscious black writers made the scene, he seems now all too prophetic, and all too relevant, majestically waiting that close, critical engagement which forms the greatest respect that can be paid to a great man and writer.

Thus, today, when we think that we know so much about black life, even down to its metaphysics and ambiguity, it is humbling to realize that the lifelong commitment of soul that was Richard Wright is of the essence of much that we think we know.

MICHEL FABRE

# Beyond Naturalism?

That Richard Wright is a naturalist writer has generally been taken for granted by American critics. In his review of *Lawd Today,* entitled "From Dreiser to Farrell to Wright," Granville Hicks proceeded, not incorrectly, to show that

> he could scarcely have failed to be influenced by James T. Farrell who was just beginning to have a strong effect on American fiction. As Farrell had learned something about documentation from Dreiser, so Wright had learned from Farrell.

When he reviewed *The Outsider* for the *New York Times,* the same critic noted:

> if the ideas are sometimes incoherent, that does not detract from the substance and the power of the book. Wright has always been a demonic writer, and in the earliest of his stories one felt that he was saying more than he knew, that he was, in a remarkable degree, an unconscious artist.

Other reviewers even seemed to regret that Wright attempted to deal with ideas. In his review Orville Prescott stated that "instead of a realistic sociological document he ha[d] written a philosophical novel, its ideas dramatized by improbable coincidences and symbolical characters." And Luther P. Jackson outspokenly lamented that the

From *American Literary Naturalism: A Reassessment.* © 1979 by Michel Fabre. Carl Winter Universitätsverlag, 1979.

words of Wright's angry men leap from the page and hit you
between the eyes. But Wright can no more resist an argument on
the Left Bank than he could a soapbox in Washington Park. The
lickety-split action of his novel bogs down in a slough of dialectics.

It is clear, then, that Wright is regarded not as a novelist of ideas or as
a symbolist, but as an emotionally powerful creator who writes from his
guts and churns up reality in a melodramatic but effective way because he
is authentic, close to nature, true to life. Conversely, the critics' displeasure
at his incursions into other realms than that of social realism proves only
that there are elements in his writing which cannot be reduced to their
favorite image of him as a hard-boiled naturalist. The question then becomes: to what extent is he part of the naturalistic stream in American
literature? Is he, in fact, sufficiently a part of it for his works to be judged,
and found satisfactory or wanting, only according to that perspective? Or is
his originality so strong that it cannot be adequately accounted for in terms
of the Dreiser/Farrell line of succession, and does this therefore necessitate
a reassessment of what is commonly held for American literary naturalism?
It is not my purpose here to reopen the long-debated question of what
exactly naturalism is. In his preface to *American Literary Naturalism, A
Divided Stream,* Charles C. Walcutt described it as "a beast of protean
slipperiness" which, soon after it had sprung from the spring of Transcendentalism, divided into rebellious, idealistic social radicalism on one side
and pessimistic determinism on the other; consequently, the assertion of the
unity of nature and spirit, the equality of intuition and reason was somewhat diminished.
If we consider naturalism as a philosophy, it is clear from the start that
Wright's perspective is only very partly akin to it. He had read Darwin's
*Origin of Species* but he probably did not even know of Herbert Spencer,
the true philosophical cornerstone of American naturalism. If he did, his
Communistic leanings set him early on the side of Marx against the
Spencerian view of the "survival of the fittest." To him, the fittest were the
productive workers, not the parasitic upper classes. Insofar as he was a
Marxist, "the organized exercise of the social will" meant the liquidation of
the bourgeoisie.
Estranged as he was from God by the oppressive religious practice of
his Seventh-Day Adventist grandmother, Wright was also prone to eschew
Transcendentalism as well as the very American belief that physical progress
reflects spiritual progress. His childhood taught him that knowledge could

indeed bring freedom, and self-education became his only means of escape from the cultural ghetto. But if knowledge can make man similar to God, he later discovered that too much knowledge can bring man beyond good and evil so that he ends, isolated from his fellowmen, in the position of a "little God" who has no right to act as one. This is the lesson in existential absurdity to be derived from *The Outsider*. Thus, at times Wright comes close to the naturalistic vision of determinism, which conceives of man as an accident, or an epiphenomenon caught in a general movement toward universal rest. This is apparent in a long (still unpublished) piece of poetry he wrote in the mid-fifties to celebrate the manifold incarnations of life. In it he deals with a force that works through man, and that inhabits him for a time, making him the vessel of a principle he cannot control. This force, though, does not tend toward static, cosmic rest; rather, it aims at self-fulfillment and unlimited expansion, it gropes toward a kind of pantheistic harmony in which matter and spirit are one. If this is transcendentalism of a kind, it represents only a transitory stage in Wright's thinking. On the whole, he is a humanist who retains the Marxist perspective as an ideological tool, and who believes in ethical responsibility, and a certain degree of free will in a world whose values are not created by a transcendental entity but by the common workings of mankind.

Insofar as naturalism is opposed to romanticism as a philosophy, it attacks the unscientific values of tradition and evinces a distrust of those natural forces that man cannot control; it thus corresponds to one facet of Wright's personality. If we look at an early short story, "Superstition," and at a later one, "Man, God Ain't Like That," we find that both denounce the obscene power that such beliefs—and Wright deliberately makes no difference between religion and superstition—can wield over the spirit of man. There, Wright is largely a rationalist. Similarly, when he advocates the cultural liberation of African nations, he still upholds the idea that what was good for Europe, insofar as rationalism and technology are concerned, should be good for the Third World: colonialism has unwittingly given Africa the tools for her own liberation from her religion-ridden ancestral past, and the new African leaders should seize that opportunity to step boldly into the twentieth century. Such is Wright's contention—an opinion which encountered strong opposition on the part of many African intellectuals at the 1956 Congress of Black Artists and Writers in Paris.

Where America was concerned, however, Wright held somewhat different views; he often regretted that his country had no past, and no traditions (however unscientific or irrational they might be).

Like many naturalists before him, Wright feared the forces that reason cannot control, forces that lie within the darkest recesses of man's soul, and his descriptions of Africa evoke at times Conrad's sense of horror in *Heart of Darkness*. Mostly he fears the forces man has unleashed and can no longer subdue, like the overpowering social systems that stifle the development of individuality.

A brief survey of Wright's many-faceted *weltanschauung* shows him to be inconclusively close to or remote from what passes for the common denominators of the various American naturalists. His position oscillates between Marxism and humanistic Existentialism.

We ought to remember that he is not primarily a thinker but a novelist, and therefore, that whatever may be characteristically naturalistic in his fiction is more likely to have resulted from his personal experience as a poor black American, or from his early readings and stands as an embattled writer. Although naturalism is as protean as a set of literary forms and techniques as it is as a philosophical view, it is, nevertheless, on these forms that the brunt of our analysis must rest.

In the often quoted episode from *Black Boy* in which he relates how he was spiritually saved by reading a few American novelists to whom he had been introduced by Mencken's *Book of Prefaces*, Wright mentions Sinclair Lewis's *Main Street*, Dreiser's *Jennie Gerhardt* and *Sister Carrie* as well as Stephen Crane:

> I was overwhelmed, I grew silent, wondering about the life around me. It would have been impossible for me to have told anyone what I derived from these novels for it was nothing less than a sense of life itself. All my life had shaped me for the realism, the naturalism of the modern novel, and I could not read enough of them.

Two things are important in this statement. First, the experiential basis of Wright's literary outlook ("all my life had shaped me for the realism, the naturalism of the modern novel"); second, the apparent lack of distinction between realism and naturalism; he seems to consider the two terms practically interchangeable. In this piece, written in 1943 after he had established his reputation as a novelist, Wright considers naturalism loosely, as simply another version of American realism; he is mostly interested in it because it provokes an authentic sense of life and an understanding of the American scene:

> *Main Street* . . . made me see my boss, Mr. Gerald, and identify him as an American type [ . . . ] I felt closer to him though still

distant, I felt that now I knew him, that I could feel the very
limits of his narrow life.

Such naturalistic novels convinced Wright that his life, hemmed in by
poverty and racism, was not the only life to be circumscribed. Even the lives
of the powerful whites that he had pictured as glamorous were restricted by
uncontrollable circumstances. All men were encompassed by the same definition of the human condition. In a sense, Wright is relieved to see that
white people don't escape man's common destiny; the racial gap artificially
established by them tends to disappear, yielding at the same time to a more
social perspective of rich versus poor, and to a universal humanistic view.
Realistic/naturalistic fiction is thus defined, through Wright's own experience, as an eye-opener, in opposition to the romantic tales, the dime novels,
the detective stories, the blood and thunder episodes he relished primarily
because they provided him with an escape from everyday life. Romantic
fiction became for him a synonym of evasion and vicarious revenge, wholly
artificial because it precluded meaningful action. Naturalistic fiction provided him with a means of liberation through understanding. Although he
sometimes read it, he contritely admits, as he would take a drug or dope, he
generally derived from it a new social perspective.

> The plots and stories in the novel did not interest me so much as
> the point of view revealed. [ . . . ] I could not conquer my sense
> of guilt, the feeling that the white men around me knew that I
> was changing, that I had begun to regard them differently.

That early impact upon his sensibilities was to last. Throughout his life,
he considered Dreiser, his favorite American master, a literary giant nearly
on the par with Dostoyevski. Nothing indicates that he had read such early
naturalists as Harold Frederic, Hamlin Garland or even Frank Norris. Yet
he knew the works of Gorki, Hauptmann, George Moore, London, Stephen
Crane, and Sherwood Anderson. Anderson appealed to him because of his
revolt against small-town life in *Winesburg, Ohio* and because of the essentially instinctive realism of his portrayals of domestic revolt. Anderson,
like Wright, neither apologized for himself nor submitted to naturalistic
despair; rather he tended to make of personal freedom a sort of mystic
quest, and to consider fiction as a substitute for religion—a thing in which
Wright also characteristically indulged.

Later, the discovery of James T. Farrell's works and his personal ac-
quaintance with him in the mid-thirties had some impact on his own writing, as is apparent in *Lawd Today*. True, Wright certainly derived more

from Conrad or Poe with regard to the expression of moods; from Henry James and Hemingway with regard to the use of symbols; from Gertrude Stein with regard to speech rhythms; and he learned from Joyce, T.S. Eliot, and above all Dostoyevski. Yet the impact of the American realists was important because it came first, and because it closely corresponded to Wright's own experience. There is a kinship between the lives of Dreiser and Wright that goes beyond literary theories. From the first, Dreiser was hard-pressed by suffering, and the destitution of the existence to which he was born suggested to him a vision of men struggling aimlessly in a society which excluded them. American life he could thus identify as a figure of distant, capricious destiny. He grew up hating the narrow-mindedness and helplessness of his family, and was so overpowered by suffering that he came to see it as a universal principle, to the point that he considered only the hand of fate where others saw the political and economic evils of capitalism.

Isn't that largely what happened to Wright? The suffering due to poverty and family disruption, the narrow-minded religion practiced at home, the subservient attitudes of the family figures of authority caused him to question and to rebel against the order of things. He too hated the threadbare woof of his spiritually deprived childhood so strongly that he tended to generalize it in his oft-criticized declaration about black life.

> I used to mull over the strange absence of real kindness in Negroes, how unstable was our tenderness, how lacking in genuine passion we were, how void of great hope, how timid our joy, how bare our traditions, how hollow our memories, how lacking we were in those intangible sentiments that bind man to man, and how shallow even was our despair . . . what had been taken for our emotional strength was our negative confusion, our flights, our fears, our frenzy under pressure.

He too disliked his father who had relinquished his responsibilities; he too deplored his mother's inefficacy; he too had a brooding boyhood and the lonely joys of wallowing in books. He too came to experience destiny as an unexpected dispensation of fate, particularly brutal in the case of his mother's stroke, and he started to build up the precariousness of his own life into a philosophy. At twelve, he held

> a notion as to what life meant that no education could ever alter, a conviction that the meaning of living came only when [he] was struggling to wring a meaning out of meaningless suffering.

He concluded:

> It made me want to drive coldly to the heart of every question
> and lay it open . . . love burrowing into psychology, into realistic
> and naturalistic fiction and art, into those whirlpools of politics
> that had the power to claim the whole of men's souls. It directed
> my loyalties to the side of men in rebellion; it made me love talk
> that sought answers to questions that could help nobody, that
> could only keep alive in me that enthralling sense of wonder and
> awe in the face of the drama of human feelings which is hidden
> by the external drama of life.

If Wright followed Dreiser along the road of pessimistic determinism and stressed the helplessness of man, it also appears that the racial oppression he suffered enabled him to find the cause for his own, and his people's, sufferings in the hatred of the surrounding white world. Severed from knowledge and from the mainstream of American culture, he tried to join it. A victim of oppression, he directed his efforts toward rebellion. Thus he partly escaped Dreiser's deep pessimism while his reverence for the invisible helped him maintain a sense of wonder and awe in front of his existential dilemma.

The fact that Wright came of age, in a literary sense, under the aegis of the Communist Party and during the depression largely accounts for the special tenor of his naturalism. The revival of naturalism in the thirties corresponded to Wright's efforts to adapt his writing to a style he could achieve relatively easily. Among the John Reeders he found for the first time a milieu akin to, and favorable to, his preoccupations. That was the time when America was being educated by shock, and the impact of the crisis on the values of American culture was probably stronger than the repercussions of the economic crash upon the capitalist system. The rational character of the social structure seemed to disintegrate, and its existential components were revealed through the alienation of the individual from a society which did not care for him. Wright had experienced this since his childhood in Mississippi, and could thus translate his own experience into general terms. His desire to use words as weapons, after the fashion of Mencken, in order to achieve some kind of liberation, had also become a nearly general tenet. The novelists of the thirties seemed heir to new obligations, and were called upon to leave their ivory towers and become politically relevant. Authenticity, which had always been Wright's criterion, was rehabilitated to stand against artiness. A comparable movement had already taken place at the turn of the century, when Frank Norris supposedly declared, as he embraced naturalism out of hatred for so-called pure

literature, "Who cares for fine style, we don't want literature, give us life."
And in Europe, the social studies of Émile Zola had developed in opposition
to the stylistic achievements of Flaubert's realism. Yet, in the thirties, a new
sense of urgency was added, and Wright felt strongly confirmed in what he
believed his mission as a writer to be.

> In their efforts to recruit masses [the Communists] had missed
> the meaning of the lives of the masses, had conceived of people
> in too abstract a manner. I would try to put some of that mean-
> ing back. I would tell Communists how common people felt, and
> I would tell common people of the self-sacrifice of communists
> who strove for unity among them.

There was indeed a deep convergence between Wright's idiosyncratic
attraction to violence (or compulsive counterviolence), and protest and, on
the other hand, the social attitude of the committed writers of the times as
Alfred Kazin has analyzed it with perspicacity. Of course, there did not
remain much of the original philosophy of naturalism in that attitude. It was
taken for granted that the writer should be a tough guy. In fact, most of the
so-called proletarian writers were the sons of the bourgeoisie, but they
considered themselves as starting from scratch and rejected literary traditions. On the contrary, Wright came from the lower classes, was largely
self-educated, and had been kept from a literary tradition; he tried to invent
one for himself, and this explains why he could endorse writers in the
thirties who, like T.S. Eliot, were often attacked by the left as "decadents."

Also, the hardness of naturalism was more or less instinctive to those
writers who tended to see life as oppression. Wright had really suffered
oppression, so he could be vehement about what he repudiated. They all
shared a common belief in social determinism, not the biological determinism of Spencer or even Dreiser, but the conviction that man is made and
crushed by his social background and environment.

As Kazin further emphasizes, proletarian naturalism generally had narrow categories and ready-made prescriptions. It was assumed that the embattled novel ought to be relatively fast-paced so that the reader could be
stimulated into active sympathy with the right cause; accordingly, thought
was often subordinate to action, and the characters developed in a predetermined way toward class-consciousness. The novelists did not pose psychological problems whose refined variations constituted the novel proper.
The strategy, Kazin argues, consisted in beginning with a state of fear or
doubt which action dissipated. One always found a great deal of facts and
documentation which answered for documentary realism.

This enumeration of the characteristics of the proletarian novel nearly amounts to a description of Wright's outstanding success of the period, i.e., *Native Son*.

Above all, Wright is conspicuous by his use and abuse of violence. This theme of violence was revived in fiction where it tended to become a demonstration of economic and social dislocation, and a reflection of the state of the American system. Wright's own inclination to violence in fiction (in life he abhorred physical violence) could mirror the violence inflicted by American society, pass for the counterviolence of the oppressed Negro, and prefigure revolutionary violence. This was also the case for Erskine Caldwell and, to a degree, for James T. Farrell, both of whom displayed real excitement in reporting capitalistic decay. One may wonder, indeed, whether those novelists—in spite of their different political affiliations, temperaments, and styles—were not united by this coming of age in a time of catastrophe, a time which corresponded to their deep need for terror. Such terror, in Wright, hardly finds release except in a kind of obsession with details of utter brutality; the endings of his novels are not cathartic. Although Bigger discovers that he is what he killed for, this does not really free him from his alienation. On the contrary it fills Max with horror at the thought of his own (and the Communists') failure. *Native Son* differs noticeably from the standard proletarian novel in that the protagonist does not achieve real social and political consciousness; as a piece of propaganda, it is much weaker than "Fire and Cloud" and "Bright and Morning Star," in spite of the opinions of the reviewers and critics of the time. The writing of violent novels thus appears, above all, to be a search for emotional catharsis, and maybe for vicarious fulfillment; this is what Wright meant when he said that writing "drained[ed] all the poison out of [him]."

Brutality is also, at times, deliberate, and calculated to shock the reader. Because bankers' daughters had wept when reading *Uncle Tom's Children* and thereby found relief, Wright says in "How Bigger Was Born" that he wanted *Native Son* to be so taut, so hard that they would have to face it without the relief of tears. This cultivation of violence often brings him closer to Dostoyevski who excells in depicting characters under extreme stress—think of Raskolnikov or Karamazov before and after the murder— than to the American naturalists. The naturalists' supposed contempt for style and their refusal of sensationalism do not apply to Wright, and is certainly better exemplified by James T. Farrell's deliberate literalness of description. Farrell renounces effects to such a degree that this becomes an attribute of his writing (his writing is far more barren and clinical than Dreiser's, whose epic imagination took him, like Zola, into wild and beautiful flights). By accumulating details with detachment and also with some cruelty to his characters, Farrell achieves a sort of stone-like solidity which is a monument in itself. Not so with Wright. There is in him a great attention to detail, but he depends much more for his effects upon the sweep and the suspense of narrative rather than upon the accumulation of revealing evidence—with the exception of *Lawd Today*.

At times, Wright's realism is quite naturalistic. He does not attempt to create simply the illusion of reality; after a careful study of life, he sometimes resorts with evident relish to nearly photographic verisimilitude. This, of course, is true mainly for descriptions and details, and is best documented by *Lawd Today*. This is also true for reactions and attitudes. For instance, while Wright was writing *Native Son*—in which he depicts in deterministic terms, "the story of a boy born amid poverty and conditions of fear which eventually stopped his will and control and made him a reluctant killer"— the Thomas Nixon case broke out in Chicago, and the novelist was quite happy to copy verbatim some of the *Chicago Tribune*'s descriptions of the murderer and to use the brief prepared by attorney Ulysses Keys. Wright also resorted to authentic sources in order to present a view of the rascist reactions of the white reporters—perhaps he did so to forestall any possible challenge by his critics. Why did he desire such literalness? One may surmise that he wanted to emulate Dreiser who had based *An American Tragedy* on the Grace Brown/Chester Gillette case. In several other instances, however, Wright goes beyond that need for undebatable proof and documentation. As I have tried to show elsewhere, even in a novella as surrealistic and existentialistic as "The Man Who Lived Underground" Wright did not use Dostoyevski's *Notes from Underground* as a source, but used instead a glaring account of the subterranean adventures of a Hollywood delinquent he had lifted from *True Detective Magazine*. Likewise, we have to go back to actual events in order to find the origin of his humorous and imaginative "Man of All Work." "The Man Who Killed a Shadow" actually comes from the Julius Fischer case which attorney Charles E. Houston had related to Wright shortly before his departure for France. Wright secured a transcript and nearly contented himself with narrating it: describing, for instance, the way the defendant had strangled and clubbed with a stick a librarian, Catherine Cooper Reardon, because she had complained about his work, Wright went as far as lifting whole sentences from the court record; even details which one could think came from his imagination and zest for horror, such as the use of the victim's pink panties to wipe her blood from the floor, are borrowed from the official transcript. Again and again, whether for details or plot episodes, Wright goes back to actual occurrences. Of course there is in this something of the painstaking search for documentary proof that he greatly admired in Émile Zola. An interview he gave to a Swedish newspaper in the late fifties shows how much he wanted to imitate the French naturalist master. Just as Zola, notebook in hand, jotted down information about prostitutes when he wanted to write *Nana,* we discover that Wright, not satisfied with copying real letters from American sailors to Spanish prostitutes in *Pagan Spain,* also tried to buy similar letters from French prostitutes when gathering documentation on GI's in France for the last volume of his Fishbelly trilogy.

To Wright, the document, designed as proof, is nearly sacred. His industrious research into the facts can sometimes be ascribed to the necessity to check actual details because of a lack of personal experience: for instance, apropos of the arraignment of Tyree in *The Long Dream,* he had to learn the details of Mississippi court procedure. In other instances his journalistic zeal seems to be a carryover from his beginnings as a correspondent for the Harlem Bureau of the *Daily Worker.* As was the case with Crane, Norris, London, Dreiser, and many muckrakers, Wright's schooling in the writing profession began partly in a newspaper office, hence his reverence for the document as objective record. Yet, contrary to Sinclair Lewis, he never turns the novel into a sort of higher journalism, and it might be truer to say that his best journalism—articles like *Twelve Million Black Voices* or "Joe Louis Discovers Dynamite"—derives its power from a nonjournalistic interest in time, locale, and dramatic sequence.

Among the many reasons for the importance of the authentic record in Wright's fiction, two seem to prevail: first, the obligation of a black writer to substantiate his most trifling indictments of the white system; second, but not least, Wright's naive pleasure in discovering that reality is often more fiction-like than fiction itself and in persuading the reader of this.

As far as form is concerned, a commonly held opinion is that the naturalists did not really care for the niceties of style. This may be true of a few proletarian novelists who disguised their ignorance in literary matters as a deliberate contempt for refined "bourgeois" aestheticism. This may be true of Farrell; and it may even be partly true of Dreiser, though his clumsier attempts at elegance are the result of a failure rather than a lack of care. This is never true of Wright, who always envinced a deep interest in style. His best-known pronouncement about writing, "Blueprint for Negro Writing" stresses the balance between content and expression. Indeed he takes writing seriously, sometimes awfully so; for him it is no gratuitous game but a weapon, a vital, self-justifying activity, a means to change the world.

In his eyes, to write well was not sufficient. He did, for instance, censure Zora Neale Hurston because the "sensory sweep of her novel [*Their Eyes Were Watching God*] carries no theme, no message, no thought." And he praised Carl Von Unruh because his comprehension of the problems of Fascism in *The End Is Not Yet* "lifts him, at one stroke, out of the class of fictionneers and onto the plane of writers who, through the prophetic power of their vision legislate new values for mankind." For Wright, the ideal for people "writing from the Left," as he does, should be to "create in the minds of other people a picture that would impell them to meaningful activity." This quest for the meaningful even leads Wright to assert that Stephen Crane's *Maggie: A Girl of the Streets* is simply a coldly materialistic picture of poverty while Jack Conroy's *The Disinherited* is the picture of men and women groping their way to a new concept of human dignity and to find Arna Bontemps's or Langston Hughes's novels more relevant, though not better, than *Sister Carrie* because their characters are "haunted with the desire to make their lives meaningful."

The strength of true fiction comes above all from the nature of the writing itself which must achieve a nice balance between form and content; "the limitations of the craft constitute its greatest virtues. If the sensory vehicle of imaginative writing is required to carry too great a load of didactic material, the artistic sense is submerged," Wright states in "Blueprint for Negro Writing." This explains why he did not hesitate to fight the attempts of CP leaders who wanted him to propagandize. He did so in the name of personal freedom, and also for the validity of an art defined by intrinsic criteria; in reply to the Jewish liberal critic David Cohn, he says:

> Mr. Cohn implies that as a writer I should look at the state of the Negro through the lens of relativity and not judge his plight in an absolute sense. This is precisely what, as an artist, I try NOT to do. My character, Bigger Thomas, lives and suffers in the real world. Feeling and perception are absolute, and if I dodged my responsibility as an artist and depicted them otherwise, I'd be a traitor not to my race alone but to humanity.

Art certainly requires a "point of objectivity in the handling of the subject matter" yet Wright will never define it through extrinsic criteria: "In the last analysis," he answers engraver Antonio Frasconi in a beautiful letter dated November, 1944, "the artist must bow to the monitor of his own imagination; must be led by the sovereignty of his own impressions and perceptions; must be guided by the tyranny of what troubles and concerns him personally. There is no other true path."

Wright himself spent hour upon hour trying to master the craft of fiction, experimenting with words, with sentences, with scenes; and with the help of other novels or prefaces after he had found grammar books and style manuals quite useless, he tried patiently to make his writing jell, harden, and coalesce into a meaningful whole. When he was successful, stories such as "Big Boy Leaves Home" or "Down by the Riverside" are proof that he was able to blend and to fuse elements and techniques borrowed from Joyce, Hemingway, Gertrude Stein, Conrad, and even James. His single-mindedness can, at times, be reminiscent of the efforts of Flaubert, whom he greatly admired. Proust's *Remembrance of Things Past* also filled him with boundless admiration, and equal despair because he felt unable to do as well. In one of the most revealing chapters of his autobiography, Wright confesses:

> My purpose was to capture a physical state or movement that carried strong subjective impressions, an accomplishment which seemed supremely worth struggling for. If I could fasten the mind of the reader upon words so firmly that he would forget words and be conscious only of his response, I felt that I would be in sight of knowing how to write narrative. I strove to master words, to make them disappear, to make them important by making them new, to make them melt into a rising spiral of emotional climax that would drench the reader with a sense of a new world. This was the single end of my living.

Here we are far indeed from the supposed naturalistic/proletarian distrust for fine writing!

The major difference between Wright's view of how fiction should depict the lives of the common people and what the believers in scientific determinism tried to achieve in fiction can be found in Wright's opinion of Nelson Algren's *Never Come Morning*. The preface he wrote for that novel considers a few of the literary strategies which could have been used for the treatment of Bruno Bicek and his friends: some writers would have resorted to satire or humor, others would have "assumed an aloof 'social worker' attitude toward it, prescribing 'pink pills' for social ills, piling up a mountain of naturalistic detail." Wright, by the way, did *not* go in for such techniques and he believed that Algren's perspective excelled all of those because he "depicts the intensity of feeling, the tawdry but potent dreams, the crude but forceful poetry and the frustrating longing for humanity residing in the lives of the Poles of Chicago's North West Side."

Here, the importance attributed to intensity of feeling over naturalistic detail, the insistence on the forceful poetry of commonplace lives is somewhat unexpected; yet, is this not what Wright attempted when he depicted

Bigger Thomas's or Jake Jackson's frustrated longings for a movie-like world? And, at the same time, is not such a statement in the very vein of a Frank Norris who considers naturalism, as incarnated by Zola, as another kind of romanticism?

In "Blueprint for Negro Writing," Wright seems to be responding to Norris's desire that ordinary characters "must be twisted from the ordinary" when he prescribes:

> The presentation of their lives should be simple, yes; but all the complexity, the strangeness, the magic, the wonder of life that lays like a bright sheen over the most sordid existence should be there. To borrow a phrase from the Russians, it should have a *complex simplicity.*

This is a way of claiming equal treatment for all in the field of literature, hence a political statement. At the same time, Wright is convinced that no literature exists without romance, without "the bright sheen" of illusion— he dedicated *Native Son* to his mother who taught him as "a child at her knee, to revere the fanciful and the imaginative." He was convinced that art had little to do with scientific objectivity (not to be mistaken for authenticity and honesty), and that:

> An artist deals with aspects of reality different from those which a scientist uses. My task is not to abstract reality but to enhance its value. In the process of identifying emotional experience in words, paint, stone or tone, an artist uses his feelings in an immediate and absolute sense.

Literature is thus less the depiction of the actual world than the representation of emotional experience through words. The world interests Wright only insofar as it affects the individual, as it is perceived, experienced, acted upon or reacted against. He places the emphasis on emotion, the emotional potential of the material, the emotion to be aroused in the reader, the emotion of the creator at work. It may be in that last domain that his intimate convictions about literary creation bring him the farthest from the theoreticians of the experimental novel and "laboratory creation." He does not view writing as a conscious production in which intellect and critical sense are unceasingly called upon to regulate fancy. His conception is rather dangerously close to the romanticists' definition of inspiration. Being a rationalist and an agnostic, if not an atheist, he confesses there is something paradoxical in such a view, and he honestly admits this contradiction:

I abhor the very notion of mysticism; yet, in trying to grasp this [creative] process in me, I encounter a reality that recedes and hides itself in another reality and, when hunted too openly, it alters its own aspect, chameleon-like, thereby escaping intro-spectional observation. I sigh, shrug, leave it alone, but still trust it, welcoming it when it comes again.

Doesn't this half-reluctant admission amount to a recognition of the contingency of visitations of quasi-divine inspiration? Further on, Wright recalls that, preceding the writing of all his books, not only fiction but even travel narratives, he had been invaded by a feeling of estrangement from his surroundings, a sense of "being possessed by a slow stirring of the emotions, a sort of haunting incitation as though . . . vainly seeking to recall some-thing long forgotten." He owns that he had no power over these creative moods, that they came when they wanted, and that no distraction could dislodge them until the writing of the piece had actually drained them off. Such a perspective defines the writer as the instrument of a power which inhabits him temporarily, coerces him to express it, and then leaves him after these strange visitations. This is strongly reminiscent of Wright's de-scription of the working of the life force in a poem of his that was mentioned previously. It corresponds to a fatalistic creation, because it becomes, in this view, a process which takes place without much actual effort on the part of the writer:

I was aware of subjective movements . . . finally being strung out in time, of events spelling a sequence, that of interlocking images shedding that kind of meaning we associate with a "story" [ . . . . ] Such moods . . . suck themselves into events, long past and forgotten, declaring them their personal property; then to my amazed delight they telescope alien and disparate images into organic wholes [ . . . . ] A crime story in a newspaper evokes a sense of excitement far beyond the meaning of the banal crime described, a meaning which, in turn, conjures up for some inex-plicable reasons its emotional equivalent in a totally different setting and possessing a completely different meaning.

Even more significant than his conception of inspiration is the defini-tion Wright provides of a "story": it is not so much an organized plot carried out through narrative, as it is a "sequence of interlocking images shedding [a] kind of meaning." "Meaning" here is emotional rather than intellectual, and the image-pattern stands for the essential element. A close reading of Wright's symbolic, often dream-like fiction reveals that the crudely apparent three-to-five-act dramatic structure is only an external framework which supports a finely woven symbolical texture. The dramatic framework is mainly a means of prodding the narrative onwards at the hectic pace required by the narrow time limits of the classical tragedy (these time limits are actually narrow in *Lawd Today, Savage Holiday,* and even *Native Son;* they are made to seem narrow in *The Outsider* and *The Long Dream* by the selection of important scenes and by glossing over several months in a few sentences). As a result, Wright's narrative derives its emotional unity not so much from the plot or even the breathless rhythm with which he carries the reader forward, as from the "complex simplicity" of its associational imagery. Again, this brings Wright closer to the expressionists (or the impressionists, for that purpose) than to the naturalists. But does not the power and beauty of *Sister Carrie* derive less from Dreiser's objective presentation or see-saw-like structure than from its weird and emotionally-laden images? Isn't this true also of the glittering world of *Nana* or Flaubert's *Madame Bovary*?

In the last resort, can't the best naturalists be declared great *because of*, not in spite of, their diffuse romanticism or epic vision? It may well be that the tendency to weave emotion and passion into documentation and reportorial accuracy is the secret of successful naturalistic writing, and that naturalism should be reassessed in that light. Rather than sheer reaction against romantic exaggeration, it would appear to be a semi-conscious attempt to rationalize the sense of doom which was so keenly felt by the romantics. Scientific theories were introduced into the naturalists' critical and conceptual views of literary creation, but did they ever turn the novel into a scientific process? On the contrary, they tended to subordinate and assimilate science to the imagination. What they considered slice-of-life authenticity, what Wright believed to be real and authentic in his novels because it rested upon documentary proof, was often only a starting point, as he admitted toward the end of his career.

> A crime story in a newspaper evokes a sense of excitement far beyond the meaning of the banal crime described, a meaning which, in turn, conjures up, for inexplicable reasons, its emotional equivalent in a totally different setting and possessing a completely contrary meaning.

If the setting and meaning are thus totally "contrary" can the original reports still be considered as relevant proof of authenticity?

Wright's conception of the artistic aim is, in the final analysis, that of a technique directed at bringing the reader, through poetic ecstasy or shock treatment, to acceptance of a new consciousness. A sort of alchemistic strategy (he actually uses and abuses the terms "to blend" and "to fuse") must be devised in order to drench the reader with the sense of something unheard, a result which could not be achieved by demonstrative logic or philosophizing. It is not surprising, then, that Wright should compliment Fritz Von Unruh because his novel is:

> a marvellous nightmare which has the power to shed light upon your waking hours. It depends for its continuity not upon the logic of two plus two equals four but upon the blooming of opposite images, upon the linking of widely disparate symbols and events, upon the associational magic of passion.

"The linking of widely disparate symbols" was the touchstone of "good" surrealistic imagery in the eyes of the French surrealists; they considered the image more successful as the symbols were more distant and unrelated. At the root of Wright's fondness for what he calls surrealism one finds not a reading of the French surrealists (although Wright liked Dali's paintings and wrote a poem in homage to Aargon) but rather the influence of his grandmother whose Seventh-Day Adventism connected in his eyes ordinary reality with remote beliefs and, even more, the influence of the blues with their typical ability to bring together seemingly unrelated elements of the American Negro's existence and blend them into a new, meaningful whole.

Another, more obvious, trend of Wright's fiction which, at times, differentiates him from the naturalists is his sensationalism. True, such sensationalism could pass for an answer to Norris's demand that a naturalistic tale must possess "a violent and energetic greatness," that the characters must be "wrenched from the quiet, uneventful round of ordinary life and flung into the throes of a vast and terrible drama that works itself out in unleashed passions, in blood and sudden death." Certainly, if the naturalists thrive on the appearance of power and gross effects (which might be defined as expressionistic), then Wright is very much of a naturalist because he retains a great deal of the awareness of American naturalism. Visceral writing is his forte; critics generally agree that he is "a born story teller" with all the implications of such a definition. Yet, if he willingly resorts to suspense, melodrama, coincidence, and subjection of character analysis to plot and story telling, does not Wright do so mostly because of his early schooling in the stock techniques of popular fiction? In his mind rawness and brutality are associated with fantasy and the gothic, i.e. another kind of romanticism.

Here, the influence of Edgar Allan Poe is prevalent; in the most gruesome episodes of *Native Son,* for example, Wright blends two such apparently irreconcilable trends as gothic horror and sadism and, on the other hand, matter-of-fact, slice-of-life reporting. Perhaps he was able to do so because of his early ability to live simultaneously on the level of everyday destitution and that of evasion through popular fiction. The tenets of naturalism would impose upon Bigger a passive character, one subject to the workings of determinism and fate; we are made to share in his subordinate behavior through a quasi-reportorial rendition of his physical and psychosomatic reactions, sensations, and half-formulated thoughts. At the same time he evolves, by implication, in a world which is more that of Dostoyevski's *Crime and Punishment* than that of Dreiser's *An American Tragedy,* and by indirection he is enlarged into a King-Kong stereotype (quite consistent with the Rue Morgue murderer)—all without losing any of his humanity, because the reader is compelled to see the whole scene from his eyes.

Wright's conception of fiction as a magic telescoping of disparate elements is certainly linked to his childhood discovery of the power of the written word. He read with the feeling that he was performing a forbidden act, and, indeed he was, given the reactions of his grandmother, who saw fiction as a creation of the devil, and the attitude of the Deep South, which banned Negroes from public libraries. As much as the educational power of fiction, its capacity to arouse wonder was always important to him. As a Communist, he emphasized the former without renouncing the latter. He made ready use of the naturalistic and proletarian perspective, but only among other possible ones. Only in the late twenties did the philosophy of social determinism answer his questions concerning the restrictions which had been imposed upon him: universal determinism posited the equality of the oppressed Negro and his white oppressor under the common sway of human destiny. Wright could then consider the absurdity of the world through the eyes of Dreiser who, he wrote, "tried to rationalize and justify the defeat of the individual in biological terms; with him it was a law of the universe." Yet he could no more accept subjection and powerlessness as a universal law, since subjection amounted to his own slow death in a racist setting, than he could his grandmother's attempt to explain his mother's illness in terms of his own impiety and God's ensuing wrath. Determinism provided him, at best, with only a transitional belief, soon superseded by the optimistic social revolutionism of the Marxist faith. When he could no longer believe in the irreversible progress of History in Communism, Wright had to face again the absurdity and precariousness of the human predicament but he did so in terms that were closer to Russian, German, or even

French existentialism. Existentialism left a way open for the creation of values by man, for individualism, and for solidarity, in a fashion that even the optimistic Spencerian brand of determinism could not. At the same time, existentialism satisfied Wright's tragic sense of life. The novel which best illustrates this shift in his philosophy (or rather the different emphasis he placed on different philosophies at different times) is undoubtedly *The Outsider.* Its first section, derived as it is from the then unpublished *Lawd Today,* is strongly naturalistic, not only in the piling up of documentary detail but in the fashion in which economic, family, and sexual ties determine both Cross Damon's and Jake Jackson's life. That Wright has to resort to violent circumstances and largely coincidental plot in order to break off with this materialistic setting and deterministic definition of Damon's life is irrelevant here. The break is significant because it represents a jump into existential freedom and into an absurd world beyond the laws of "normal" causation. Cross will lie, kill, burn a church, drive to suicide the woman who loves him, act like one of those "little Gods" he so vehemently condemned for their ruthless use of power, only to discover finally the necessity of human solidarity and some kind of moral law. The break in the style is itself a significant transition from naturalistic reportage in didactic, philosophical prose, somewhat in the fashion of Sartre's *Les chemins de la liberte.'* Although Wright's contribution to that type of fiction is of historical importance, we must confess that he is not at his best as a stylist when he resorts to such long-winded arguments, and that the jump from naturalism to the philosophical novel does not always suit his talents.

He, on the contrary, effected the change from naturalism into what he would call surrealism quite successfully in "The Man Who Lived Underground." It is revealing that the piece was begun as a novel, in whose naturalistic first part the protagonist was a victim of circumstances: the police arrested him and beat him up on suspicion of a crime he had not commited. This part (which was suppressed from the published novella) ended with Fred Daniels's literal jump outside reality into the underground world of the sewer. Chance allowed him to escape in the way Cross Damon later did, but necessity and a search for an emotional relationship also drove him back above ground and into the hands of his torturers. In the same way, Damon owns on his deathbed that man cannot bear absolute solitude, that he must establish a bridge with other men, that the necessity of man's determinism must, in some way, be acknowledged. As a change from naturalism into another kind of literary strategy "The Man Who Lived Underground" is a success because surrealism, as we tried to show, better suits Wright's passion for gothic detail and violence than philosophical didacti-

cism. It appears that Wright functions best as an artist whenever, in his own
words, he is able to

> fuse and articulate the experiences of man, because his writing
> possesses the potential cunning to steal into the inmost recesses
> of human hearts, because he can create the myths and symbols
> that inspire a faith in life.

To that end, American naturalism, both as a philosophy and as a
literary technique in the line of Dreiser and James Farrell, provided him only
with a starting point; then either, as we suggested, a larger definition of
naturalism must be given—if it is to encompass the many facets of Wright's
writing—or it must be recognized that he often overstepped its boundaries.
Wright's attraction to the fanciful, the mysterious, the irrational always
proved too strong for him to remain attached to his self-declared rationalism and deliberate objectivity. His heavy reliance upon visceral and violent
emotions may account for this inability. Far from being a limitation, it turns
out to be one of the major resources of his narrative power, in the same way
that his obstinate refusal to submit to authority and his insatiable curiosity
concerning everything human certainly led him to ask some of the most
relevant questions of our time.

ROBERT B. STEPTO

# I Thought I Knew These People: Wright and the Afro-American Literary Tradition

One of the curious things about Richard Wright is that while there is no question that his best works occupy a prominent place in the Afro-American canon, or that a survey of Afro-American literature would be incomplete without him, many, including myself, find it difficult to describe his place in the Afro-American literary tradition. Part of this feeling may be attributed to a growing concern over how often "canon," "survey," and "tradition" have been casually treated as synonymous terms and unthinkingly interchanged. We all have distinctive, "working" definitions for these terms, but frequently in our teaching, if not so much in our writing, they are blurred and offered, perhaps in the same discussion or lecture, as three verbal lunges at a single vague but tacitly understood idea. When we try to clarify them and teach accordingly, teaching becomes infinitely more difficult, especially when one assumes the task of illuminating a tradition as opposed to following blindly dates of publication or of biography, or proceeding along the slightly more arduous path of identifying what are commonly held to be the "best" texts. An author's place in a tradition depends on how he reveals that tradition. It is not simply a matter of when his works were published but also of how they illuminate—and in some cases honor—what has come before and anticipate what will follow. In Afro-American literature particularly, the idea of a tradition involves certain questions about the author's posture not only among his fellow writers but also within a larger artistic continuum which, in its exquisite commingling of materials spoken, played,

From *Chant of Saints*. © 1979 by Robert B. Stepto. University of Illinois Press, 1979.

and written, is not the exclusive property or domain of the writer alone. Richard Wright is a fine writer, perhaps a great one; he has influenced, in one way or another, almost every important black writer who has followed him. But Wright forces us to face a considerable problem: to what extent may we qualify his place in the artistic tradition and still submit that he is unquestionably a participant in it? I don't pretend to be able to solve this problem, but I can explore three of the questions involved: What was Wright's posture as an author, and how did it correspond with models provided by the tradition? How do his works illuminate or complement those Afro-American texts preceding them? And, what has been his effect on our contemporary literature and culture? In answering these we will be a little closer to understanding Wright's place—of lack of one—in the tradition.

## I

Many passages in Wright's works illustrate the issues concerning his authorial posture, but the following one from "I Tried to Be a Communist" seems particularly appropriate, partly because it is autobiographical and partly because it raises all the familiar arguments regarding Wright's posture toward his audience. In the passage, Wright describes what happened when he spoke before a unit meeting of black communists in Chicago (*The God That Failed*).

> The meeting started. About twenty Negroes were gathered. The time came for me to make my report and I took out my notes and told them how I had come to join the Party, what few stray items I had published, what my duties were in the John Reed Club. I finished and waited for comment. There was silence. I looked about. Most of the comrades sat with bowed heads. Then I was surprised to catch a twitching smile on the lips of a Negro woman. Minutes passed. The Negro woman lifted her head and looked at the organizer. The organizer smothered a smile.

When the organizer finally breaks the silence, Wright recoils from his comments, significantly remarking, "His tone was more patronizing than that of a Southern white man. . . . I thought I knew these people, but evidently I did not." Then Wright informs us:

> During the following days I learned . . . that I . . . had been classified as an *intellectual* . . . that the black Communists in my unit had commented upon my shined shoes, my clean shirt, and

the tie I had worn. Above all, my manner of speech had seemed
an alien thing to them. . . . "He talks like a book," one of the
Negro comrades had said. And that was enough to condemn me
forever as bourgeois.

Wright's ambivalent attitude toward his race and its rituals is amply revealed here, and, while it is not a matter which should enter into our
evaluations of his art, it does haunt and becloud our feelings concerning his
place in the tradition. Aware of the vivid scenes in *Black Boy,* wherein racial
bonds are shown to be either hypocritical or forms of submission, and
recalling as well how he argues in "Blueprint for Negro Writing" . . . for
Negro writers to transcend "the nationalist implications of their lives," we
are able to comprehend his behavior at the unit meeting but not necessarily
approve of it. What brands him an intellectual in this instance is not, strictly
speaking, his clean clothes or his articulateness. If this were the case, then
most of the black preachers in America—whom Wright termed "sainted
devils"—would bear the same mark and be cast from church and pulpit.
That Wright "talks like a book" is closer to the heart of the matter, for it is
Wright's *mode* of articulation, and the related matter of how he did not (or
could not) acknowledge kinship with his black brethren while articulating
the Party line, which most troubled his black audience and, in turn, bothers
us.

Wright's refusal to partake of the essential intra-racial rituals which the
situation demanded suggests that he was either unaware of, or simply refused to participate in, those viable modes of speech represented in history
by the preacher and orator and in letters by the articulate hero. The question
of articulation does not rest exclusively with matters of verbal facility, but,
on a higher plane, with the expression of a moral consciousness which is
racially-based. And of course this involves a celebration of those honorable
codes of conduct among one's kin.

Wright's dilemma reminds one of Du Bois's short story in *The Souls of
Black Folk* entitled "Of the Coming of John," in which the "black" John,
John Jones, comes home from college to teach school and "rescue" his black
townspeople from their "backwardness." His chance to address neighbors
and kin occurs at the black Baptist church, and despite his college-honed
elocution he fails miserably in his purpose, partly, one imagines, because he
attempts to assault those rituals of behavior which the humble building in
which he speaks both represents and reinforces. Divorced from the community, condemning blindly all intraracial codes as formulae for submission, speaking an oddly-cadenced tongue, John Jones fails because of his

inarticulateness; and as the story unfolds, he becomes the prototype for Bigger Thomas when he finally expresses himself by bludgeoning the "white" John, John Henderson, kissing his momma, and running away. Jones would have done well to take Wright's advice in "Blueprint" that one only transcends what is "national" in their lives by first embracing it. But he did not, and it is questionable whether Wright did either.

In both the story of John Jones and Wright's "I Tried to Be a Communist," the failure to articulate is at once a matter of the voice assumed and of how that voice relates to the audience at hand. While Jones did not speak to or of his audience, Wright compounded Jones's error by speaking beyond his immediate audience to another, which in this case was Big Brother. We might see our way to calling a truce and sounding a grace note if, when Wright states that the blacks condemned him as "bourgeois," we could be certain that he is employing both the party line and "black culture-based" senses of the term. This might have suggested his awareness, in retrospect, of the violation of intraracial codes. But the evidence is, if not exactly to the contrary, at least unconvincing.

The "unit meeting" passage hints at many complaints laid at Wright's door, but none loom larger than Ellison's lament (*Shadow and Act*) . . . that Wright "could not for ideological reasons depict a Negro as intelligent, as creative or as dedicated as himself." The charge pertains particularly to Bigger Thomas, but as we see in *Black Boy* and in "I Tried to Be a Communist," Wright's limited depiction of the Negro extends occasionally to self-portraits as well. It is hard to believe that the bumbling black writer alienating black folk and performing a poor job of propagandizing for the Party is supposed to be Wright himself, but for reasons neither wholly self-effacing nor wholly aesthetic it is, alas, poor Richard.

The issue is really Wright's idea of the hero, although I believe none of his critics put the matter quite this way. If we assume, as I do, that the primary voice in the tradition, whether in prose or verse or music, is a personal, heroic voice delineating the dimensions of heroism by either aspiring to a heroic posture, as do the voices of Douglass and Du Bois, or expressing an awareness of that which they *ought* to be, as we see Johnson's Ex-Colored Man and Ellison's Invisible Man doing, then the mystery of what is unsettling about Wright's voice (and protagonists) begins to unfold. Bigger Thomas is hardly the only maimed or stunted or confused figure in Afro-American literature; this is not what makes him different. What *does* is his unawareness of what he *ought* to be, especially as it is defined not by the vague dictates of the American dream but by the rather specific mandates of a racial heritage. When Ellison complains (*Shadow and Act*):

> Wright could imagine Bigger, but Bigger could not possibly
> imagine Richard Wright. Wright saw to that.

his lament is really that Wright did not place Bigger in the tradition. Inter-
estingly enough, placing *Wright* in the tradition was exactly what Ellison
tried to do in 1945 (but later renounced in "The World and the Jug" in
1963) when he argued that *Black Boy* was a blues in prose (*Shadow and
Act*).

All in all, Wright's authorial posture is much like that of Booker T.
Washington. Both men are, to use George Kent's phrase, "exaggerated
Westerners" (*Blackness and the Adventure of Western Culture*), especially
with regard to the voice and posture each perfected in order to reach those
whom they perceived to be their audience. Responding to what might be
termed the literary offences of Washington, Du Bois argued in *The Souls*
that part of what was wrong with the Tuskegee Spirit was the degree to
which "the speech and thought of triumphant commercialism" was indeed
*becoming* that spirit, or at least the *expression* of it. Ellison makes a smiliar
point about Wright when he says, ". . . Wright found the facile answers of
Marxism before he learned to use literature as a means for discovering the
forms of American Negro humanity" (*Shadow and Act*). In the case of both
men, the speech and thought they espoused led to a necessary denial, at least
in print, of certain Afro-American traditions. Hence, they were, in their
authorial posture, exaggerated individuals alienated from their race and, to
some degree, themselves. Even when they are about the task of creating
themselves in autobiographies, their vision is shaped and possibly warped
by this state of "exaggeratedness." Thus, in *Up from Slavery*, Washington
models himself as the ideal fundraiser and public speaker and defers to the
facile portraits of himself by journalists, while Wright, in *Black Boy*, sup-
presses his own extraordinary human spirit by rendering himself a black
"biological fact" (see Kent, *Blackness*).

But as with most comparisons there are distinctions to be made. Beyond all questions of era and place rests the simple fact that Washington
was in control of the implications of his authorial posture while Wright was
not. When, for example, Washington rebukes the models and motifs of the
slave narratives by casting *Up from Slavery* in the vein of the Franklinesque
source book and, to some degree, the Horatio Alger tale, we sense that this
was the price he willingly paid to exchange his full life story for funds for
Tuskegee and other, sometimes clandestine, projects. He knew what he was
about and the dollars most certainly came rolling in. When Wright, on the
other hand, even in the writing of *Black Boy*, embraces the example of

Dreiser, Lewis, and Mencken far more than that of Toomer, Johnson, Hughes, or Hurston, we want to know what was the trade-off, what the exchange or sacrifice comparable to Washington's? In sum, Wright was more the victim of his posture than the master of it, and in this he is not alone in Afro-American letters. If he indeed occupies a prominent place in the tradition because of his views on author and audience, it is because the founders set aside a large space for confused men.

## II

Turning to the question of how his books may confirm Wright's place in the tradition, we find ourselves on what seems to be surer ground but in the end is not. Despite Wright's apparent ignorance of Afro-American literature during his youth and rise to literary prominence, there are distinct links between certain preceding narrative types, the slave narrative and plantation tale in particular, and his own writings. But the question remains as to whether these links are mere repeated patterns or of the resilient stuff that establish author and text in an artistic continuum.

*Native Son*, for example, may be viewed as a plantation tale, not only because there are ties between it and the "revisionist" plantation tales of Charles W. Chesnutt, but also because certain features of setting, action, and character are recognizably those of a nineteenth-century American plantation society. The setting is roughly that of a plantation, with the slave quarters west of Cottage Grove Avenue, a respectful long block from the Big House of the Dalton's on Drexel Boulevard. Dalton may not be a slave-holding captain of early agri-business, but his immense profits do come from the land and from the hard toil of blacks in that, as president of the South Side Real Estate Company, he landlords over hundreds of over-priced rat-infested tenements, including that in which Bigger and his family lead their sorry lives. This provides the essential irony of the famous cell-block scene where Mrs. Thomas kneels before Mrs. Dalton and begs for her intervention, saying (*Native Son*):

> "Please don't let 'em kill my boy! You know how a mother feels! Please, mam. . . . We live in your house. . . . They done asked us to move. . . . We ain't got nothing . . . I'll work for you for the rest of my life!"

Mrs. Thomas's plea is in part one for Mrs. Dalton to honor a sense of commitment initially established by the covenant between master and slave. Her offer to work for the Daltons the rest of her life is, under the circumstances, a gift she has already given and will continue to give as long as she is trapped in one or another tenement of Dalton's ghetto.

Besides the Daltons and Mrs. Thomas, there are other minor characters such as Britten, who in his functions as a private eye turns out to be more and more like an overseer. And of course there are the major characters, Bigger, Mary Dalton, and, I would argue, Attorney Max. When George Kent writes that "A major source of the power of *Native Son* derived from Wright's ability to articulate the relevant rituals of black and white cultures—and Bigger's response to them," he refers to those rituals emphasizing the presence or absence of "rational drive, curiosity, revolutionary will, individualism [and] self-consciousness" (see *Blackness*). But he should have also mentioned those ritualized postures of the black male and white female which, one imagines, have prevailed in the mainstream of the culture since the races first came into contact. Despite her flirtation with communism. Mary Dalton is still the young, white, and (as her Christian name implies) virginal belle on the pedestal. She might at first sit alongside Bigger in the front seat of her father's car, but in the end, she removes to the rear with her boyfriend, Jan, only to reinforce the distance by reminding Bigger to cart her trunk to the station in the morning. And so the shuttle is set in motion, orders one moment, her drunken head on Bigger's shoulder the next. If Bigger is confused, the police and newspapers are not: Mary is the white beauty, Bigger the black brute.

These postures are, unfortunately in our world, timeless, and we would be wrong to suggest that they are in some way the exclusive property of the antebellum South. And because Mary and Bigger are in this sense conventional types, we must wonder whether the third major character, Attorney Max, is as well. Like Mary's boyfriend, Jan, Max resembles the sympathetic white found in the slave narratives who is somewhat removed from the system. But while Jan remains within the type—and is therefore as one-dimensional as are most of the novel's characters—Max's status is more problematic. While he never gains the intimacy with Bigger he so desperately seeks, Max does nevertheless, more than any other, spark Bigger's fleeting glimpse of the possibilities of life and of human communion. Moreover, as his courtroom speech implies, he sees, more than the rest, how America has made Bigger far more than Bigger has fashioned himself. Max's use of language is what allows him to break out of the plantation tale type. It contrasts not only with Bigger's verbal deficiencies and with the corruption of language by the State's Attorney and the press, but also, on a subtler scale, with Mary and Jan's insensitive verbal gropings across the racial chasm ("Isn't there a song like that, a song your people sing?") which only fill Bigger with "a dumb, cold, and inarticulate hate."

Indeed, what most distinguishes *Native Son* from its antecedent plantation tale texts is not its bleak urban landscape but the fact that the traditional heroic modes of transcending travail in this world, such as the gift of uncommon insight and speech, have been given not to Bigger but apparently to Max instead. Thus, the issue of Bigger's sub-heroic posture is further confused by the question of whether Wright intends Max to be the novel's heroic voice and, by extension, Wright's voice as well.

All this brings us to Max's celebrated courtroom speech. If Max speaks for Wright, we must assume that he specifically does so in the courtroom episode where he is not only eloquent but forthright and compassionate. Yet this poses a considerable problem, for in implicitly espousing the classic liberal notion that truth will invariably foster justice, Max blunts the raw revolutionary fervor which Bigger generated and which first seduced the communists to come to his aid. In doing so, Max exchanges his credentials as a radical for a heroic posture which is very much in the American grain. Thus, while transcending the character type in the slave narratives which he first resembles, Max soon takes on the features of a familiar turn-of-the-century type, the "white moral voice," of whom Charles W. Chesnutt, in Afro-American letters, provides us with at least four examples. Max is, then, a revolutionary manqué; a reformer possessing a grand but ineffectual idealism which leaves him horror-struck before the fact of Bigger's pending execution.

If Max is *not* Wright's voice, or at least not the heroic voice in the novel, then we would expect him to be sketched ironically, with the stress falling on what may be less than heroic in his words and character. But this is not the case. What we have instead is a confusion of political language and purpose, compounded by the troublesome fact that Wright seems to have bestowed the gift of eloquence on Max with no clearly discernible end in mind.

The problem with Max seems to be a fictive equivalent of Wright's own dilemma in "I Tried to Be a Communist." In each case, the speaker's articulateness does not meet the needs of the occasion and in that sense is a kind of illiteracy, especially of the sort that is enforced by America's rituals along the color line. If, in *Native Son,* Max is indeed Wright's voice, it is not because of the content of his speeches but rather because he shares with his author a misperception of audience, grounded in what we may term an extraordinary and almost myopic innocence. Thus, despite the novel's many and varied images of American slave society, the absence of an articulate hero whose posture and language tends to modulate the forces of a hostile environment renders *Native Son* a most problematic novel in Afro-American letters.

*Black Boy,* on the other hand, is more clearly conceived and is hence the better of Wright's two greatest published works. The dominant voice of the book seems to be finally that of its author precisely because it has a fair measure of human proportion. To be sure, we are almost overwhelmed by those relentless passages in *Black Boy* in which Wright fashions himself a black "biological fact." But countering these are the moments of marvelous self-assertion, the Whitmanesque catalogs of sensual remembrances, and overall, the presence of a questing human being seeking freedom and a voice. Here, a hostile environment *is* modulated by an emerging, extraordinary figure, and the resulting narrative establishes a place for itself in the continuum founded by the slave narrative.

One may list a number of motifs *Black Boy* shares with the slave narratives—the violence and gnawing hunger, the skeptical view of Christianity, the portrait of a black family valiantly attempting to maintain a degree of unity, the impregnable isolation, the longing and scheming to follow the North Star resolved by boarding the "freedom train"—but the most enduring link is the motif (and, one might argue, the narrative form) of the narrator's quest for literacy. Frederick Douglass provides the most compelling statement (*Narrative of the Life of Frederick Douglass, An American Slave*) of how literacy and freedom are entwined goals when he relates:

> Very soon after I went to live with Mr. and Mrs. Auld, she very kindly commenced to teach me the A, B, C. After I had learned this, she assisted me in learning to spell words of three or four letters. Just at this point of my progress, Mr. Auld found out what was going on, and at once forbade Mrs. Auld to instruct me further, telling her, among other things, that it was unlawful, as well as unsafe, to teach a slave to read. To use his own words, further, he said, "If you give a nigger an inch, he will take an ell. A nigger should know nothing but to obey his master—to do as he is told to do. Learning would *spoil* the best nigger in the world. Now," said he, "if you teach that nigger (speaking of myself) how to read, there would be no keeping of him. It would forever unfit him to be a slave. He would at once become unmanageable, and of no value to his master. As to himself, it would do him no good, but a great deal of harm. It would make

him discontented and unhappy." These words sank deep into my
heart, stirred up sentiments within that lay slumbering, and called
into existence an entirely new train of thought. It was a new and
special revelation, explaining dark and mysterious things, with
which my youthful understanding had struggled in vain. I now
understood what had been to me a most perplexing difficulty—
to wit, the white man's power to enslave the black man. It was
a grand achievement, and I prized it highly. From that moment,
I understood the pathway from slavery to freedom.

While Wright's quest for literacy was hardly this arduous, it was nevertheless difficult and, especially by the time he was nineteen and in Memphis,
fraught with danger. As he intimates in *Black Boy,* there were white men
who might have killed him had they known he was reading Mencken and
Sinclair Lewis and absorbing their indictments of America. Unlike Douglass,
Wright did not have to dupe white boys in the streets in order to learn how
to cipher, but he did have to discover a sympathetic Irishman who secretly
lent him his library card before he could break the isolation and read ". . .
books that opened up new avenues of feeling and seeing. . . ." And it was
this reading, as well as the writing of stories and even commencement
addresses, which prompted young Richard to follow the North Star and, in
a supreme act of self-assertion, free himself.

   All in all, our comparison of *Black Boy* and *Native Son* provides us
with a number of strong, revealing contrasts, but none presses with greater
urgency and portent than that of the self-assertive, self-aware narrator of
*Black Boy* seeking literacy and a voice appositioned against the image of
Bigger and his inert cohorts assaulted by the mindlessness of B-grade Hollywood films and the rhetoric of propaganda emanating not only from the
communists but also from the Daltons, the government, and the press.
Clearly, Wright could match his model of the writer described in "Blueprint" who is "something of a guide in [our] daily living," but it is remarkable that he did so only in the writing of his autobiography.

## III

   Despite what we've previously said about Wright's distance from the
race and his problems concerning voice and audience, there is considerable
evidence of his influence on, and enshrinement by, the contemporary black
writer and critic. In 1964, while participating in a symposium on Wright,
Saunders Redding declared: "Certainly, if we are in a renaissance, as it
were, more or less similar, though very, very different from the renaissance

of the twenties, it is because of Richard Wright." Given the year in which Redding made this statement, one may assume that he was referring to the ascending careers of several writers, of whom Baldwin and Ellison might very well have topped the list. Their protests to the contrary, Baldwin and Ellison *were* influenced by Wright; one might even argue that a significant part of their drive to write derived from a desire to "humanize" Bigger. A great deal of ink has been spilled on this subject, and I won't contribute mine. Rather, I would like to explore briefly Wright's influence on the critics and authors of Afro-American literature of the last decade.

Perhaps the most obvious evidence of Wright's influence is provided by the titles of several widely disseminated studies of Afro-American literature published in the 1950s and 1960s. In addition to Baldwin's *Notes of a Native Son* (1955) and Cleaver's "Notes on a Native Son" in *Soul on Ice* (1968), we have Edward Margolies's *Native Sons: A Critical Study of Twentieth-Century Negro American Authors*. Yet another quasi-sociological survey of Afro-American writing, and one which systematically excludes black women writers (the title is no reasonable rationale for this), Margolies's book is hardly a ground-breaking performance. One imagines that it was rushed to print, as were many other titles, to meet the needs of the new market created by the rise of Afro-American Studies. But it is worth our attention because Margolies attempts, in a very modest way, to forge a critical approach to Afro-American literature based on the example and impact of *Native Son*. He writes in his introductory chapter:

> The example of *Native Son* enabled others to deal with a body of subject matter they had hitherto warily skirted. Wright opened up for Negro writers not only the bitterness of their lives, but other taboo matters as well—miscegenation, homosexuality, the white-Negro power structure, and even the singular freedom a Negro feels in a society that denies him any recognition of his humanity. The courage to "tell it the way it is" is the prime requisite of artistic integrity. Human revelation is the business of the artist; he must write about what he *knows* to be true—imaginatively or otherwise—and the first truths he must know are about himself. *Native Son* provided many Negro authors with these precedents. In its way it liberated them as no other book has done since.

We are not entirely happy with this statement; one hopes, for example, that Margolies's list of "taboo matters" beginning with miscegenation and ending with the "singular freedom" of the Negro is not supposed to reflect the

order of their importance. But the idea of treating *Native Son* as some sort
of watershed in Afro-American literature is not altogether amiss, especially
if one wishes to investigate the course of Afro-American literary *art*. However, Margolies is centrally concerned with "the Negro's evaluation of his
historical and cultural experience in this century"; for him, *Native Son* is a
point of departure more for social scientific evidence than for the discovery
of an artistic tradition.

As the black aesthetic critics and writers surfaced in the late sixties,
partly in response to the critical inadequacies of approaches like Margolies's,
they embraced Richard Wright as a novelist and also as an aesthetician. In
some instances, however, it was not so much Wright but Bigger Thomas
who, strangely enough, was promoted as the black artist's model. For example, Sarah Webster Fabio writes in her contribution to Addison Gayle's
*The Black Aesthetic:*

> No turning back, though. This is the day of Biggers and the
> ghosts of Biggers. Black writers—most of them poets plus—have
> always been barometers, even when America kept the bell jars on
> them. Have always been/still are/will be. Always traveling with
> ears to the ground; attuned to the drumbeats of the age.

One assumes that Fabio, who usually makes better sense, is being rhetorical.
Buried in here somewhere is the notion that black writers, armed with
poems and novels for weapons, must "kill" as Bigger did in order to feel the
pulse of time and, for the first time in their lives, feel free. As rhetoric this
may be powerful and, for some, inspiring, but it hardly suggests a viable
aesthetic ideal, nor does it pay proper credit to Richard Wright. Addison
Gayle, however, offers a more fruitful line of inquiry when he correctly
turns to the example of Wright, not Bigger, and argues:

> The task of pointing out northern duplicity was left to the black
> artist, and no writer was more effective in this undertaking than
> Richard Wright. When Wright placed Bigger Thomas and Mr.
> Dalton in a northern setting and pointed up the fact that Bigger's
> condition resulted from Dalton's hypocrisy, he opened up a
> Pandora's box of problems for white liberals and Negro leaders,
> neither of whom could bring themselves to share his vision. . . .
> The liberal ideology—both social and literary—of the northern
> Daltons has become the primary target of the Afro-American
> writer and critic.

Above and beyond the issue of how Gayle views contemporary black writers and critics pursuing their muse, this statement is questionable as a "political" reading of *Native Son*. The total picture of liberal thought in the novel includes, as we've indicated before, the words and deeds of Attorney Max, even though it is through him that the most explicit and vitriolic condemnation of the Daltons is expressed. If a critic values such features in literature and actually intends to build an aesthetic upon such foundations, as Gayle apparently does, then Wright's inability to portray Max as a "pure" radical should conceivably becloud his view of *Native Son* as a seminal book. But apparently this is not a problem for Mr. Gayle. Our point is, however, that here is another attempt to trace a pattern in Afro-American literature which has *Native Son* as its source. As Margolies emphasizes the socio-cultural, Gayle, albeit with greater attention to the Afro-American artist's posture in society, stresses the political, the literary war against an ideology. Since each of these patterns has a considerable history beginning well before the publication of *Native Son* in 1940, one might say that both Margolies and Gayle are trying, from what often seems like opposite corners of the earth, to move toward an articulation of a tradition. But patterns aren't traditions, and even a combination of Margolies and Gayle approaches does not illuminate all we want to know about books like *Native Son* and *Black Boy*. If indeed, as some are saying, the black art-as-sociology and black aesthetic theories of the 1960s are outmoded, it may be because the latter is but an extension and political radicalization of the former, and neither approach is fully in tune with the heartbeat of the artist and his art.

By and large, the chief limitation to most of the criticism of *Native Son* is that the critics have dwelled on what we may loosely call the novel's content. Whether *Native Son* actually shocked the proverbial banker's daughter (who might identify, one supposes, with Mary Dalton) as Wright hoped it would remains unclear. What *is* clear, however, is that Wright's critics have been preoccupied by those very features of the novel which are presumably distressing to proper young ladies. Generally, most of the criticism of *Native Son* falls into one of two categories: predictable, journeyman-like studies of imagery (light and dark; animal references) and symbolism (the soaring airplane, various timepieces, the Christian crosses); or, responses to those features which, as Baldwin has written, "whet the notorious national taste for the sensational." The problem, we discover, is that these approaches unduly isolate the text from the corpus of American and Afro-American literature and direct discussion of *Native Son* toward yet another ritualized, pseudo-scientific rehash of the black man's plight.

As I have tried to indicate earlier in these pages, Wright's influence on the contemporary critic may lead to the pursuit of other types of questions. Our sense of an Afro-American literary tradition can be sharpened and enhanced, for example, by assaying Wright's departures from it. We need to develop what has already been ventured about Bigger and Wright's entanglement in the web of double-consciousness so that we may come to know them and the place of *Native Son* in the artistic continuum. We need to assess why, from the standpoint of artistic and even aesthetic considerations, Wright earnestly desired to become a jazz critic in the twilight of his career. Above all, we must not hesitate to discover the Americanness of Richard Wright. Such an activity is actually part of the legacy handed down by such pioneering Afro-American critics as William Stanley Braithwaite and Sterling A. Brown. Wright's departures from Afro-American traditions generally serve to confirm his place in the mainstream of American letters, and, for the moment, it seems like the knowledgeable Afro-Americanist critic is best suited to articulate Wright's stature in both literary worlds.

Turning to Wright's influence on the contemporary black writer, especially those writers first published during the last decade, we find a predictable array of responses ranging from celebrations of Bigger to what we can only deem more thoughtful considerations of Wright's work which frequently reexamine those rituals of black and white cultures of which we've already spoken. The celebrations of Bigger more often than not represent the exploitation of these cultural rituals, and seem to be generated by psychological needs surfacing as strategies for political power, or by unadulterated greed. Writers are often found in the former camp (Eldridge Cleaver, for example), while the would-be artists behind the spate of "blaxploitation" films may be designated to the latter. If indeed, as Kichung Kim writes, "For many Black Americans . . . Bigger is probably the one character they find most authentic in all of American literature," we need not wonder why these writers and filmmakers have a considerable audience. None of this is Wright's doing or intention. The man who split the atom did not drop the bomb. However, like the scientist who foresaw the holocaust of Hiroshima, Wright, in his portraits of Bigger fantasizing at the movies and dreamily reading detective stories, seems to have prophesied what is a lamentable feature to our present cultural state. What he understandably could not foresee is that today not only is Bigger still in the audience, but his fantasized self is on the screen.

A far more honorable and direct response to Wright may be discovered in the recent fiction of black women authors. We have alluded to the effort to "humanize" Bigger but the attempts to revise and redeem Mrs. Thomas and both Bessies (the one in *Native Son* and the one in *Black Boy*), launched mostly by black women writers, must be mentioned as well. There is little written discussion of this; but looking at the literature itself, we can find types of Mrs. Thomas and both Bessies leading richer lives and having more going for them than a false church, a whiskey bottle, and, as Wright says of the Bessie in *Black Boy,* a peasant mentality.

Ann Petry's *The Street* (1946) and Toni Morrison's *The Bluest Eye* (1970) are two novels from what may be termed the antipodes of the contemporary period which support our point. Although Lutie Johnson in *The Street* is ultimately defeated by the dimensions of racism and sexism at work and at home in Harlem, she, unlike the Bessie in *Native Son,* possesses a fair measure of pride, will, and grace. The fact that near the end of the novel she kills her black lover, not to silence him, but because of the continual sexual and psychological assault he has made on her life, would suggest that Petry was about the task not only of redeeming Bessie but of revising Bigger as well.

In *The Bluest Eye,* virtually all of the black women, whether they be prostitutes or keepers of the hearth, are far more compelling, complex, and differentiated than Wright's. Mrs. Pauline Breedlove and her daughter, Pecola, may be likened to Mrs. Thomas and her daughter, Vera. Both sets of women are entrapped by the burdens of being poor, black, and female. But for all their woes, or perhaps because of them, Mrs. Breedlove and Pecola are the dreamers in Morrison's novel. Their dreams may be false and irredeemably warped—Mrs. Breedlove covets Jean Harlow's hair, Pecola desperately searches for blue eyes—but they dream just the same; they have an inner life. Most importantly, in terms of the tradition of the articulate hero, the arresting story of all the Breedloves (Pauline, Pecola, Sammy, and the father, Cholly) is told by a young woman, Claudia MacTeer, whose accumulation of the facts and rendering of the tale softens our horror while yielding her a special knowledge with which she can face and endure adulthood.

All in all, the black women novelists of our age seem to be agreeing with Alice Walker that "black women are the most fascinating creations in the world." Thus, out of necessity, they are turning to Toomer, Hurston, Brooks, and Petry, and not to the majority of black male writers for their models and encouragement. In this light, the rise of a feminine and sometimes feminist voice in contemporary Afro-American fiction may be directly related to the narrow and confining portraits of black women in earlier modern fiction, including that of Wright.

Besides the revision of characters, we also find evidence of the contemporary writer treating the aforementioned cultural rituals as lore handed down; as essential metaphors to be combined with others such as the heroic black athlete and the veil. For example, in "Heartblow," Michael Harper's series of poems for Wright in *Debridement* (1973), we find this poem entitled "Afterward: A Film":

> Erect in the movies
> with a new job,
> *Trader Horn*
> and *The Gay Woman*
> unfold in a twinbill:
> drums, wild dancing,
> naked men, the silver
> veils on the South Side.
> He imagines nothing:
> it is all before him,
> born in a dream:
> a gorilla broke loose
> from his zoo
> in a tuxedo: baboon.
> You pick your red bottom
> The Daltons are the movies.
>
> On my wall are pictures:
> Jack Johnson, Joe Louis,
> Harlow and Rogers:
> "See the white god and die."
>
> Underground I live in veils,
> brick and cement,
> the confession beaten out,
> slung with hung carcasses,
> a bloody cleaver grunting,
> a dead baby in the sewer:
> "all the people I saw were guilty."
>
> Marked black I was shot,
> *double-conscious brother in the veil*—
> without an image of act or thought
> *double-conscious brother in the veil*—
>
> The rape: "Mrs. Dalton, it's me,
> Bigger, I've brought Miss Dalton
> home and she's drunk":

to be the idea in these minds,
*double-conscious brother in the veil—*
father and leader where is my king,
veils of kingship will lead these folks
*double-conscious brother in the veil—*
"see the white gods and die"
*double-conscious brother in the veil—*

The opening stanzas take two of Wright's most effective images of Bigger the empty vessel being inundated and filled by the celluloid flotsam of popular culture, and integrate them into one flowing portrait of assault, first at the theatre and finally in his quarters at the Dalton home. All this is done with careful and loyal attention to the text. The gorilla reference is, for example, almost a quotation of Jack's playful response to Bigger's musings over what it would be like to attend a party like that in *The Gay Woman*, only now the self-debasing racial comment at the heart of Jack's joking is fully exposed and relentlessly pursued. Furthermore, in the second stanza, mention of the photos on Bigger's walls at the Daltons' serves to remind us of how, according to Wright's vision, Bigger and Mary will encounter each other in a dance designed by warped yet powerful cultural and historical forces; a dance of psycho-sexual and racial ritual along the color line. In short, stanzas one and two present those cultural forces affecting Bigger in book 1 of the novel as much as stanza 3 captures Bigger's mood in book 2.

In the third stanza, the series of images transports us back to the scene of Mary's dismemberment and forward to Bigger's confession while immersing us in Bigger's flight underground in Dalton's ghetto. The primary image is that of a hellish landscape, peopled by the victimized and oppressed, which the poet places in a historical continuum, not so much as Wright did by means of economic and political reference, but rather by ancient metaphor, the veil. Through this metaphor, Harper can now expand upon his image of Bigger until it approximates the fullest dimensions of the artistic continuum. Thus, in the remaining stanzas, the line *"double-conscious brother in the veil"* becomes at once a musical refrain and, like a repeated color in African woven cloth, the agent and source for a compelling visual rhythm.

In poems such as these, Wright, I feel, is restored to his proper stature as a participant in Afro-American letters. Harper's mining of Wright's primary images and placement of them in the continuum, as well as his implied suggestion that Wright deserves a place in the pantheon where we find Du Bois, yields the kind of evidence which balances all we know of Wright's shortcomings. And it is this balanced view of Wright, as an author who could argue "Tradition is no longer a guide. . . . The world has grown huge and cold" while providing us with archetypes which generations of writers would in turn place *in* the tradition he rejected, that begins to define his stature in the Afro-American tradition.

ROBERT B. STEPTO

# *Literacy and Ascent:* Black Boy

*I was poised for flight, but I was waiting for*
*some event, some word, some act, some*
*circumstance to furnish the impetus*
        —RICHARD WRIGHT, *Black Boy*

    *He leaps, board wings clum—*
*sily flapping, big sex*
    *flopping, falls.*

    *The hawk-hunted fowl*
*flutter and squawk;*
    *panic squeals in the sty.*

    *He strains, an awk-*
*ward patsy, sweating strains*
    *leaping falling. Then—*

    *Silken rustling in the air,*
*the angle of ascent*
    *achieved*
—ROBERT HAYDEN, "For A Young Artist"

[E]lsewhere,] we saw how a modern or epiloging text, *The Autobiography of an Ex-Coloured Man* achieves a place for itself in the Afro-American narrative tradition by binding the rhetorical conventions of the authenticating narrative to the narrative impulses of the immersion ritual, creating what is, in effect, an aborted narrative of immersion. [Here,] we shall discover how another modern text—Richard Wright's *Black Boy* (1945)—achieves a comparable integrity within the tradition by fusing a different set

From *From Behind The Veil: A Study of Afro-American Narrative.* © 1979 by the Board of Trustees of the University of Illinois. University of Illinois Press, 1979.

of conventions and impulses from the authenticating form to the narrative properties of the ascension ritual, creating what is fundamentally a narrative of ascent that authenticates another, primary text by the same author. *Black Boy* has the responsibility of revoicing Wright's own *Native Son* as well as harking back to certain primary tropes in the Afro-American narrative canon, and the fact that *Black Boy* meets both of these responsibilities is cause enough (although not the most often cited cause) for the narrative's great fame.

Of course, the "official" and sanctioned authenticating text for *Native Son* is not *Black Boy*, but the pulsing and affecting shorter piece, "How Bigger Was Born." Written within a few months after *Native Son* saw print in 1940 and promptly published by *Harper's*, "How Bigger Was Born" soon replaced *Native Son*'s original and innocently vapid preface by a "white guarantor" (Dorothy Canfield Fisher), and in that way took over the responsibilities of not only introducing but also authenticating Wright's greatest novel. On its surface, this development had all the marks of a great personal and artistic triumph: the opportunity for Wright to introduce his own text suggests a high level of earned and sanctioned authorial control. But while "How Bigger Was Born" answered one question—how Wright came to know Bigger—it unintentionally posed another: How did Wright come to escape *becoming* a Bigger?

At first glance, this latter question appears exceedingly irrelevant and extraliterary, but it is not—primarily because of the compulsions in the Afro-American letters that prompt the question, and because the question need not be answered (as the example of *Black Boy* attests) in a nonliterary way. Despite Wright's brave assertion in "Blueprint for Negro Writing" (1937) that "tradition is no longer a guide," there can be no doubt that tradition guided him: in the 1940s, after he finally read most of the corpus of Afro-American literature, and became aware of, if not thoroughly imbued with, the demands of its tropes and traditions, Wright had to write *Black Boy* (indeed, all of *American Hunger*) because "How Bigger Was Born" is not a full and complete authentication of *Native Son,* and neither text authenticates the extraordinary articulate self that lies behind them. Once that self *was* authenticated in *Black Boy*, Wright could expatriate to France (or just about anywhere, save Mississippi) and pursue new projects, including new modes of writing. And that is exactly what he did.

In "How Bigger Was Born," Wright deftly sketches the various "Biggers" he encountered in Mississippi, Memphis, and Chicago who collectively provided the wellsprings, as it were, from which he drew the archetypal Bigger Thomas. Of course, missing in that essay is Wright's acknowledgment of the Bigger who resides in the shadows and deeper recesses of his own personal past, the Bigger who once had a powerful grip on the thoughts, actions, and even the debilitating inarticulateness of Wright's daily life as a youth. In *Black Boy* Wright finally makes this acknowledgment or confession, and his remarks are often as self-serving as they are informative. For example, in chapter 3 of *Black Boy* we discover that Wright's own youthful experiences gave him a firsthand knowledge of the cockiness and restlessness that typically characterize streetcorner or poolhall gangs like Bigger Thomas's in *Native Son*. Wright did not have to draw exclusively upon his experiences as a WPA-sponsored youth worker in a south side Chicago Boys' Club—as reported in "How Bigger Was Born"—in order to capture the prevailing ambiance of Bigger's world. The following passage from the beginning of the chapter describes Wright's own coterie of restless and pubescent seekers, but the feelings, rituals, and persons sketched are hardly unique to Wright's childhood:

> Having grown taller and older, I now associated with older boys and I had to pay for my admittance into their company by subscribing to certain racial sentiments. The touchstone of fraternity was my feeling toward white people, how much hostility I held toward them, what degrees of value and honor I assigned to race. None of this was premeditated, but sprang spontaneously out of the talk of the black boys who met at the crossroads. . . . We had somehow caught the spirit of the role of our sex and we flocked together for common moral schooling. We spoke boastfully in bass voices; we used the word "nigger" to prove the tough fibre of our feelings; we spouted excessive profanity as a sign of our coming manhood; we pretended callousness toward the injunctions of our parents; and we strove to convince one another that our decisions stemmed from ourselves and ourselves alone. Yet we frantically concealed how dependent we were upon each other.

Clearly, these words describe Bigger Thomas's world in book 1 of *Native Son*, a world that Wright evidently once shared, modally if not literally, with his most famous protagonist. But this passage is not nearly so much about shared (and, hence, authenticated) experience as it is about profound differences in degrees of literacy, or the chasm between literacy and its absence. The passage is unique to *Black Boy* because of the voice displayed, rather than the detail deployed; the voice is that of a former "Bigger" who has transcended both a woeful circumstance and an illiterate self. Put another way, the voice displayed in *Black Boy* is that of an Afro-American articulate hero who has learned to read the "baffling signs" of an oppressing, biracial social structure.

Wright's compulsion to exhibit his hard-won literacy is amply documented as the chapter continues. He glosses or annotates what he remembers to be the kind of conversation in which his gang perennially engaged.

> "Hey." Timidly.
>
> "You eat yet?" Uneasily trying to make conversation.
>
> "Yeah, man. I done really fed my face." Casually.
>
> "I had cabbage and potatoes." Confidently.
>
> "I had buttermilk and black-eyed peas." Meekly informational.
>
> "Hell, I ain't gonna stand near you, nigger!" Pronouncement.
>
> "How come?" Feigned innocence.
>
> " 'Cause you gonna smell up this air in a minute!" A shouted accusation.
>
> Laughter runs through the crowd.
>
> "Man, them white folks oughta catch you and send you to the zoo and keep you for the next war!" Throwing the subject into a wider field.
>
> "Then when the fighting starts, they oughta feed you on buttermilk and black-eyed peas and let you break wind!" The subject is accepted and extended.
>
> "You'd win the war with a new kind of poison gas!" A shouted climax.
>
> There is high laughter that simmers down slowly.
>
> "Man, them white folks sure is mean." Complaining.
>
> "That's how come so many colored folks leaving the South." Informational.
>
> "And, man, they sure hate for you to leave." Pride of personal and racial worth implied.
>
> "Yeah. They wanna keep you here and work you to death."
>
> "The first white sonofabitch that bothers me is gonna get a hole knocked in his head!" Naive rebellion.
>
> "That ain't gonna do you no good. Hell, they'll catch you." Rejection of naive rebellion.

"Ha-ha-ha . . . Yeah, goddammit, they really catch you, now."
Appreciation of the thoroughness of white militancy.

"Yeah, white folks set on their white asses day and night, but
leta nigger do something, and they get every bloodhound that
was ever born and put 'em on his trail." Bitter pride in realizing
what it costs to defeat them.

"Man, you reckon these white folks is ever gonna change?"
Timid, questioning hope.

"Hell, no! They just born that way." Rejecting hope for fear
that it could never come true.

"Shucks, man. I'm going north when I get grown." Rebelling
against futile hope and embracing flight.

"A colored man's all right up north." Justifying flight.

"They say a white man hit a colored man up north and that
colored man hit that white man, knocked him cold, and nobody
did a damn thing!" Urgent wish to believe in flight.

"Man for man up there." Begging to believe in justice.

Silence.

Wright's recomposition of these exchanges and his reading of them as the
signs of a culture from which he has triumphantly removed himself constitute a moment heretofore unheralded in *Black Boy* and, quite likely, in
Afro-American narrative letters as a whole. Johnson's Ex-Coloured Man
proves to be incapable of expressing a single retrospective thought, partly
because his development as an individual is essentially an illusion, and
partly because his tongue is bound to an ahistorical rhetoric. In contrast,
Wright's persona is, along with Frederick Douglass's, the essential retrospective voice in the tradition. Whereas James Weldon Johnson draws on
the example of Booker T. Washington's *intentional* minimalization of the
distance between past and present, creating a narrator who *unintentionally*
pursues such minimizing activities through his language, Wright takes the
other path and fashions a voice who, if anything, exploits the reach between
past and present. The reasons for this act of exploitation are clear and
extend beyond the confines of *Black Boy*'s narrative line. The past is the
southern black belt bound to the northern ghetto by the aimlessness and
inarticulateness of the Biggers in us all, while the present is, in the terms
*Black Boy* affords, the increasingly unchartable realm of the articulate survivor.

And so the grand narrative strategy of *Black Boy* is set in motion.
Expressions of literate mobility slowly take form, then accompany, and then

supersede expressions of illiterate immobility; the new triumphing expressions gain their greatest resonance when we perceive how they counterpoint certain major antedating images in *Native Son*. While the preceding example regarding Bigger's and Wright's gangs and their coded speech suggests the kind of mobility Wright eventually achieves through language, we mustn't overlook the fact that mobility, for Wright, is very much a physical matter as well. He wanted to improve his mind, and he nearly worshipped the mysteries of language that afforded "new avenues of feeling and seeing"; but he also wanted to get the hell out of Dixie. All this is captured magnificently, I think, in the theater episode late in *Black Boy*, which the careful reader must counterpoint with that in *Native Son*.

The episode in *Black Boy* depicts Wright's short career as a movie theater ticket-taker. In that capacity, and because of an abiding desperation for enough money to leave what he calls elsewhere "the gross environment that sought to claim [him]," he conquers his fears and joins in a scheme to resell tickets and pocket the profits. Of course, the theater is a "colored" theater; as such, it takes its place in a continuum of symbolic constructions in Afro-American letters, including the various theaters in Toomer's *Cane* and the once-elegant Regal in which Bigger Thomas and his soulmates view "The Gay Woman" and "Trader Horn." What makes this theater episode a relatively fresh expression in the canon is the same thing that creates the counterpoint between it and the antedating event in *Native Son*. In *Native Son* Bigger is in the theater, viewing the celluloid flotsam of what Wright calls "a culture not a civilization," and although he and his brethren pose questions and issue taunts, they are far more encased by than removed from the cultural images flashing before them. On the other hand, in *Black Boy* Wright is outside the theater, removed from a technological culture's crudest propaganda; he is desperately but bravely putting together the last few dollars needed to buy the only kind of ticket that interests him and *should* interest Bigger—that train ticket (so magnificently a fresh expression of Douglass's "protection" pass) to what he hopes will be a better world. In terms of the orchestrated dialectic between Wright's two greatest works, this particular episode in *Black Boy* revises a major moment in *Native Son* by affirming that arresting images of illiterate immobility and literate mobility may be contextualized in the same symbolic space.

In this way, before embarking for Europe and his second great journey in quest of a civilization and not a culture, Wright erected the antipodes of the black world upon which his best literature is strung. It is a rather complete world when seen whole, chiefly because it is ordered less by political persuasion and economic law than by a quintessentially Afro-

American notion of literacy in communion with artistic vision. When his oeuvre is viewed in this way, it seems remarkable that so many writers and critics (encouraged, perhaps, by certain celebrated remarks from Baldwin and Ellison) have persisted in the essentially Du Boisian enterprise of exposing the "partial truth" broadcast by *Native Son,* when it is clear that Wright "completed" that "truth" eventually. In the long run, the charge that a writer of Wright's talent should have been able to present the literate and illiterate (and mobile and immobile) dimensions of the world he knew in the harmonic as well as dissonant tropes of *one* exquisite expression may tell us less about aesthetic value than about those moments in literary history when aspects of intertextuality are largely forsaken, when the compulsions of a given tradition function more as dictates than as guidelines. Blinded as we have been by the searing light of *Native Son,* we have rarely seen how *Black Boy* completes that novel; nor have we always seen how *Black Boy* revoices certain precursing tropes in Afro-American letters, tropes that reach back at least as far as the slave narratives. In the former instance, the narrative performs the duties of an authenticating narrative, while in the latter it assumes the shape and fiber of a narrative of ascent. These activities are not distinct in image and episode, because they are not distinct or opposing activities in the narrative as a whole. For Wright as for others, including most notably Frederick Douglass, literacy and ascent are the interwoven contours of the road to freedom. Every expression of literacy in *Black Boy* that revises an expression of illiteracy in *Native Son* inevitably advances the narrator's ritualized ascent. This, if nothing else, assures a space for *Black Boy* in the Afro-American narrative tradition.

As in all the great Afro-American narratives of ascent, a primary feature of *Black Boy* is Wright's persona's sustained effort to gain authorial control of the text of his environment. The first phase of such an effort is always the identification of the enveloping culture's "baffling signs," which are to be read and, in some sense, transcended by the questing figure. In *Black Boy* the three catalogs of boyhood remembrances that provide such welcome relief from the relentless depiction of assault are also the means by which Wright can enumerate his culture's coded references in a concentrated way. The first catalog appears in chapter 1; it is sorely needed even at that early point in the narrative, because it offers a legato bridge after Wright's furious opening riff on how, when he was four, he almost burnt the house down, and as a consequence was beaten until he lost consciousness and wandered day and night, in dream and without, in a "fog of fear." This catastrophic childhood event immediately calls to mind that which begins *The Autobiography of an Ex-Coloured Man,* and one can make useful comparisons between the two. Both narrators conduct experiments with forms that are primary expressions of family or community: in *Black Boy*, Wright fires the fluffy white curtains, but behind this lies his wanton mischief with the hearth; in *The Autobiography*, the Ex-Coloured Man uproots the "spirit in glitter." Furthermore, while both are soundly beaten for their violations, the Ex-Coloured Man retreats from the outdoor arena of his crime to the interiors of his boyhood cottages, while Wright's persona reverses this movement and flees from his home to outside. These two opposing treatments of a primary scene come into sharper focus when we observe the ways in which they speak to one another. The utter finality and completeness of the Ex-Coloured Man's dedication to knowing, and hence controlling, the world signified by his boyhood interiors is clarified by Wright's comparable ambition to know and control a world that initially has no definition, other than that it is outside and beyond a taut and bepeopled structure afflicting him.

It is virtually foretold that, when each narrative continues, the Ex-Coloured Man will identify the enveloping and engaging signs of his interior world (the glittering coins, the soft shined leather, the first of several pianos), while Wright's persona will list the equally significant signs belonging to an exterior space. Wright's catalog begins this way:

> Each event spoke with a cryptic tongue. And the moments of living slowly revealed their coded meanings. There was the wonder I felt when I first saw a brace of mountainlike, spotted, black-and-white horses clopping down a dusty road through clouds of powdered clay.
>
> There was the delight I caught in seeing long straight rows of red and green vegetables stretching away in the sun to the bright horizon.
>
> There was the faint, cool kiss of sensuality when dew came on to my cheeks and shins as I ran down the wet green garden paths in the early morning.
>
> There was the vague sense of the infinite as I looked down upon the yellow, dreaming waters of the Mississippi River from the verdant bluffs of Natchez.

The list builds in much the same evenhanded way, laying languorous image upon languorous image until we come upon the first (and only) sign involving kin—a sign that places someone who theoretically should be a part of the oppressing interior structure outside that structure, and indeed out-of-doors: "There was the experience of feeling death without dying that came from watching a chicken leap about blindly after its neck had been snapped by a quick twist of my father's wrist."

After this, the catalog of remembrances is characterized far more by small terrors and afflictions than by enrapturing pleasures and balms:

> There was the thirst I had when I watched clear, sweet juice trickle from sugar cane being crushed.
>
> There was the hot panic that welled up in my throat and swept through my blood when I first saw the lazy, limp coils of a blue-skinned snake sleeping in the sun.
>
> There was the speechless astonishment of seeing a hog stabbed through the heart, dipped into boiling water, scraped, split open, gutted, and strung up gaping and bloody.
>
> There was the hint of cosmic cruelty that I felt when I saw the curved timbers of a wooden shack that had been warped in the summer sun.
>
> There was the cloudy notion of hunger when I breathed the odor of new-cut bleeding grass.
>
> And there was the quiet terror that suffused my senses when vast hazes of gold washed earthward from star-heavy skies on silent nights.

In this way Wright inaugurates the anti-pastoral strain in *Black Boy*. There is no mistaking the extent to which his feelings toward his father (in the context of the narrative) are at the heart of this development. Unlike the Ex-Coloured Man, who pursues his father's signs, if not precisely his father, after the latter leaves him and his mother almost paradoxically comfortable but adrift, Wright's persona rejects all that his father signifies. Especially after the father abandons his family, fails in his own flight and ascent to Memphis, and returns to work the Mississippi soil as a sharecropper, the son considers him the first of several elder kinsmen who are "warnings," not "examples." All this cannot be said explicitly in the catalog, but the positioning of the father outdoors (recall here that the father is the only one who can *see* and capture Richard after he flees outside and under the house during the fire) and the sudden change in the remembrances after this positioning tell us much and anticipate the first chapter's closure.

The Ex-Coloured Man gains momentary control over his father by playing the piano exquisitely—only to be controlled in turn (as the new expensive piano that soon arrives suggests) by his father's "signs." Likewise, Wright's voice seeks a measure of control over (and distance from) his father by effectively and defiantly declaring war on the most clear and obvious implied meanings in his father's daily address—as if such assaults might somehow dim the feverish glow of the premonition his father embodies. All this is made most evident in the famous kitten episode, wherein Wright's father, desperate for sleep after night work, is kept awake by the "loud, persistent meowing" of a stray kitten. He angrily yells, "Kill that damn thing! . . . Do anything, but get it away from here!" Young Richard responds, we will recall, by fashioning a noose and stringing up the kitten. The kitten's deathly gyrations—"It gasped, slobbered, spun, clawed the air frantically"—transport us back to the "leap" into death of the chicken whose neck was snapped by his father's hand. Ironically, Wright bests his father but reenacts an unsavory memory of him in the process.

At this point, aspects of the afflicting, and mostly female, interior world of *Black Boy* assert themselves—his mother devises a punishment that is as devastating psychologically as the first punishment was physically—but, as the chapter continues, the father remains the focus of Wright's youthful wrath. After the father leaves his wife and children to fend for themselves, Wright's persona soon remarks, "As the days slid past the image of my father became associated with my pangs of hunger, and whenever I felt hunger I thought of him with deep biological bitterness." While the immediate source of this bitterness is a grievous circumstance in the present, it is fed by hidden, less immediate energies. Modally, the image of the father being, while in Memphis, a pitifully inadequate provider is but a link in a chain of highly charged figurations that begins with the chicken-killing and ends with the sorrowful sight of him "standing alone upon the red clay of a Mississippi plantation, a sharecropper, clad in ragged overalls, holding a muddy hoe in his gnarled, veined hands." Collectively, the images present Wright's youthful impressions of immobility, hunger, and death. As his father appears in his memory's eye, with hoe in hand like some diminished king still grasping his impotent scepter, the Wright in *Black Boy* recoils from the death-in-life signaled by the red clay soil, much as Du Bois's and Johnson's narrators did before him, and seeks a realm characterized at least in its nearest reaches by flight, sustenance, and survival. Speaking in retrospect, a quarter-century after his first Memphis years, Wright's persona puts the matter this way:

> As a creature of the earth, he [his father] endured, hearty, whole, seemingly indestructible, with no regrets and no hope. He asked easy, drawling questions about me, his other son, his wife, and he laughed, amused, when I informed him of their destinies. I forgave him and pitied him as my eyes looked past him to the

unpainted wooden shack. From far beyond the horizons that bound this bleak plantation there had come to me through my living the knowledge that my father was a black peasant who had gone to the city seeking life, but who had failed in the city; a black peasant whose life had been hopelessly snarled in the city, and who had at last fled the city—the same city which had lifted me in its burning arms and borne me toward alien and undreamed-of-shores of knowing.

With these unrelenting words, Wright's persona does not so much slay his father as bury him alive. The jangling present that they once shared with such great discomfort is swiftly dismantled: for the father, the present is "a crude and raw past" that imprisons him; for the son, it is a vibrant future of living and knowing that sets him free. Just as they no longer share the same pulse of time, it is clear that they also no longer inhabit the same space, the same point of departure. The race has been run, and the plantation-bounding horizons that entomb the beaten man do not touch, let alone encompass or intersect, the "area of living" to which the victor has ascended. With the literal and figurative geography of *Black Boy* clarified in this way, the narrative's anti-pastoral strain—rooted as it is in similar motifs in antedating narratives—is finally unveiled and writ large. Furthermore, the city, a new and far more hopeful social structure erected upon what had been the site of departure for father and son alike, evolves and assumes an aggressive posture in the narrative's machinery, in triangular competition with the oppressing domestic interior and the ambiguous but unsnaring out-of-doors. Once the particular attractions of urban life for a truly questing figure are thus established, Wright's persona's flight to larger, grander, and hopefully more promising urban situations (such as Chicago) seems not just likely, but inevitable. (In real life, as we say, Wright's flight to Chicago, then to New York, and then to Paris was just as determined and heroic; and it is interesting to note, given the associations just discussed, that he did not live "upon the land" again until he expatriated to France.)

The second catalog appears fairly early in chapter 2 of *Black Boy*. As suggested in the catalog's opening phrase—"The days and hours began to speak now with a clearer tongue"—this catalog is meant to represent a later stage along the path to literacy, beyond that in which events "spoke with a cryptic tongue." Nevertheless, many of the entries, especially at the beginning of the catalog, record the wonders and pleasures young Richard continues to discover outdoors. In that way they are virtually interchangeable with similar items in the first catalog:

There was the breathlessly anxious fun of chasing and catching
flitting fireflies on drowsy summer nights.

There was the drenching hospitality in the pervading swell of
sweet magnolias.

There was the aura of limitless freedom distilled from the
rolling sweep of tall green grass swaying and glinting in the wind
and sun.

There was the feeling of impersonal plenty when I saw a boll
of cotton whose cup had spilt over and straggled its white fleece
toward the earth.

With the eighth entry, however, where Wright describes "the drugged, sleepy
feeling that came from sipping glasses of milk," the catalog begins to focus
loosely but distinctly upon signs of food and sustenance that occasionally
assume manna-like qualities:

There was the slow, fresh, saliva-stimulating smell of cooking
cotton seeds.

There was the puckery taste that almost made me cry when I
ate my first half-ripe persimmon.

There was the greedy joy in the tangy taste of wild hickory
nuts.

There was the dry hot summer morning when I scratched my
bare arms on briers while picking blackberries and came home
with my fingers and lips stained black with sweet berry juice.

There was the relish of eating my first fried fish sandwich,
nibbling at it slowly and hoping that I would never eat it up.

There was the all-night ache in my stomach after I had climbed
a neighbor's tree and eaten stolen, unripe peaches.

After leaving Memphis with his mother, young Richard finally got something to eat while living briefly with his Granny and Grandpa Wilson in
Jackson. For this reason it is quite appropriate to say that the signs cata-
loged above not only represent a large portion of what was "enchanting"
about the post-Memphis world of Granny's house (he will reverse his opinion about her domain as the narrative progresses), but also respond to the
signs of that aspect of his American hunger imposed by his father's many
failures. Physical hunger in the past is not the only catalyst for these images
of sustenance; while in the Wilson home, amid the plenty and pleasure of
nature's full fare, Wright learns of another hunger when Ella, the school-

teacher boarding with the family, whispers to him, after much cajoling, the story of Bluebeard and His Seven Wives.

As Ella relates the tale, young Richard is transported to another world— a world that is not charted by the vital geometry of food or its absence:

> She whispered to me the story . . . and I ceased to see the porch, the sunshine, her face, everything. As her words fell upon my new ears, I endowed them with a reality that welled up from somewhere within me. . . . The tale made the world around me be, throb, live. As she spoke, reality changed, the look of things altered, and the world became peopled with magical presences. My sense of life deepened and the feel of things was different, somehow. . . . My imagination blazed. . . . When she was about to finish, when my interest was keenest, when I was lost to the world around me, Granny stepped briskly onto the porch.

Students of Afro-American narratives in general and of Frederick Douglass's 1845 *Narrative* in particular need not wonder about what Wright is experiencing, or about what comes next. At the heart of the episode is the ancient call of literacy's possibilities, occasioned by the narrator's first fleeting glimpse of the vibrant word—and the equally ancient response of admonition or suppression, made by a representative of the most immediate oppressing social structure. When Granny Wilson abruptly appears upon the scene, shouting that Ella is an "evil gal," that Richard is "going to burn in hell," and that what Ella and Richard are doing is "the Devil's work," she becomes for us (albeit within the confines of a black world) the latest manifestation of the archetypal oppressor initiated in Afro-American letters by Frederick Douglass's Mr. Auld. Indeed, this bond between Granny Wilson and Mr. Auld, which vilifies her far more than any oath we can imagine, is reinforced, perhaps unwittingly or subconsciously, by Wright's curious aside on how "white" Granny looked when she was angry: "My grandmother was as nearly white as a Negro can get without being white, which means that she was white. The sagging flesh of her face quivered; her eyes, large, dark, deep-set, wide apart, glared at me. Her lips narrowed to a line. Her high forehead wrinkled. When she was angry her eyelids drooped halfway down over her pupils, giving her a baleful aspect." More to the point, however, is the fact that Granny Wilson, like Mr. Auld before her in the tradition, interrupts and effectively bans as evil a fundamental activity in the narrator's quest for literacy. The "hunger" her behavior prompts in Richard is, in his telling of it, of a piece with the "torment" plaguing Douglass at a comparable point in his career.

The word of caution suggested above probably should be made more explicit: in reading *Black Boy* and observing its indebtednesses to tropes established by the slave narratives, we must remind ourselves that what places *Black Boy* in the tradition is not Wright's "enslavement" (which, despite its horrors, is finally not of the same weight and scale as, say, Douglass's), but the debt-laden rhetoric he brings to the task of describing it. With this in mind, we may thrill at Wright's concluding remarks about the Bluebeard episode, akin as they are to Douglass's declaration of his discovery of "the pathway from slavery to freedom"; yet at the same time we can recognize and measure them as part and parcel of a rhetorical strategy:

> Not to know the end of the tale filled me with a sense of emptiness, loss. I hungered for the sharp, frightening, breath-taking, almost painful excitement that the story had given me, and I vowed that as soon as I was old enough I would buy all the novels there were and read them to feed that thirst for violence that was in me, for intrigue, for plotting, for secrecy, for bloody murders. So profoundly responsive a chord had the tale struck me that the threats of my mother and grandmother had no effect whatsoever. They read my insistence as mere obstinacy, as foolishness, something that would quickly pass; and they had no notion how desperately serious the tale had made me. They could not have known that Ella's whispered story of deception and murder had been the first experience in my life that had elicited from me a total emotional response. No words or punishment could have possibly made me doubt. I had tasted what to me was life, and I would have more of it, somehow, someway . . . I burned to learn to read novels and I tortured my mother into telling me the meaning of every strange word I saw, not because the word itself had any value, but because it was the gateway to a forbidden and enchanting land.

As the chapter continues, young Richard learns the full consequences of hungering after words, and of employing them without knowing all that they might mean or imply. I refer here, of course, to the bathing scene, wherein Richard reminds Granny to be sure to kiss his behind after she has toweled it off—a scene that is as darkly hilarious as those in the slave narratives, where an unknowing slave effectively asks his master to do the same and is beaten within an inch of his life. One such consequence is that Ella is blamed and forced to move, and that an avenue to reading and knowing—to sustenance of a particular sort—is thereby closed to Richard. The second catalog of signs to be read (and in that sense savored) is thus a response to multiple kinds of hunger; images of tasting and eating are but tropes for the pleasures of reading newly found, minute particulars. Despite all the admonitions the narrator hears or discovers regarding how "forbidden and enchanting" lands often bear strange fruit, the episode of Ella and Granny concludes on a hopeful note, because the catalog of signs at its end posits a familiar but nonetheless exhilarating correlation between manna and the word.

The third catalog also appears in chapter 2 of *Black Boy,* and is in some ways the most interesting of the three. The events leading up to the catalog depict a perennial concern—Wright's hunger as a boy, especially during those times when he, his mother, and his brother are not living with kin— and also a more immediate crisis, the death of his dog, Betsy. As often happens in *Black Boy,* these two dilemmas are bound as one. A week earlier, young Richard had been unable to bring himself to sell Betsy for money for food; with the dog's death, that possibility is irrevocably closed to him. The episode is important in the narrative because Wright's persona learns at least two lessons from it. The obvious one is expressed quite simply and directly by his mother's sole remark, " 'You could have had a dollar. But you can't eat a dead dog, can you?' " The less obvious (but perhaps more important) lesson is that stubbornness expressed outwardly and somewhat ingeniously by an insistence upon the literal meaning of words is still stubbornness. Something links the Betsy episode with the earlier events in which young Richard hangs a kitten, supposedly at his father's behest. In each instance the persona attempts to assert a sense of pride and self-worth by insisting upon the literal meaning of words: He told me to kill the kitten, didn't he? The ninety-seven cents the white woman offered me for Betsy wasn't a dollar, was it? But those attempts always lead to little more than the animal's death and the evocation of his mother's wrath. Clearly, in each case the persona has some elementary idea of how to manipulate words and meaning, but no idea of how to control the contextualizing event.

Here the narrative machinery of *Black Boy* oils itself and, in a sense, exposes itself, allowing us in turn to both construct and partially deconstruct the narrative as a whole. What is exposed, I believe, is the feigned innocence that must lie behind any scheme of vindictive literalness, no matter how simple or spontaneous. If the persona is capable of assuming such a posture, then our belief in his actual innocence and his subsequent inability to pursue certain kinds of verbal strategies is undercut. The obvious counterargument is that the innocence feigned in the kitten and Betsy episodes does not compromise the person's character—that, indeed, it displays his character by portraying his willingness, even as a youth, to fight a losing battle for a good if personal cause. But that leaves us where we began. The fact remains that *Black Boy* requires its readers to admire Wright's persona's remarkable and unassailable innocence in certain major episodes, and to condone his exploitation of that innocence in others. This, I think, is a poorly tailored seam, if not precisely a flaw, in *Black Boy*'s narrative strategy.

What is oiled is that part of the machinery which presents the evolution of Wright's persona's quest for authorial control. As I have suggested before—and as the 1845 Douglass *Narrative* instructs—authorial control of a personal history is achieved when the author's persona not only becomes the definitive historian (or fictionizer) of his past, but also finds a voice that is articulate enough to at least modulate, if not absolutely control, the pressing forces of a hostile environment. In *Black Boy* the kitten and Betsy episodes, marked as they are by the persona's youthful attempts to modulate or control person and event through language, represent the point of departure for whatever measure of authorial control the persona will achieve in his quest for literacy and freedom. In this way the third catalog of the narrative assumes a special weight and meaning: after the failures and rebuffs resulting from his inability to sell Betsy upon his own terms (monetary, but also verbal), young Richard is prompted quite naturally to speculate on what he may control—and on what terms.

> If I pulled a hair from a horse's tail and sealed it in a jar of my own urine, the hair would turn overnight into a snake.
>
> If I passed a Catholic sister or mother dressed in black and smiled and allowed her to see my teeth, I would surely die.
>
> If I walked under a leaning ladder, I would certainly have bad luck.
>
> If I kissed my elbow, I would turn into a girl.
>
> If I heard a voice and no human being was near, then either God or the Devil was trying to talk to me.
>
> Whenever I made urine, I should spit into it for good luck.
>
> If I covered a mirror when a storm was raging, the lightning would not strike me.
>
> If I stepped over a broom that was lying on the floor, I would have bad luck.
>
> If I walked in my sleep, then God was trying to lead me somewhere to do a good deed for Him.

While entries such as these unquestionably present the narrator initiating or embodying certain causes for certain effects, we must be aware (as Wright was undeniably aware) of the narrow limits of a world in which such acts have great meaning. On one hand, the catalog champions sign-reading of a fundamental sort, and that is an important step up the ladder to literacy for the sign-reader. On the other, the catalog can be seen as a mere listing of folk beliefs or events into which the narrator projects his own hypothetical participation—the point being that opportunities for personal modulation or control of events are nil, because the sequence and *form* of the "folk event" are always prescribed and hence pre-known. The fact that immersion in the enactment (or reenactment) of a "folk event" creates only an illusion of authorial control gives us pause in reading this catalog; but even more germane is the argument which Wright sustains in his own way, in "Blueprint for Negro Writing," that literacy *vis-à-vis* superstition rarely has any bearing on literacy *vis-à-vis* the word. With all this in mind, the purpose and place of the third catalog in *Black Boy*'s narrative strategy becomes ringingly clear, especially when we remind ourselves of Wright's other famous dictum in "Blueprint" that what is national (or "folk") in our lives must first be embraced in order to be transcended. The catalog marks that point on the path to literacy at which Wright's persona becomes proficient in the initiation and dispensation of "tribal" interpretations of the environment, and at which the persona may quite understandably rationalize such a proficiency by arguing, "Because I had no power to make things happen outside of me in the objective world, I made things happen within. . . ." But of course this way-station on the path is far more a point of departure than a destination: once the persona embraces and knows the signs and tongue of his "folk" world, he can only relinquish the quest and be defined by that world or, especially if he aspires to literacy *vis-à-vis* the word, courageously travel on. That Wright's persona will indeed travel on is made clear by two points on which the chapter ends. First, he returns to school; second, he sights for the very first time an airplane soaring in the sky. True to his limited experiences, and perhaps to the "reading" level documented by the catalog, the narrator's response is, "It's a bird . . . I see it." At that point— a point which affects much of the Afro-American canon to come—a man lifts our hero up upon his shoulder and solemnly enlightens him by saying, " 'Boy, remember this, . . . you're seeing man fly.' "

The three catalogs in the opening chapters of *Black Boy* are three systems of signs to be read en route to literacy. Once he reads them, young Richard knows something of the delight and terror, range and limitation, and literacy and illiteracy of the world into which he is born. Once that world is read and in that sense embraced, he is not just prepared but fated for the fresh space to be gained by additional knowing and seeing. All this is substantiated and reinforced in a wonderful way by the already discussed passage in the very next chapter, where Wright re-creates and glosses a typical conversation conducted by his boyhood gang. The entire conversation is a fourth catalog in the narrative in which every entry is, before it is glossed, a sign of the oppressing culture that necessarily must be read, and in that sense controlled to some degree, by anyone aspiring to be a literate survivor. In the first catalog Wright's persona is assaulted by the signs; in the second the assault continues, but is defused somewhat by the countering idea that signs may be read as well as felt; in the third the persona attempts to control the signs by entering them, but, since they are of a particular tribal sort, acts of entry are not full and complete acts of reading and control. In what I am calling the fourth catalog, each gloss is the kind of articulate response to a cultural sign that the persona has been working toward all along (by gathering a word hoard, finding a voice, discovering a perspective, seeing, feeling). The glory of Wright's construction is that the catalogs depict a progression not only from muteness to voice, and from stasis before assault to mobility found in response to assault, but also from "formless forms" bereft of counterpoint to highly formal ones rich with counterpoint—especially of an Afro-American persuasion. In the third catalog the "If/then" formula of the inherited and essentially static folk beliefs or events establishes the idea of counterpoint as an aspect of literacy in a fundamental, if not entirely invigorating, way; but it is in the fourth catalog, where response becomes a matter of personal articulation, that counterpoint is not simply enacted formulaically but sung. Here we may finally take the next step beyond Ralph Ellison's now classic definition of Richard Wright's blues (that, like any covering cherub, has guided us but inhibited us for so long) and locate that blues in a discrete counterpointing linguistic structure within the narrative. In the fourth catalog, each unit of exchange between an adolescent's wail or bark of misery bound to humor, and a mature voice's *reading* of the signs contained therein, is a blues stanza rendered improvisationally in literary terms; the articulate response is, of course, the requisite coda to the whole unit. The achievement of these improvised blues stanzas, at a time when most Afro-American writers (including Langston Hughes) were barely doing more than "transcribing" the blues onto the printed page, is remarkable in itself. But even more extraordinary is the fact that Wright, in this one rare, rhythmic moment in his art, could make those stanzas say so much. The key, I think, lies in the fact that each stanza is initiated in the past (the youthful wails, barks, growls, and riffs) and completed in the present (the mature voice's gloss). In this exaggerated way, Wright reminds us that reading—the completion of the stanza, as it were—depends on seeing and knowing and gaining perspective, and that art—once again, the completion of the stanza—is equally dependent upon the discovery of a mature voice. If *Black Boy* were an immersion narrative, it could end right here, and glory in the fact that indigenous art forms so vigorously and yet so partially sung in our hero's youth finally have been completed. But of course *Black Boy* is not an immersion narrative, but one of ascent. The great satisfaction which Wright's persona receives from singing the blues with skill is that, in direct contradiction to one famous blues line, he *can* get out of "them blues" *alive*.

In the preceding sections of this [essay] . . . I have mentioned some of the tropes and conventions found originally in the slave narratives and sustained in *Black Boy*. This section—which could be entitled "Reading, Writing, and Ascent"—focuses on another strain of indebtedness in the narrative, one that is rooted far more in turn-of-the-century literature than in what came before. The strain to which I refer links *Black Boy* to antedating texts such as Sutton Elbert Grigg's *Imperium in Imperio,* Du Bois's *The Souls of Black Folk*, and Johnson's *The Autobiography of an Ex-Coloured Man,* and establishes *Black Boy* as an antedating text for many recent narratives, including Ellison's *Invisible Man* and Toni Morrison's *The Bluest Eye*. What all these narratives share (or rather, participate in) is a primary scene in Afro-American letters: the schoolroom episode, which is often accompanied by its chief variant, the graduation episode. The significance of this scene has less to do with the extraordinary frequency of its appearance or even with its "logical" place in a prose literature dominated by autobiographical and bildungsroman impulses, and more to do with how it characterizes and shapes—in literary terms—a discernible period in Afro-American literary history. Schoolroom and graduation episodes in Afro-American literature begin to assume their proper stature when we recall not only the laws and race rituals that enforced a people's illiteracy (*vis-à-vis* the written word) but also the body of literature, including most obviously the slave narratives, that expresses again and again the quest for freedom *and* literacy achieved regardless of the odds, regardless of the lack of sanctioned opportunities such as school attendance. When familiar images in the early narrative literature, such as that of a Frederick Douglass or a William Wells Brown having to dupe white urchins in order to learn the rudiments of reading and ciphering, give way to fresh if not altogether joyous expressions of black youths in one-room schoolhouses, high schools, institutes, colleges, and even universities, then we may say truly that a primary configuration in the tradition is being systematically revoiced, and that these expressions are almost singlehandedly creating a new contour in the tradition's history. To place *The Souls of Black Folk* or *Black Boy* in this contour, for example, is to say more about either text (especially about their relations to one another) than can be said when they are relegated to categories largely imposed by other disciplines, such as "literature of accommodation" and "literature of protest."

One point to be made regarding Richard Wright's participation in these activities is that his greatest novel, *Native Son*, is totally bereft of any schoolroom or graduation episode—unless one wishes (somewhat perversely) to assign those properties to the cell or courtroom scenes, or to Bigger's "tutorials" with Attorney Max. In contrast, *Black Boy*'s middle chapters are one sustained schoolroom episode; furthermore, the graduation episode that completes chapter 8 is unquestionably a major event in the narrative, and perhaps *the* event young Richard seeks when he earlier confides that he is "waiting for some event, some word, some act, some circumstance to furnish the impetus" for his flight from what he calls elsewhere "that southern swamp of despair and violence." The resulting contrast between the two volumes should not be viewed in any qualitative way—for example, the absence of the schoolroom scene from *Native Son* does not categorically make it a superior or inferior work of literature. But it should be examined, nevertheless, if for no other reason than to receive its suggestion of the full reach of the Afro-American landscape charted by Wright's oeuvre. Once this reach or territory is explored (and the space between Bigger's world and Wright's persona's world is indeed of continental proportions), the glories and failures of Wright's transtextual artistic vision becomes newly manifest. The glory is primarily and fundamentally the territory itself, a space full of nightmare and misery that is finally bounded only by the seemingly limitless horizons of living and knowing. The failure is essentially that Wright's antipodal construction of the landscape unwittingly positions his supreme fiction of himself—not just as a man or even as an articulate survivor, but as an artist—*within* an antipode, and hence removes it from whatever mediating postures might be available to him. Much has already been said about this particular failure or dilemma; Ralph Ellison and George Kent explore this issue in their own way when they remark respectively that "Wright could imagine Bigger, but Bigger could not possibly imagine Richard Wright," and that Wright's "deepest consciousness is that of the exaggerated Westerner." My interest here, however, lies less with investigating Wright's resulting posture as an artist and more with exploring the way stations and stretches of road that constitute the pathway to whatever posture Wright's persona in *Black Boy* achieves. And it seems clear that the persona's school experiences provide a proper place to begin.

Since the world of *Black Boy* is so relentlessly hostile, we should not be surprised to discover that most of young Richard's learning situations are pockets of fear and misery. Certain features of the schoolroom scene, such as the persona's first efforts to acquire a (written and spoken) voice, are sustained here and there, providing a few bright moments. However, when these features occur, they are usually contextualized in the narrative as the spoils of bitter battles; their piercing light may be attributed as much to the flash of weapons as to the lamp of learning. Wright's persona is so embattled in his school experiences partly because, until he enters the Jim Hill School at the age of twelve, most of his schooling occurs at home or in classrooms that are formidable extensions of that horrific and inhibiting domestic world. When Ella (who is, we recall, a schoolteacher) clandestinely tells young Wright the spirited tale of Bluebeard, transporting him to new worlds beyond whatever he had previously dreamt and felt, the porch where they sit becomes momentarily a schoolroom complete with globe, primer, and, most important, a teacher sensitive to a child's hunger for knowledge. But that porch is first and foremost—as well as finally—Granny Wilson's porch, and Granny, with her particular ideas about the extraordinary reach of the Devil's hand, seems always just beyond the doorway, ready to pounce upon any "mischief" invading her domain. Another construction of this situation is offered when Aunt Addie returns from the Seventh-Day Adventist Religious School in Huntsville to open her own church school. Unfortunately, young Richard has no choice but to matriculate there. From the start, it is clear that things couldn't be worse if the class were taught by Granny Wilson herself: Richard and Addie square off right away, and when the battle of wills leads to a pitched free-for-all, replete with biting and kicking, in which Richard brandishes a kitchen knife in much the same fashion that he will later grab a razor blade in each fist to ward off his Uncle Tom, we cannot possibly be surprised to learn that Addie stopped calling on Richard in class, and that "Consequently [he] stopped studying."

Not all of Richard's "home learning" in *Black Boy* is this violent or unfulfilled. The rare moments of learning from kin are provided by his mother, usually during those brief interludes when they are living neither with his father nor with Granny Wilson—the prime representatives of the narrative's oppressing exterior and interior spaces. Quite typically, given Wright's drive to achieve literacy *vis-à-vis* the word, the best example of his mother in a teaching role involves diction—the choice of certain words for certain conditions and circumstances. And, quite appropriately, given the violent world of the narrative, the words he learns to use are "whip" and "beat" and, less directly, "boy" and "man":

> When word circulated among the black people of the neighbor-hood that a "black" boy had been severely beaten by a "white" man, I felt that the "white" man had had a right to beat the "black" boy, for I naively assumed that the "white" man must have been the "black" boy's father. And did not all fathers, like my father, have the right to beat their children?
>     . . . But when my mother told me that the "white" man was not the father of the "black" boy, was no kin to him at all, I was puzzled.
>     "Then why did the 'white' man whip the 'black' boy?" I asked my mother.
>     "The 'white' man did not *whip* the 'black' boy," my mother told me. "He *beat* the 'black' boy."
>     "But why?"
>     "You're too young to understand."

To be sure, young Richard does not understand completely—but when does one ever pick up a grain of truth, in or out of school, and understand it completely upon first hearing? Sad as it may be, it is through exchanges such as this one that young Richard is taught about his environment, his place in it, and about *how* words mean as well as *what* they mean. Although his mother is unquestionably a part of the domestic structure afflicting and oppressing him, she is also, possibly because she is his mother, the best teacher his circumstances afford him: she explains words, she tells him stories, she helps him learn how to read. For this reason—and perhaps, too, because his semi-invalid mother often appears to be as ensnared by the household as he is—young Richard cares for her, is not violent with her, and grieves for her in his own stolid way during her many illnesses. Still, there is an underlying tension between Richard's deep feeling for his mother and his compulsion—based not on whim or fancy, but on a rather accurate assessment of his circumstances—to take his neophyte stories and sketches outside the home, to show them to others including, in the first instance, an incredulous neighbor woman who most certainly turns out not to be the surrogate mother, aunt, or grandmother that Richard is obviously searching for. The abiding presence of this dilemma offers one more reason why Richard must leave the South—and take his mother with him. While flight may not allow mother and son to recapture those special moments when the home was a site of learning, it will at least extract them from Granny's lair and allow them to begin again.

Significant schooling outside the home environment in *Black Boy* begins only when young Richard enters the Jim Hill Public School. The only earlier public school experience reported in the narrative occurs in Memphis, shortly after his father "disappears." Richard's brief report serves mainly to depict the point of departure for his ascent, first and most immediately in his school world and then in the larger circumferences of his life beyond the South:

> I began school at Howard Institute at a later age than was usual; my mother had not been able to buy me the necessary clothes to make me presentable. The boys of the neighborhood took me to school the first day and when I reached the edge of the school grounds I became terrified, wanted to return home, wanted to put it off. But the boys simply took my hand and pulled me inside the building. I was frightened speechless and the other children had to identify me, tell the teacher my name and address. I sat listening to pupils recite, knowing and understanding what was being said and done, but utterly incapable of opening my mouth when called upon. The students around me seemed so sure of themselves that I despaired of ever being able to conduct myself as they did.

In this way, in a context removed from the domestic interior, Wright's persona initiates a motif that we know from the slave narratives: the ascent to find a voice which can, among other things, guide conduct and name itself. But the ascent is not immediately forthcoming; all of the episodes described above involving Granny Wilson and Aunt Addie—episodes marking young Richard's forced return to the domestic interior—intercede between his all-too-few days at Howard Institute and his three years at the Jim Hill School. When he finally reenters the school world, his longing to begin the ascent has become an unfathomable energy, and his hunger for learning and for exploring the realm beyond Granny Wilson's doorstep is even more acute than his perpetual desire for food. Indeed, as he tells of his first days at Jim Hill School and of his willingness to go without his usual miserable fare at home in order to see "a world leap to life," he remarks, "To starve in order to learn about my environment was irrational, but so were my hungers."

Although this may suggest that the school world of *Black Boy* is, in comparison to the narrative's other structural spaces, a kind of paradise, such is hardly the case. In fact, the school world is truly the second circle of Wright's southern hell, just as the oppressing domestic interior is the first circle, and the white world of the narrative, to which young Richard will be introduced shortly, is the third. The school world is not as physically violent as the domestic interior, but it has its own array of punishments and afflictions which display themselves fully in both of the signal episodes in which Wright's persona takes a symbolic step toward freedom and literacy.

In the first episode, young Richard writes a short story ("The Voodoo of Hell's Half-Acre") which the mature Wright describes in retrospect as being "crudely atmospheric, emotional, intuitively psychological." The youth instinctively shows it to someone outside the hostile environments of home and school, the editor of the local Negro newspaper. The happy result is that the story is printed—young Richard has indeed come far from that day when he shared his first sketch with a neighbor. But any joy or inspiration that he experiences is quickly stifled by what he calls elsewhere "the tribe in which [I] lived and of which [I was] a part." After family, schoolmates, and teachers pummel him with their questions and condemnations, he is left thoroughly alone and abused—"I felt that I had committed a crime"—but charged all the more with the self-generated energy needed to continue his ascent. It is quite significant that the episode ends with Wright's persona's first expression of the North as a destination and a symbolic space, and that his emerging fantasy of what he will do there involves acts of literacy on a grand scale: "I dreamed of going north and writing books, novels. The North symbolized to me all that I had not felt and seen; it had no relation whatever to what actually existed. Yet, by imagining a place where everything was possible, I kept hope alive in me." These imaginings keep young Richard valiantly on the move for many years, but their immediate and much-needed effect is to offer him enough resilience to endure another year of tribal rigors at home and at school.

During the next year (and chapter) of the narrative, young Richard takes his second symbolic step toward freedom and literacy while at Jim Hill School, and that step is described in the graduation episode. While the first step involving his storywriting may be said to be an indebted and inverted rendering of the Ex-Coloured Man's reception as a youthful artist within his community, the graduation episode is a comparably indebted and inverted expression of many prior moments in the literature, but especially perhaps of that day in 1841 when Frederick Douglass rose to the podium and found his voice in Nantucket. In each of Wright's episodes, his inversion of antecedent expressions is not total—"The Voodoo of Hell's Half-Acre" is probably no less flawed than the Ex-Coloured Man's youthful interpretations of romantic melodies, and Wright's persona's graduation speech is certainly no worse than Bernard Belgrave's in *Imperium in Imperio* or Shiny's in *The Autobiography*. But that is not the point. It is rather that Wright seems intent upon revising certain abiding expressions within the literary tradition of communal succor and of potential immersion in community, in order to place *Black Boy* within the ranks of the narrative of ascent. Put another way, his effort is to create a persona who experiences major moments of literacy, personal freedom, and personal growth while in a kind of bondage, and yet who maintains in a very clear-headed way his vision of a higher literacy and a better world.

As one might expect, the heart of the graduation episode is not the delivery of speech or its reception—that would suggest that communal bonds between speaker and audience are possible, and that the persona is satisfied with the stage of literacy he has achieved. Rather, the episode focuses on the series of tempestuous events that precede the "great day." Of these, none is more important than young Richard's conversation with the principal of the Jim Hill School. The scene that ensues should be familiar to students of Afro-American literature, because the principal is clearly an intermediate manifestation of a character type most visibly inaugurated by Jean Toomer in *Cane*'s figure of Hanley, and most formidably completed (for the moment) by Ralph Ellison in *Invisible Man*'s Bledsoe. In that scene young Richard is forced to choose between his principal and his principle: whether to accept and read a speech "ghost written" by a "bought" man, or to go ahead with a speech written by himself, on his own, and probably in the same tattered but secretly dear notebook that produced "The Voodoo of Hell's Half-Acre." He chooses the latter course, and there ensues a predictable response amongst the tribe—from the principal on down to his schoolmates and, at the level of his home life, his worn-out and retired kinsman, Uncle Tom. After the barrage of assaults and cajolings, including bribes, Richard doggedly pursues his righteous course and describes the resulting event in this way:

> On the night of graduation I was nervous and tense; I rose and faced the audience and my speech rolled out. When my voice stopped there was some applause. I did not care if they liked it or not; I was through. Immediately, even before I left the platform, I tried to shut all memory of the event from me. A few of my classmates managed to shake my hand as I pushed toward the door, seeking the street. Somebody invited me to a party and I did not accept. I did not want to see any of them again. I

walked home, saying to myself: The hell with it! With almost
seventeen years of baffled living behind me, I faced the world in
1925.

Several aspects of this statement interest me greatly, and I would like to
offer two additional quotations from other sources by way of beginning to
remark upon them. The first is quite recognizably from the 1845 Douglass
*Narrative:*

> But, while attending an anti-slavery convention at Nantucket, on
> the 11th of August, 1841, I felt strongly moved to speak. . . . It
> was a severe cross, and I took it up reluctantly. The truth was, I
> felt myself a slave, and the idea of speaking to white people
> weighed me down. I spoke but a few moments, when I felt a
> degree of freedom, and said what I desired with considerable
> ease. From that time until now, I have been engaged in pleading
> the cause of my brethren—with what success, and with what
> devotion, I leave those acquainted with my labors to decide.

The second quotation, as much a part of the tradition as the first, is from
Langston Hughes's "The Negro Writer and the Racial Mountain," published in *The Nation* in 1926, within a year after Wright's persona made his
commencement speech at the Jim Hill School:

> We younger Negro artists who create now intend to express our
> individual dark-skinned selves without fear or shame. If white
> people are pleased we are glad. If they are not, it doesn't mat-
> ter. . . . If colored people are pleased we are glad. If they are not,
> their displeasure doesn't matter either. We build our temples for
> tomorrow, strong as we know how, and we stand on top of the
> mountain, free within ourselves.

By citing these very different passages, I want to suggest that the voice
Wright's persona assumes—the voice found and honed presumably through
experiences such as those surrounding and including the graduation—is
very much in the Afro-American heroic grain. The hard-won freedom that
Wright's persona acquires from the ordeal of the entire valedictory event is,
at root, much the same as the "degree of freedom" Douglass's voice experiences while addressing the throng. Furthermore, while Wright's persona
has neither reached the top of his idea of the "racial mountain" nor designed the temple to be situated in that space (that "Blueprint" will
come twelve years later), he clearly shares Hughes's conviction that one
must ascend beyond the "low-ground" of oppressive—interracial and

intraracial—social structures to gain one's voice on one's own terms and, in that sense, be free. Like Du Bois before them, Wright and Hughes both seek the heights of a "Pisgah" soaring above the "dull . . . hideousness" of a structural topography that is racially both black and white.

What is new about Wright's rendering of this familiar event is not the voice achieved, but the positioning of the event in the narrative itself. Unlike Douglass, Wright is not trying to end his narrative; instead, he is attempting to move his persona from one world of the narrative to another. He does not want to suggest (as Douglass does) that the achievement of voice may yield even a fleeting sense of personal ease and of community, for that would disruptively suggest that his persona has found a measure of comfort and stability in the very world he is about to leave. And so Wright's persona moves on with his stride unbroken—handshakes are barely acknowledged, invitations to parties are cast aside—and with only one small anchor fixing the occasion in official time: he mentions the year, and it is 1925. One notes this latter point partly because, in accord with the Du Boisian model in *The Souls,* few dates are recorded in *Black Boy,* and partly because 1925 is such a watershed year in Afro-American literature. What this suggests about the graduation episode in *Black Boy* is that Wright is concerned not only about positioning the event in the narrative itself, but also about placing the event in Afro-American literary history. At the very time when the New Negro "renaissance" was under full sway in Harlem (*The New Negro,* edited by Alain Locke, made the pages of *Survey Graphic* in 1925) and, tangentially, in places such as Washington, D.C. (let us not forget Georgia Douglas Johnson, Jean Toomer, Sterling Brown, and Edward "Duke" Ellington), Richard Wright was belatedly but triumphantly graduating from the Jim Hill School and, according to the exquisite fiction of his personal history, thinking much the same thoughts that a bona fide renaissance hero (Langston Hughes) would publish within a year.

Wright gets the maximum mileage out of the graduation episode, and he does so in accord with his particular vision of how he must revise and at the same time honor tradition in order to assume a place within it. His revision of Douglass's model episode allows his persona to travel on, having achieved a voice and vision comparable to Douglass's; and with his revision of Afro-American literary history *vis-à-vis* 1925 he makes a place for himself within that history well before any of his major texts were written—let alone, saw print. With these ingenious undertakings completed, it is hard to believe that *Black Boy* has not run its course—although, in a very real sense, it has only just begun.

Given all of the affinities we have discovered between a modern text like *Black Boy* and a slave narrative like Frederick Douglass's 1845 *Narrative*, we must ask whether Wright merely duplicates narrative strategies inaugurated by the slave narratives, or whether he employs those strategies as a foundation for his own expressions of assault and ascent. This fascinating question liberates us from the need to examine further such obvious narrative features as the quest for freedom and literacy and the requisite mystification of the North, and directs us toward what turn out to be *Black Boy*'s most controversial passages. By and large, these are the passages in which Wright's persona aggressively demystifies the "black world" of the narrative or rejects what is tribal in his life. While this feature is unquestionably anticipated by certain slave narratives (recall here Frederick Douglass's distant and nearly cold-blooded attitude toward his fellow slaves in his opening chapters), Wright's revoicing of the motif is so strident and sustained that we may say that he is striving to create something new.

The slave narratives contain countless acts of rejection of the "black world" as it is configured by life in the slave quarters and among kin. However, these acts are nearly always presented by the narrators as difficult compromises that the fleeing slave must make, and as additional expressions of slavery's assault upon the slave family and community. When it is made clear, for example, that neither Henry Bibb or William Wells Brown can successfully escape to freedom while bringing loved ones in tow, we are encouraged to grieve for their lot and to admire the courage and determination that prompt them to cut even the most tender bonds, leaping for what may be only an idea of a better life. Indeed, the Bibb and Brown narratives are so successful in this regard that when Bibb's wife resignedly becomes her master's favored concubine (complete with her own cottage in the clearing) and when Brown's mother is ruthlessly sold downriver, we hardly blame Bibb or Brown for being far away and free; instead, we grieve all the more for their continuing hardship.

While Wright's persona in *Black Boy* does what he can (as soon as he can) to have his mother accompany him in his northward ascent, the narrative's energies and strategies are not directed toward suggesting that this is a great triumph by black humanity over oppressive social forces, or that the flight north involves any sort of conflict or compromise occasioned by tribal feelings. On the contrary, *Black Boy* picks up where Douglass's 1845 *Narrative* leaves off, rationalizing the flight to freedom by portraying the "black world" known to the persona as another phase and form of slavery. Wright uses the new resulting portrait for its own narrative ends. Nowhere in the slave narratives do we find a passage comparable to the following famous one in *Black Boy,* partly because Wright is consciously and aggressively attempting to clear a space for himself in Afro-American letters:

> After I had outlived the shocks of childhood, after the habit of reflection had been born in me, I used to mull over the strange absence of real kindness in Negroes, how unstable was our tenderness, how lacking in genuine passion we were, how void of great hope, how timid our joy, how bare our traditions, how hollow our memories, how lacking we were in those intangible sentiments that bind man to man, and how shallow was even our despair. After I had learned other ways of life I used to brood upon the unconscious irony of those who felt that Negroes led so passional an existence! I saw that what had been taken for our emotional strength was our negative confusions, our flights, our fears, our frenzy under pressure.

The passage goes on for another paragraph and includes language that anticipates everything the persona will soon say about his search for a civilization and not a culture: "Whenever I thought of the essential bleakness of black life in America, I knew that Negroes had never been allowed to catch the full spirit of Western civilization." But by the end of the quoted section, Wright has already made his point and exposed his underlying concerns. Some readers might argue that Wright is attempting to "shock" his way into Afro-American literary history, and, to a degree, they have a point. But the fact of the matter is that Wright's extraordinary assertions have less to do with his opinion of how to arrest the attention of an American reading public than with his abiding struggle to define himself in relation to the most persistent spectres in both his private and his literary imagination: his father, Bigger Thomas, and the "Bigger" in his past.

One notes a strange but distinct and exacting correspondence between the above-quoted passage and that earlier one in which Wright's persona recalls and pities his father's condition as a Mississippi sharecropper twenty-five years after his failure in Memphis. The opening phrases of both are specifically fashioned to distance the persona, in time and achievement, from the black "specimen" he is about to dissect. "After I had outlived the shocks of childhood, after the habit of reflection had been born in me" is but a restatement of "A quarter of a century was to elapse between the time when I saw my father sitting with the strange woman [in Memphis] and the time when I was to see him again, standing alone . . . a sharecropper." In the earlier passage, the persona goes on to describe his father as a "black peasant" (and hence, for Wright, a denizen of America's trough). Given the fact that the persona senses some lingering bonds with his father ("I could see a shadow of my face in his face . . . there was an echo of my voice in his voice"), there is no mistaking why such extraordinary and virulent energies are used to condemn the father to a well-bounded time frame and geography: Wright wants his father out of his life, shelved in the space he has created for him. My suggestion here, prompted in part by the proximity of the passages to one another, is that the new or second passage can be easily read as yet another strident attempt by Wright's persona to condemn and obliterate the haunting image of his father. Every failing with which Negro America is charged is, at base, a failure he has witnessed within his family circle; each phrase employing the word "our"—our tenderness, our joy, our traditions, our memories, and especially our despair, our negative confusions, our flights, our fears, our frenzy—is fundamentally in reference to his relations with his kin, his father in particular. Surely Wright's persona has his family and father as much as his race in mind when he concludes the second half of his remarks: "And when I brooded upon the cultural barrenness of black life, I wondered if clean, positive tenderness, love, honor, loyalty, and the capacity to remember were native with man. I asked myself if these human qualities were not fostered, won, struggled and suffered for, preserved in ritual *from one generation to another*" (italics added). With these words, kin and a culture are summarily dismantled as a price willingly paid so that a once-distant civilization may be envisioned and achieved.

Of course, whenever Wright, even in the creation of his autobiographical narrative, broods upon the cultural barrenness of black life, images of Bigger Thomas soon appear in our minds, and apparently in his as well. I have suggested before that one reason why Wright had to write *Black Boy* was so that he could lay to rest the question of how he escaped becoming a Bigger. While the passage being discussed does not precisely answer that question, it does offer one of Wright's strategies for displacing himself from Bigger's world. The issue of whether life in Negro America is as stunted as Wright's persona proclaims it to be is finally irrelevant, since the passage describes the black world of Wright's oeuvre in general, and of *Native Son* in particular. Indeed, the passage is something of a key to a full and complete understanding of all that Bigger represents: unlike his author (or at least his author's fiction of himself), Bigger never "outlives" the "shocks of childhood." As the cell-block scenes so convincingly report, he never acquires the "habit of reflection." The failures amongst Negroes involving real kindness, tenderness, genuine passion, great hope, joy, traditions, memories, and all the rest of Wright's bristling list are as rampant as the rats in Bigger's world; "the unconscious irony of those who felt that Negroes led so passional an existence" is clearly Wright's signal concerning how he wants us to receive the words and deeds of Mary Dalton, Jan, and possibly Attorney Max; and finally the phrase "our negative confusions, our flights, our fears, our frenzy under pressure" is but a compressed revoicing of what we know of Bigger's life, a line that virtually restates the title of each book within *Native Son*—Fear, Flight, Fate. While this "key" to *Native Son* is useful, the passage as a whole is finally even more useful to its author as a rhetoric (if not wholly a rite) of purgation or exorcism. One suspects, however, that the dim outline of all *three* of Wright's demons—his father, Bigger Thomas, and the Bigger in himself (or at least his past) who is almost simultaneously resurrected and buried in *Black Boy*—will always be before him. Even when he methodically dissects and shelves both Biggers and his father in the same morgue of his imagination, he is but reenacting Bigger Thomas's disposal of both the idea and the remains of Mary Dalton and Bessie. By writing *Black Boy* Wright may have learned that demons can reside in one's actions, as well as in one's mind.

At the beginning of this section I remarked that passages such as the one under discussion are controversial, and this is evident from the response they have occasioned amongst the writers who follow Wright in the tradition. Ralph Ellison, James Baldwin, Ernest Gaines, Cyrus Colter, Toni Morrison, James Alan McPherson, Al Young, Leon Forrest, Alice Walker, Gayl Jones, and Ishmael Reed are among the fiction writers who immediately come to mind, whose best work dispels the deathlike chill of Wright's (albeit rhetorical) vision of Negro America; in the context of this discussion, what I take to be Ellison's response interests me most. I should say at once, with Ellison's phrase "antagonistic cooperation" in mind, that the conversation between literary sensibilities which I am about to suggest has less to do with "anxieties of influence" (a subject which has been energetically explored *vis-à-vis* Wright and Ellison by Joseph Skerrett) and more to do with how one contour in literary history occasions another. The distinction forwarded here is one that Ellison himself encourages when he tutors Irvin Howe, in "The World and the Jug," by explaining: "perhaps you will understand when I say he [Wright] did not influence me if I point out that while one can do nothing about choosing one's relatives, one can, as artist, choose one's 'ancestors.' Wright was, in this sense, a 'relative'; Hemingway an 'ancestor.' " As his remarks continue, Ellison embellishes his distinction between "relative" and "ancestor" in general, and between Wright and Hemingway in particular, to a point where his final word on the subject is that Wright, as a "relative," was "a Negro like myself, and perhaps a great man"; Hemingway, as an "ancestor," was "in many ways the true father-as-artist of so many of us who came to writing during the late thirties." The phrase "father-as-artist" undoubtedly rings some critics' chimes, but I for one am quite unwilling to declare that I know the melody or the hour. I am more interested in the fact that Ellison is attempting a plausible explanation for his assertions, an explanation that is far more personal and atextual (and therefore, as history has shown, more vulnerable to attacks from the intelligentsia and not-so-intelligentsia) than necessary. Had Ellison gone ahead and pinpointed a textual source for the "antagonistic cooperation" between his art (and artistic sensibility) and Wright's, he could have avoided some of the confrontations that afflicted him in the 1960s. He did not have to look very far: the passage in *Black Boy* which is under discussion is a (perhaps *the*) textual source that clarifies Wright's and Ellison's artistic relationship, and it seems likely that Ellison was aware of the passage, since he quotes the second half of it in "Richard Wright's Blues."

While there can be no doubt that much or all of Wright's damning list of the Negro's shortcomings rankles Ellison, the crowning affront has to be: "After I had learned other ways of life . . . I saw that what had been taken for our emotional strength was our negative confusions, our flights, our fears, *our frenzy under pressure*" (italics added). I have suggested before that what Wright is up to here is, in part, a deliberate re-creation of the "black world" of *Native Son* (complete with references to the novel's section titles), prompted by a desire to distance his questing, articulate persona ("After I had learned other ways of life") from that world, and hence from Bigger Thomas. I want to suggest now that Wright is also about the task of defining a contour in literary history and placing himself in it—for certainly that is one momentous potential effect of his self-serving revision of Hemingway's famous credo, "grace under pressure." Once Wright bravely revoices that phrase as "frenzy under pressure" while planting obvious allusions to his most celebrated novel, not only is Afro-American life peremptorily typed, and possibly stereotyped, but a distinct idea of Afro-American literature—complete with maps of its foundations, abiding tropes, and central texts—is also aggressively launched. At the heart of either radical construction is the apparent conviction that Hemingway's creed must be turned inside out before it has any relevance to Afro-American life or art. This, I believe, is unquestionably a source-in-text for Ellison's differences with Wright, not simply because one of Ellison's "ancestors" has been mugged, but more profoundly because the idea of Afro-American life and art promulgated by Wright's assertions effectively excludes *his* life and art.

All in all, the relationship between Wright and Ellison is not unlike that between Washington and Du Bois. In either case, the issue is not whether the younger artist believes that the established figure is truly committed to the partial truthfulness of his rhetoric. Du Bois never argued that; and Ellison makes a point of writing, in "Richard Wright's Blues," that "Wright knows perfectly well that Negro life is a by-product of Western civilization, and that in it . . . are to be discovered all those impulses, tendencies, life and cultural forms to be found elsewhere in Western society." Nor does either Du Bois or Ellison assert that the narratives displaying Washington's and Wright's rhetorics (*Up from Slavery* and *Black Boy,* even more than *Native Son*) are such formidable artistic creations that they leave little or no space in Afro-American letters for their own work and that of others. Du Bois and Ellison are terribly proud men, but each would argue that the partial truths from which *Up from Slavery* and *Black Boy* derive their power occasion more good literature than they stifle. Both Du Bois and Ellison rightly came to feel that the older writer's rhetoric was quickly and disastrously becoming a race's and nation's language at large, instead of remaining one of many languages in text; which is to say, the rhetorics of Tuskegee and of Protest, as the latter came to be called, assumed tyrannical holds upon a nation's idea of a race's and culture's humanity. In response, in *The Souls of Black Folk* Du Bois reworked numerous features of *Up from Slavery* which I have already cited, and in *Invisible Man* Ellison obviously recast certain components of *Black Boy*—the persona's father, grandfather, and school principal, as well as his encounters with Mrs. Moss and young Harrison from the rival optical company. In Du Bois's and Ellison's cases, what we witness is not artistic envy—partly because the arena is not exclusively that of art—but "antagonistic cooperation" creatively forged between literary texts and kinsmen. To their credit, Du Bois and Ellison appear to have realized that the creation of such conditions—much like a properly functioning system of checks and balances—is fundamental to a nation's health, and possibly a step toward the ideal of *communitas* that lies beyond the lockstep of interracial and intraracial rituals. Aware that language at large must be a medley of many tongues, they raised their voices accordingly.

A. ROBERT LEE

# *Inside Narratives*

*All my life had shaped me for realism, the naturalism of the modern novel, and I could not read enough of them.*
                                                                —Black Boy (1945)

*I picked up a pencil and held it over a sheet of white paper, but my feelings stood in the way of my words. Well, I would wait, day and night, until I knew what I wanted to say. Humbly now, with no vaulting dream of achieving a vast unity, I wanted to try to build a bridge of words between me and the world outside, that world which was so distant and elusive that it seemed unreal.*
                                                                —American Hunger (1977)

Both these observations, each without doubt something of a flourish with which to round out his two volumes of autobiography, nonetheless serve their purpose well enough: they underscore how momentously Richard Wright regarded his call to a literary career. The first directs us less to the kind of fiction he himself would eventually write than to the liberating shock of recognition he experienced on reading the likes of H. L. Mencken and Theodore Dreiser and others of the first current of American literary realism. For in their different anatomies of America he saw not exactly the mirror of his own life—how could any of them have written with authority of a complex black Southern boyhood lived hard against the colour line and under the permanent threat of white racist violence?—but human existence depicted as an oppressive power-web able to damage and often consume the individual.

The later observation belongs to Wright's 1930s Depression and Chicago years, the era of his vexed membership in and departure from the

---

From *American Fiction: New Readings.* © 1983 by Vision Press Ltd.

American Communist Party which together with his increasing disenchant-
ment with America and subsequent F.B.I. and State Department harassment
led to his permanent European exile in 1947. His sense of elation on opting
out of the Party's *dicta,* for all that it had helped him towards what then
seemed a credible ideology of racelessness and anti-capitalism, almost exactly parallels the sense of self-possibility he reports in *Black Boy* on leaving
the Dixie South for his own northwards migration. To "build a bridge of
words" between himself and America (and worlds beyond), for a veteran of
Mississippi-style racial custom and a former CPUSA activist, must indeed in
the light of that background have seemed an unreal notion. For in claiming
the right to use words to his own design Wright not only gave notice of his
chosen path as a writer, he also affirmed that he intended nothing less than
to take on and beat at its own game the white-run and proprietary world
accustomed as if by ancient decree to doing the very defining of reality.

To emphasize Wright's passage into authorship—his belief in writing
as a crucial liberative and existential rite—is, I hope, equally to imply a great
deal about his fiction itself. For so committed a writer (and committed in a
manner distinct from the customary Marxist and Sartrean senses) and for
whom from the outset fiction clearly meant more than writing in any one
single key, it must have been an irritatingly inadequate praise which on
publication of *Native Son* (1940), the novel which most established his
name, confidently pronounced him America's first "Negro protest writer,"
its "black Dreiser," the custodial voice of "black anger." For though Wright
rarely did other than assume a departure-point of deep abiding dissent, a
personally endured bitter intimacy with American racial hypocrisies, this
kind of phraseology, well-intended or not, ultimately proves unhelpful. It
has locked his and a whole tradition of Afro-American writing into too
reductive an opposition: white oppression as against black protest, a sim-
plified dialectic in which black and white play out their predictable adver-
sary racial roles. As in the cases of Ralph Ellison and James Baldwin after
him, Wright recognized from the start that so easy a version of race and
human ways would not take him or his reader very far. Some "anger" might
indeed get ventilated. Black grievances might or might not win a sympathetic hearing, especially where white liberal guilt was involved. But the
fiction as such would get rendered down into something akin to diagram-
matic sociology, treatise or sermon rather than worlds taken from life yet
transformingly re-imagined. Equally the real complexities of race—its elusive sexual and psychological components, the fine nuance and built-in
taboos and patterns of offence and defence—given that Wright as a black

writer could hardly not write out of his historic blackness, simply would get bypassed.

Yet Wright's grasp of these complexities, and often in truth his own individual complexity, rarely won notice. Throughout the Depression years and even into the 1940s he was regularly taken to reflect the Communist Party view that Marxism pointed a way "beyond race" and towards the holistic view of history he calls the "vast unity" in *American Hunger*. Then, during the Eisenhower Tranquil '50s, as an expatriate in Paris and where read at all, he found himself castigated as some kind of literary dissident, an ungrateful black anti-American voice in league with an intellectual class still enamoured of Soviet Russia and unacceptably out of sorts with the nation's taste for the Cold War and its middle-America WASP consensus. In turn, in the 1960s, having for years played Dean of the expatriate black colony in Paris, he was claimed by yet another image. The generation raised on Civil Rights and then marches like that into Selma and inner-city explosions and the rhetoric of Malcolm X and the Panthers seized on him as an exemplary spokesman for Black Power, an early standard-bearer of either-or black militancy. In this, too, his name was to be set off against assumedly acquiescent Native Sons like Ellison or Baldwin or pacifist Christian black leadership in the mold of Martin Luther King. None of these accounts, however convenient and understandable for their time, went near to meeting Wright's overall measure.

All of these versions of Wright, furthermore, to one degree or another, persist. His "bridge of words," despite the massive debate about "realism" from Zola onwards to today's Derridean and post-Modern polemic, goes on being referred to some implied generic (or at least Dreiserian) standard of realism/naturalism. Nor has Wright won, free of his slightly antiquarian Marxist armature, the mind forged on *New Masses* and "scientific" history and Afro-America's equivalent of Mike Gold or John Reed. With Black Power and the 1960s came the Black Aesthetic view of Wright, the author of *Native Son* and volumes like *Twelve Million Black Voices* (1941) and *The Color Curtain* (1956) as the voice of a self-referential black culture, a domain of separatist black consciousness and value inaccessible to prying white eyes. But though Wright himself nowhere argued for so exclusive a standard of judgement, the rediscovery in the 1960s of a usable black cultural past did help to relocate his work as a point both of contrast and continuity with the interwar New Negro and Harlem Renaissance for which Alain Locke's anthology *The New Negro* (1925) served as a manifesto. Even so, rarely did the proponents of the Black Aesthetic adequately confront Wright's own cultural eclecticism, the Southern-born Black Boy to be sure but also the author who acknowledged among other departure-points Heidegger and nineteenth-century European existentialism and a writerly line which lists Poe, Hawthorne, Kafka, Dostoyevski, and Melville among its luminaries. Nor did it meet Wright's many ambivalences about pan-Africanism and global notions of blackness, not to mention his own ambiguous position as a black guest-exile in still colonialist France. These different versions also tend to cross and overlap, one or another part truth taken for the whole. Oddly, the deceptive clarity of Wright's work has played its part here, its ease of access tempting the incautious into too ready a final version both of the man and his writing. For an author, certainly, almost taken by rote to lack the finish of, say, a Hemingway or Fitzgerald, or later an Ellison or Baldwin, Herman Melville's drily sage observation in *Moby-Dick* offers just the right cautionary note: "I have ever found your plain things the knottiest of all."

## II

Loosening Wright and his fiction from these interconnecting personal and racial myths becomes even more difficult in the light of the role he became called upon to play for other Afro-American writers. First, there has been the question of his "school," the constellation which includes among its preeminent names Chester Himes, Ann Petry and Willard Motley, and at a slightly later remove, figures like William Gardner Smith, John O. Killens, and John A. Williams. All of these, however markedly different in interests and manner, somehow have to be thought Wrightian realists, the composite literary voice of a black America writing stock "Negro protest." That Wright, for sure, whether during the Chicago and *New Masses* 1930s or as the presiding resident of the Paris black literary colony or as the subsequent Third World apologist, did exert an extraordinary influence does not have to be doubted. His style as a realist, too, obviously did make its impact. But to credit him with some coercive or patriarchal direction over the imagination of writers as insistently self-propelled as Chester Himes or Ann Petry amounts to serious distortion. Himes's relation with Wright, for example, especially as set out in his two-volume autobiography, *The Quality of Hurt* (1972) and *My Life of Absurdity* (1976), pays a far more complicated tribute to his fellow exile—for like Baldwin he both loved and found himself frequently warring against Wright—than formula allusions to a Wrightian school anywhere near allows.

Wright's relationship with his supposed two principal "sons," James Baldwin and Ralph Ellison, similarly tells an altogether more freighted story.

Baldwin's two well-known essays, "Many Thousands Gone" (1951) and "Alas, Poor Richard" (1961), in all their stylish self-disaffiliation from Wright, need to be decoded as an act of the most especial intimacy, a freedom sought as much from Wright's strange hold on the white world's version of American blackness as from Wright himself. Ellison, too, for his part, has given an equally complex account of his relationship with Wright. On the one hand, in "Richard Wright's Blues" (1945) and his subsequent "The World and the Jug" (1963), he speaks of simply "stepping round" Wright, perhaps understandably the remark of the creator of so richly endowed a novel as *Invisible Man* (1952). Yet just as *Invisible Man* transforms for its own purposes the many backward glances to Dostoyevski, Melville, Poe, Joyce, Malraux, and the other figures Ellison has mentioned in *Shadow and Act* (1964) and in several interviews as influences (not to mention his echoing of Jazz and black folklore), so it calls up Richard Wright also and in particular the most powerful of his short stories, another adroitly subterranean narrative of identity and revelation, "The Man Who Lived Underground" (1945.)

The saga of Wright as assumed black literary touchstone continues most dramatically into the 1960s in Eldridge Cleaver's *Soul on Ice* (1968) where in "Notes of a Native Son" he uses the Wright of *Native Son* as he sees him—"the Richard Wright [who] reigns supreme for his profound political, economic, and social reference"—to berate James Baldwin as the incarnation not only of sexual but political effeminatization, ever willingly knee-bent to the white man in a damning two-way sense. But Cleaver's admiration of Wright as the tough heterosexual black warrior and condemnation of Baldwin as castratus and the hater of his own blackness, however eye-catching, also will not serve as anything like the whole case. With just cause Cleaver might have been seeking a mythology suited to the polemical needs of the Black Panther challenge to America—the call to Afro-Americans to cease being the compliant and all too literal prisoners of a history begun in slavery and continued in the nation's ghettos and penitentiaries—but a mythology indeed is what it was and not one to capture the full human ambiguity of either Wright or Baldwin.

From another angle there has been the Wright of John A. Williams, both the fictive Harry Ames of Wright's major racial-political thriller, *The Man Who Cried I Am* (1967), the wise but sacrificial figure whose legacy is offered as one of necessary total vigilance against destruction from white power interests, and Wright the subject of a tender biography for children, *The Most Native of Sons* (1970). Williams's depiction of Ames as the victim of F.B.I. and C.I.A. machinations working in some kind of harness with various white-supremacist groups also points forward to the Wright Addison Gayle has revealed in *Richard Wright: Ordeal of a Native Son* (1980), a piece of excavation (however dully written) to complement Michel Fabre's standard biography, *The Unfinished Quest of Richard Wright* (1973). By gaining access to most of Wright's Government files under the Freedom of Information and Privacy Acts of 1966 and 1974 Gayle shows how, in cold sober fact, Wright did suffer from McCarthyist red-baiting and racist government officialdom. The rumour still persists, indeed, in some Paris and black circles, that his death did not come about by natural causes. Gayle's account also yields another important significance; it was written by a leading Black Aesthetic critic and assumes a stance towards Wright which suggests that only another black American with the right "blackness" of outlook could understand Wright's place within an America directed by its white police and Intelligence agencies.

Finally, and if it is not dutifully insisted that he wrote only unembellished naturalism, the long shadow of Wright can again be detected in an absolutely contemporary "post-realist" body of Afro-American fiction in which realism becomes phantasmagorical and Bosch-like in its imagining. Among the best and most symptomatic of this kind of work have to be Chester Himes's pyrotechnic Coffin Ed/Gravedigger Jones *romans policiers* first published in French as part of Gallimard's *Série Noire,* in which Harlem becomes both a literal black world and a magical shadow-territory shot through with violence and *bizarrerie.* To these should be added the versatile pastiche fiction of Ishmael Reed beginning from *The Free-Lance Pallbearers* (1967), William Melvin Kelley's highly Ellisonian *dem* (1967), and novels like Hal Bennett's *Lord of the High Places* (1970), Robert Deane Pharr's *S.R.O.* (1971), Cyrus Colter's *The Hippodrome* (1973), and John Wideman's *The Lynchers* (1973). In this legacy, not one always granted to Wright, the implicit surreal ingredients of his own fiction become palpably more central, realism turned inside out, absurdist and often bitingly macabre and funny.

Given, thus, these extraordinary thickets which have enclosed Wright and most likely still kept his true self just out of view—whether the Richard he himself invents in *Black Boy* and *American Hunger* (and deftly perpetuates in reportage like *Black Power* (1954), *The Color Curtain* (1956), and *Pagan Spain* (1957), or the veteran of that intimidatory Mississippi and Arkansas black upbringing, or on the evidence of his contribution to *The God That Failed* (1949) the half-in half-out Chicago Marxist, or the Greenwich Village and New York personality and shock author of *Native Son,* or still later the Paris expatriate and internationalist Third World advocate—

it can hardly do harm to concentrate yet more attention on the subtlety of imagination actually at work in the fiction.

It may well be that Wright's fiction can no longer be read clear of his several legends or his impact on almost all subsequent Afro-American writing. Further, the turbulent politics of race, particularly as they evolved through the civil rights era and after, would seem to have claimed him as part of a black American pantheon which reaches well beyond things literary. Certainly for anyone still inclined to seek in Wright's fiction the unencumbered storyteller, it has become pretty well impossible not to be conscious of reading one or another "Richard Wright," most of all the major forebear of contemporary black American literary narrative. In other words, Wright as mythic founder-figure and the giver of black-realist testament has settled like a dense blanket over the fiction, adding yet further layers of complexity to an achievement already in itself hedged with racial and political complication.

## III

As Wright himself has been made over into legend so to a disturbing degree has his fiction been imprisoned inside a set critical vocabulary. This agreed account continues to interpret him in terms of Dreiserian naturalism or Protest, albeit updated in some cases by Addison Gayle and others still anxious to evaluate according to Black Aesthetic writ. Without denying Wright's inclination towards naturalism and the location of his stories within a solid contour of social reality, I want to underline just as much the somewhat different writer he himself hypostasized and nowhere more clearly than in his celebrated preface to *Native Son*, "How Bigger Was Born." There, as in essays like "The Literature of the Negro in the United States," he insists on his equal inclination to see in black history not only a literal past scarred by oppression but a matchingly inward and emblematic drama, one remembered within the collective Afro-American psyche and in Blues and black oral tradition as much as in the punitive outer record of racial gains and defeats. The last paragraph of "How Bigger Was Born" especially insists on this double inheritance:

> We have in the Negro the embodiment of a past tragic enough to appease the spiritual hunger of even a James; and we have in the oppression of the Negro a shadow athwart our national life dense and heavy enough to satisfy even the gloomy broodings of a Hawthorne. And if Poe were alive, he would not have to invent horror; horror would invent him.

In so claiming James, Hawthorne, and Poe as *semblables* (again an essay like "The Literature of the Negro in the United States" which avers that "The Negro is America's metaphor" shows how conscious he was of *black* literary tradition), he points precisely to what the half-title of Melville's *Billy Budd* most helpfully calls "inside narrative," that which for Wright is the inner other story being told under the outward guise of realism.

In this respect, the stories collected in *Uncle Tom's Children* (1938) and *Eight Men* (1961) offer especially useful points of illustration, each at once "naturalist" yet at the same time parabular and imbued with recognizably deeper memories of racial encounter and phobia. The note I refer to is struck, for instance, in "Big Boy Leaves Home," the first of the tales in *Uncle Tom's Children,* by the protagonist Big Boy when he says of the events which have left his friends Lester, Buck, and Bobo dead and himself a terrified Northwards-bound fugitive from Dixie lynch law: "It all seemed unreal now." On the surface the story appears to offer a straight (if highly dramatic) episode of Southern racist violence, the account of four black boys whose swim at a summer water hole leads on to death and flight. But the story's virtual every detail activates far more ancestral resonances from deep within Southern racial history, the rites whereby black manhood is killed or at least mutilated for its supposed desiring of white womanhood and in which "the South" as sometimes in William Faulkner's mythical kingdom of Yoknapatawpha becomes both a bucolic river and pinewood Heaven and a brute Inferno.

Told as a classical five-act sequence, the story opens with the boys' banter, their snatches of black bawdy and the "dozens" and the general roughhousing, all of which represent the marks of time spent at adolescence. The landscape of the woods, the "cleared pasture" and the "tangled vines" thus serve as actual landscape and as Nature's seeming stamp of approval. At the swimming hole, they encounter the first discord within this summery boyhood harmony, the sign put up by Ol' Man Harvey, "NO TRESPASSIN," its frank illiteracy at one with the intrusion of white property ownership into natural free space. With the arrival of the white woman and her soldier lover, the story calls into play the South's even more familiar racial equation: Big Boy, "black and naked"; a screaming belle; and the avenging white manfolk with blood on his lips after the first tussle with the gun vowing death to "you black sonofabitch."

Paradise thereby turns to nightmare, pleasure to pain. Big Boy flees after the death of Harvey's soldier son back to family and community (to the Bluesy chorus of his mother "This is mo trouble, mo trouble") and then away again into hiding at the kilns to await his latterday Underground

Railway escape in a truck owned by the emblematic Magnolia Express Company. Big Boy's journey down into this kiln-pocked Hell is heralded by "six foot of snake," racism's devil serpent made incarnate, which he kills with his stick, even though he imagines in his Dantean hiding place "whole nests of them," each "waiting tensely in coil." His underground hole, like Fred Daniels's in "The Man Who Lived Underground" and that of Ellison's unnamed narrator in *Invisible Man,* particularizes the larger historical hole into which Big Boy and his three friends and the black race in general have been cast since slavery. He thinks back across his benigner past of home, school, the train, the songs and "long hot Summer days," the terrain of the twelve-string Blues guitar and the briar-patch. And against this deep, comforting place of memory he plays out in imagination his fantasy-revenge on the white race, would-be heroism of the kind he thinks will make headlines like "NIGGER KILLS DOZENS OF MOB BEFO LYNCHED." Yet even as he dreams, the posse hunts down and captures Bobo in the refrain of "We'll hang ever nigger t a sour apple tree." Bobo, in turn, burns to the chorus of "LES GET SOURVINEERS" and "HURRY UP N BURN THE NIGGER FO IT RAINS!" As he dies, another black boy martyred to white hate, so Big Boy chokes the Cerberus-like dog belonging to his white pursuers, token redress for the butchery of his friend and yet also the necessary murder of his own prior innocence.

As he then makes his escape, his insides drawn "into a tight knot," he senses rightly that the "home" he is leaving is both his own corner of the South and the whole serried history which lies behind it and also the self which for him has now passed out of innocence into experience and been fashioned by the same "horror" and "shadow" which will mark his near-namesake Bigger Thomas. Big Boy, as it were, has internalized the historic penalty of being black and a sexual fantasy figure within the white American South. Wright's story thus operates on a number of double bases: it tells a latterday escape narrative to recall past nineteenth-century slave narratives, and it shows how each "fugitive" black American carries on the pulse and deeply within the larger communal scars of racist brutality. Behind its surface, too, looms the memory of even older destruction, Biblical and also dynastic, Cain against Abel replayed as white against black. Wright deposits these layers of "inside" meaning within the story's ostensible outer detail, whether the contrast of black and white, or Day and Night, or Nature as in turn kindly and hellish. To call a story like "Big Boy Leaves Home" simply naturalistic leaves out its genuine command of tone, Wright's organizing pattern and cadence; in effect it leaves almost all the work still to be done.

Each of the other pieces in *Uncle Tom's Children,* even if one does not think them in equal measure successful, operates in similarly double manner. In "Down by the River," true to the classic Blues from which Wright borrows his title, the ostensible story of a black drowning and white ingratitude for help given during a Southern flood encloses an inward parable of how the black protagonist—perhaps too obviously called Brother Mann—here, as so often under Southern auspices, is in every sense "sold down the river" by unfair racial odds. As Mann drowns, the story describes his body as "encased in a tight vase in a narrow black coffin that moved with him." Such detail implies that this Flood doubles as the Flood of History itself, Southern-style, a murderous "white" stream of time in which black skin has become the garment of death. Similarly, in "Long Black Song," we again enter mythy Blues terrain as languidly Southern in atmosphere as the Georgia of Jean Toomer's *Cane* (1923), in which a black woman gets tricked into giving her sexual favours to a white salesman. Her husband, Silas, finally chooses to burn to death rather than be hanged cravenly for the revenge he enacts on the white order of things which has so cheated him. He follows "the long river of blood," but for once a martyr of his own choosing and not of the system which both literally and figuratively has denied him (and black men before him) their rightful manhood. "Fire and Cloud," a story again full of mythic association though weakened by Wright's too sentimental wish to envisage shared black-white resistance to racism, tells the story of an Uncle Tom preacher and black community leader who after a vicious beating comes to reject passive black Christianity in favour of implacable opposition to arbitrary white authority in his Southern small town. The beating itself, which Wright dramatizes powerfully as a Klan-style crucifixion, serves both as an instance of brutality and a rite of deepest inward liberation for the Reverend Taylor and the past standard he represents. The story also reflects Wright's own move from nominal Christianity into a more Marxist view of real salvation, change through solidarity.

In "Bright and Morning Star," another of Wright's stories with a Marxist and interracial element (which appropriately was published as a separate piece in *New Masses* in May 1938), he sets the warm maternal presence of Aunt Sue, the black mother of two activist sons, against white Southern law-and-order thuggery. An' Sue, to give her her black name, represents Faulkner's Dilsey no longer available as black choric servant figure for white people, but the black woman as fierce protectress of her own. In shooting the stool pigeon who has brought on the torture and death of her son Johnny Boy and thereby in turn bringing on her own death from the racist villainy about her, she becomes the very incarnation of the death of Uncle Tomism, or as the story puts matters "the dead that never dies."

She becomes legend, the exemplary myth. Wright's language throughout works literally yet also iconically, whole pharases so pitched as to call up black Bible cadence and a past racial history told and retold to the point where it becomes parable. Typical is the following:

> But as she had grown older, a cold white mountain, the white folks and their laws, had swum into her vision and shattered her songs and their spells of peace.

The inside narrative of "Bright and Morning Star" resides exactly in Wright's lexicon of "cold white mountain," "songs" and "spells of peace," black pictographic community speech which belongs to the world of Blues and known deeply in the heart. Aunt Sue indeed dies in fact but lives on in myth.

In this respect, Wright wrote no better story than "The Man Who Lived Underground," the centre-piece to *Eight Men.* Its journey form rightly has won praise for how it calls up Dante's *Inferno* and Dostoyevski's *Notes from Underground,* and for how, too, it cannily anticipates *Invisible Man* and LeRoi Jones/Imamu [Amiri] Baraka's *Dutchman.* For in Fred Daniels's underground odyssey, Wright develops both a literal-seeming drama of escape—a manhunt no less—and a parable of the black American as at once underground man and yet also witness, at once forced into hiding his own true self yet able to see all. In descending via the manhole cover down into his underground, Daniels sees the America into which he has been born as a land of both plenty and waste, a nation which simultaneously offers and withholds its abundance. Each glimpse of this America he experiences as one previously denied access, a kind of black underworld trespasser or scavenger forced to live at the margins of or underneath the presumed white mainstream of the nation's history. Little wonder that his first sight is that of a glistening sewer rat, a rat also to anticipate that which Bigger Thomas kills at the beginning of *Native Son* and which prefigures his own rodent-like fate in the final police chase. Everything Daniels sees, and on occasion steals, Wright sets against the spirituals being sung by the black congregation, America's black history as carried by the historic power of its music and the story's touchstone against which to locate white reality.

As Daniels flees down into the sewer, he appears to step free of time itself and to become a traveller through all single versions of time. The story's questions ask: "How long had he been down here? He did not know." Plunged thus into a time beyond any one time, each thing he sees takes on a weight well in excess of the literal. He sees first the dead abandoned baby "snagged by debris and half-submerged in water," a Blakean Innocent, eyes closed, fists clenched "as though in protest," and its mouth "gaped black in soundless cry." Such mute human frailty links directly to Fred Daniels's own fate, his self also essentially still-born and an object of repudiation. As he "tramps on," one particular black figure in history yet also the personification of all past black "tramping," he next sees an embalmer at work, his "establishment" ice-cold, white and diabolic. The embalmer's own "throaty chuckle" underlines the point trenchantly, whiteness as Hell.

In turn, each subsequent encounter works in similar double manner, actual scenes yet far more, America and reality as parts of a coded, visionary landscape. The coal bin conjures up not only literal fuel but the whole underground fire of black life itself. The movie house and its flickering screen offers an analogy with Daniels's own miasmic perceptions of the world as seen from his black underground, life in truth seen as if on a cinema reel. The fruit and vegetables he steals become almost painterly, food transposed from actual to surrealist nourishment as on a Dali or Impressionist canvas. Similarly, the jewels he takes glisten hypnotically in the dark, real plunder yet also Gatsbyesque fantasy wealth. Even the newspaper heading, "HUNT NEGRO FOR MURDER," assumes an air of disjunctness, language as some foreign cryptogram which encodes reality to its own system. The same note applies in the Aladdin's Cave Fred makes of the stolen banknotes, and in his tentative first efforts to write out his name. In writing *freddanniels* and the other words he becomes the like of the first cave-dwellers, a human presence obliged by history to begin again in the path towards finding his signature.

The world thus seen from the black underground both patently exists as fact yet equally as hallucination. Daniels himself resembles as much as anyone Melville's Bartleby, a fellow-prisoner of walls:

> What was the matter with him? Yes, he knew it . . . it was these
> walls; these crazy walls were filling him with a wild urge out into
> the dark sunshine above ground.

He is finally shot because the story he resurfaces momentarily to tell cannot be credited by the police, any more than can be that of Ralph Ellison's narrator in *Invisible Man* or Baraka's Clay in *Dutchman*. Wright's naturalism again secretes inside narration, the elusive underground sediments of black American history. "The Man Who Lived Underground" undoubtedly offers the best of *Eight Men*'s stories, yet each of the others (and especially "The Man Who Was Almost a Man" and "Man of All Work") operates to a decipherably similar doubleness of purpose. As so often Wright's surface functions as the equivocal outward show of the other narrative being told deep within.

## IV

These double purposes of Wright's fiction apply equally, if not more so, to his longer work. All five of his novels—*Lawd Today* (post. 1963), *Native Son* (1940), *The Outsider* (1953), *Savage Holiday* (1954) and *The Long Dream* (1958)—blend and interweave different skeins of narrative within the story ostensibly on offer. *Lawd Today,* to take Wright's probable first novel which ironically was not published at the time of writing because of its lack of a "clear" Marxist orientation, outwardly tells a representative twenty-four hour day in the life of Jake Jackson, black Chicago postal worker. Its lively surface detail has all to do with the Lincoln Day Holiday, Wright's informed sense of Chicago's South Side street and bar life, community dreams of magical Numbers fortunes, black talk and rap, down-home food and sexual opportunism. In other words, it maps black urban style, the energies of a major black city-within-a-city. At the same time, *Lawd Today* explores wholly more inward terrain, Jake Jackson as a man close to psychological split and collapse. The increasing hatred he shows his wife, the valetudinarian Lil, and his inability to keep rein on his temper, mark a man going steadily out of control. Jake in fact veers increasingly towards murderousness, the victim of a process which has locked him into that internalized ghetto Chester Himes once eloquently termed "the prison of my mind." Reality might apparently reside in a Chicago Lincoln Day Holiday with extracts from Roosevelt Firesides on the radio, 1930s popular songs and a busy scenario of commercial hustle. But for Jake, fissured, dangerous, reality also lies far more inward, in the realms of the beleaguered psyche which can erupt into violence at the barest provocation. *Lawd Today* uses its documentary format to depict history as both daytime reality and incipient interior nightmare.

The same, I would maintain, largely holds true of *Native Son,* for all its assumed status as a naturalist classic of a kind with Dreiser's *An American Tragedy* and Steinbeck's *The Grapes of Wrath*; it also is an "inside" story and precisely as "dense and heavy" and full of "shadow" as Wright himself hoped it might be in "How Bigger Was Born." At the immediate level *Native Son* tells of the tenement upbringing of Bigger Thomas, his half-witting murder of his white patron's daughter, the subsequent disposal in the furnace of Mary Dalton's body and in turn his flight, the murder of his girl Bessie and his trial and defence as developed in the top-heavy dialectics of Mr. Max, the Jewish and Marxist lawyer. So much, to be sure, added to the "realist" urban background of Chicago, half-locates Wright's novel: but it also leaves the fuller achievement of *Native Son* seriously unacknowledged.

It has been objected to *Native Son*, in part by James Baldwin, that it reads as though set in something of a historical vacuum, its principal characters unsatisfactorily one-dimensional and without sufficient human resonance. To the extent that this is true, it suggests not so much weakness as the fact that Wright was attempting narrative markedly different from that assumed to be naturalistic; he was in fact as much writing his own version of the kind of narration he mentions as the line of Poe, Hawthorne, and Dostoyevski. The landscape of the novel, for instance, certainly proposes a real Chicago but also and in matching degree a Chicago of the mind and senses, the bleak outward urban landscape of *Native Son* as the correlative of Bigger's psyche. His violence, from the opening episode with the rat and his bullying of his poolhall friends through to the murder and incineration of Mary and his flight, takes its course as the expression of his turbulence within. It serves as his one form of self-articulation. *Native Son* thus should be read as exploring psychology and human personality in a manner as close to, say, Kafka, as to Dreiser or Steinbeck, the Chicaco of the novel as much the expression of the displaced city pent up inside Bigger as the Windy City of actuality. In arguing for this more "shadowed" reading of *Native Son,* three supporting kinds of allusion must do duty for the novel's procedures as a whole: they have to do with sight, with the image of Bigger as rat, and with exactly the kind of city depicted in *Native Son.*

Not only "The Man Who Lived Underground" but *Native Son,* too, calls up *Invisible Man* in its handling of seeing and sightlessness, typically in a passage like the following in which Bigger considers the implication of having killed Mary:

> No, he did not have to hide behind a wall or a curtain now; he had a safer way of being safe, an easier way. What he had done last night had proved that. Jan was blind. Mary had been blind. Mr. Dalton had been blind. And Mrs. Dalton was blind; yes, blind in more ways than one. . . . Bigger felt that a lot of people were like Mrs. Dalton, blind.

Just as Bigger's black world sees him one way—merely wayward if his hard-pressed mother is to be believed, a tough street-companion according

to his poolhall buddies, a lover in Bessie's eyes—so, too, to the white world
he is seen only through part of his identity, as some preferred invention like
the recipient of Mr. Dalton's self-serving largesse, or the proletarian black
worker imagined by Mary and her lover Jan, or Mr. Max's example of how
"scientific" history shapes the individual consciousness. Even the final chase
scenes across rundown wasteland Chicago against which he is silhouetted
by the police cross-lights show him only in part, the formulaic rapist-
murderer. Bigger's full human self, even at the end probably ungrasped by
the victim himself, lies locked inside "the faint, wry bitter smile" he wears
to his execution. Perhaps the true self lies teasingly present in the white cat
which watches him burn Mary's body (an episode to recall the duplicitous
intentions of stories like "Ethan Brand" or "The Masque of the Red Death"),
in part the emissary of the white world which has hitherto so defined Bigger
but just as plausibly the rarest glimpse of his own fugitive and "whited"
identity.

The rat killed by Bigger in the opening chapter also sets up a motif
which resonates throughout the novel. Its belly "pulsed with fear," its "black
beady eyes glittering," the rat points forward to the figure Bigger himself
will become, the part-real part-fantasy denizen of a grotesque counter-
Darwinian world in which human life—his own, Mary's, Bessie's—seems to
evolve backwards into rodent predation and death. Whether in pursuit or
the pursued, Bigger becomes damned either way, just as he victimizes others
while doubling as both his own and society's victim. These inner meanings
of the novel also lie behind Wright's three-part partition of "Fear," "Flight,"
and "Fate," as much notations of *Native Son*'s parabular meanings as the
apparent drama at the surface. Bigger's parting words to Mr. Max suggest
that he has some first glimmerings of the process which has metamorphosized
him into a human rodent, but he goes to his death still trapped by the
predatory laws which he sought to repudiate by throwing the skillet at the
rat in the opening chapter.

In "How Bigger Was Born," Wright speaks of Chicago as "huge,
roaring, dirty, noisy, raw, stark, brutal," that is as the city of the historic
stockyards, oppressive summer humidity and the chill polar winds of the
mid-Western winter. He also speaks of Chicago as a city which has created
"centuries-long chasm[s] of emptiness" in figures like Bigger Thomas.
*Native Son* depicts Chicago in just that way: as a literal instance of
colour-line urban America but also as the more inward City of Dreadful
Night, for Bigger both the world among whose tenements and on whose
streets he has been raised and the city which he has internalized, one of
violence and half-understood impulses to revenge. To discern in *Native Son*

only an urban-realist drama again evades the dimension of the novel Wright himself knowingly calls "the whole dark inner landscape of Bigger's mind."

V

Though by no means disasters, both *The Outsider* and *Savage Holiday* go seriously adrift and for connected reasons. In the former, Wright cannot resist loading his story of Cross Damon as the black twentieth-century man of alienation *par excellence* with an accompanying (and intrusive) set of explanations about *angst* and the whole eclectic tradition of outsiderness. Not only does he actually name time and again founding figures like Heidegger and Kierkegaard, but he glosses Damon's different murders and assumptions of identity with allusions to Dread, Will, the legacy of the Absurd. To this end, too, he imports into the novel Damon's fellow outsider, the hunch-backed District Attorney Eli Houston, to whom it falls as it does to Mr. Max in *Native Son* to analyse the processes which have made Damon what he is, the perfect instance of the amoral, alienated man of will. In *Savage Holiday,* Wright's touchstone becomes Freud, human personality in the form of Erskine Fowler, an ex-Insurance Man eased out of his job to make way for the boss's son and the victim of an almost absurd turn of events which results in the death of a neighbour's young boy. His own glaring sexual repression eventuates in murder, the stabbing of the boy's voluptuous mother whose easy sexual style torments Fowler. As in *The Outsider,* Wright can be lively, but more often he turns essayistic and tutorly. The failure of both books lies in the fact that Wright simply will not trust his own tale to do the work; whether the keystone is Existentialism or Freudianism, the inside narrative is made damagingly explicit. Wright's philosophical interest thereby throws the drama of his novels out of balance, their inside direction far too available from the outset.

Fortunately, though not without other faults, Wright's last novel *The Long Dream* (a sequel *Island of Hallucination* remains unpublished) shows no blemish of this kind. In part this most likely has to do with Wright's return to the materials he drew from so convincingly in *Black Boy,* the Deep South and its haunting memory as a place of origins. For the story *The Long Dream* tells, that of Fishbelly Tucker's childhood and passage into adult identity, Wright organizes without the directing hand which breaks into and flaws *The Outsider* and *Savage Holiday.* Indeed, the sheer full-plottedness of the novel could hardly have left too much scope for that kind of intrusion.

A major part of the novel's success lies in Wright's meticulous recreation of Fishbelly's childhood, at once the wholly individual childhood of a black boy in the South whose undertaker-father takes care to educate him as best he knows into the wiles needed to survive in the treacherous world of small town Dixie, and at the same time a version of Black Childhood itself, the dynastic re-enactment of what it means to be black, curious, and permanently at risk from white authority. Fishbelly, from the first acquiring of his folk name (which Wright does marvellously) through to his first sexual awakenings, does learn from Tyree his father, but he also comes to know that his father's business exists on deals struck with the Chief of Police, Cantley, and that the town's tacit and demeaning lines of agreement have been arranged on the basis of white superiority and black inferiority. Further, Fishbelly perceives that his father, by running a Numbers racket and brothel, is also embalming his people figuratively just as he embalms them literally in his undertaking business. The chain of events which finally kills Tyree and leads to Fishbelly's jailing on a trumped-up sex charge involving a white woman thus again assumes a double set of meanings. Fishbelly's story, in all its twists and detail, offers the chronicle of one life: but it also absorbs the ritual of black coming-of-age, the perception of what it is to be man and nigger, self and shadow.

Fishbelly's story undoubtedly plays off Richard Wright's own. And like the story Wright successfully fictionalized into *Black Boy* and *American Hunger,* it refracts through the one life the more collective story of black community as experienced in the American South. The impress of that South, its deeply inward story as well as literal geography and the past as shaped below the Mason-Dixon line, Fishbelly carries with him as he flees not as Big Boy and others to the Northern city but as Wright himself to Europe. Wright persuasively locates this double memory in "the locked regions" of Fishbelly's heart. The novel, too, rightly makes vivid use of dream and memory, forms of imagined life which work to deepen the impression of "inside narrative" and which play against the "actual" history being told at the surface. *The Long Dream,* then, offers the seeming literal history of Fishbelly, but as the title suggests and the last chapter makes explicit a history which is also "dream" and "nightmare." Both stories lie within Fishbelly's mind, the South as at once the realm of literal phobias and outrage and his own troubled growth into adulthood and the matching other realm of all the "shadows" which have settled within his personality.

In his introduction to George Lamming's *In the Castle of My Skin* (1953), Wright explicitly calls attention to the ancestral racial layerings which have marked out black experience in the white West. He also implies how impossible it would be to render that experience to any single measure, be it that of Protest, or one or another version of naturalism, or even of Marxism or Existentialism or Freudianism. One observation in particular helps to locate the multiple reaches of his own fiction:

> the Negro of the Western world lives, in *one* life, *many* life-times. . . . The Negro, though born in the Western world, is not quite of it; due to policies of racial exclusion, his is the story of *two* cultures: the dying culture in which he happens to be born, and the culture into which he is trying to enter—a culture which has, for him, not quite yet come into being. . . . Such a story is, above all, a record of shifting, troubled feelings groping their way towards a future that frightens as much as it beckons.

Such a story, we might want to say, amounts to exactly the inside narrative on offer in Richard Wright's fiction.

HOUSTON A. BAKER, JR.

# Reassessing (W)right:
# A Meditation on the Black (W)hole

*I strove to master words, to make them disappear.*
WRIGHT, *American Hunger*

*What is to be avoided above all is the reestablishing of "Society" as*
*an abstraction vis-à-vis the individual. The individual is the social*
*being. His life, even if it may not appear in the direct form of a com-*
*munal life carried out together with others—is therefore an expres-*
*sion and confirmation of social life.*
MARX, *Economic and Philosophical Manuscripts*

*I tried to find the usual ladder that leads out of such holes, but there*
*was none.*

ELLISON, *Invisible Man*

The reassessment of *The Sport of the Gods* which yields the foregoing interpretation of the novel is simply an instant—one blues moment, as it were—in the project of deciphering an American form. Dunbar's effort was early, and its inscriptions of the vernacular matrix are revealed only through subtle analysis.

The same does not hold for a mid-twentieth-century black author like Richard Wright. For the blues energies of theme and narrative structure that Dunbar preserved and passed on in *The Sport of the Gods* were magnified by the efforts of the Harlem Renaissance of the 1920s—a time of extraordinary production in Afro-American writing.

From *Blues, Ideology and Afro-American Literature.* © 1984 by The University of Chicago Press.

When he commenced his autobiography *Black Boy* (1945), in fact, enough narrative instances existed to make available for Wright options that are implied in his essay "How Bigger Was Born." In this interpretive essay, Wright insists that he might have followed a genteel, integrationist line in the novel *Native Son* (1940), endearing himself thereby to the Afro-American middle class and amusing Anglo-America with polite observations on life among the black lowly. To have followed such a line would have been to rank himself with a great many Afro-American predecessors. Instead, he chose to take the lid completely off the seething cauldron of Afro-American vernacular culture and show the indigenous folk in both their glory and their squalor—but, certainly, in their resonantly energetic capability for disruptive expressive action. In this latter course, too, Wright followed a classic line in Afro-American expression, a line suggested, for example, by *Narrative of the Life of Frederick Douglass* with its uncompromising portrayals of vernacular dimensions in the life of the "slave community."

The point, surely, is that Dunbar and the Harlem Renaissance—as well as writers of the thirties such as Zora Hurston and Waters Turpin—provided options for Wright *vis-à-vis* a dream of American form. And like his more energetic predecessors who absorbed into their conscious lives and creative styles the rhythms of train-wheels-over-track-junctures, he chose to provide yet another installment in the project of achieving a blues book most excellent. Wright's place in the project, however, can be understood only through the deconstruction of quite familiar (and lamentably narrow) modes of assessing his corpus that have held sway for decades. Tropological energy is de rigueur if one would comprehend the signal black (w)holeness of Richard Wright.

The word "reassessment" implies a shift in axiological determinants that prompts reconsideration of the type and amount of use one hopes to extract from familiar objects and events. To reassess Richard Wright, therefore, would be to alter prevailing conceptions of the value to be extracted from such characteristic fictions as, say, "Big Boy Leaves Home" and "The Man Who Lived Underground." Such an alteration would constitute a beneficial cognitive shift, for traditional evaluative accounts of Wright and his corpus have been grounded on a theoretical model that has generated a quite limited set of explanatory terms. This well-rehearsed model is a discourse predicated on *lack*. It is, in fact, a model which proceeds almost entirely in terms of a capitalistic economics' "need" and "lack." And it inscribes, in each evaluative instance, the effects of a decidedly bourgeois orientation. The polarization that it privileges, as my subsequent discussion will make clear, stands in marked contrast to Wright's own iconography of "absence" and "desire."

In such classic instances of traditional evaluation as James Baldwin's controversial essays and Ralph Ellison's engaging "The World and the Jug," the author of *Native Son* is adjudged a rebellious Southerner psychologically deprived by the Jim Crow ethics of a Mississippi upbringing and intellectually denied by the vagaries of an incomplete formal education. Baldwin insists, for example, in an extraordinarily derogatory postmortem entitled "Alas, Poor Richard" that Wright's "notions of society, politics, and history . . . seemed . . . utterly fanciful." Only at the close of his life, asserts Baldwin, did Wright begin to acquire "a less uncertain esthetic distance, and a new depth." Yet he never achieved, in his successor's venomous accounting, an informed, artistic comprehension of the modern world, remaining through all his days "a Mississippi pickaninny, mischievous, cunning, and tough." Baldwin's evaluation of Wright is incomparably more malevolent than Ellison's. The latter merely refuses to grant Wright the status of "artist," insisting that his predecessor adopted a fixed, ideological perspective before he had achieved the technical mastery requisite for genuine creativity.

Wright's own creative self-portrait in *Black Boy* is to some extent responsible for the assessments of Baldwin and Ellison. The narrator of the autobiography depicts himself as largely autodidactic, attracted to "words as weapons," and uncommonly fierce in his appropriation of literature as a form of social action. Wright's successors seem to read this portrait, not as a figuration of the deconstructive writer at work or as an implicit condemnation of the shortcomings of a warped system of southern injustice. Rather, both Ellison and Baldwin interpret the autobiography's portrait of denial, lack, and fierce appropriation as an inscription of the artist *maniqué*. Wright's successors see him as a writer bereft of rich intellectual endowments and committed to a limiting form of engaged literary action. The craftsman of "The Man Who Lived Underground" is characterized in traditional evaluative discourse as a "protest" writer. "Lack," thus, generates "protest" in the familiar discourse. And "protest" stands as both an indictment and a levy, signaling to the initiated a realm of quite problematic expressive value. James Baldwin provides the classic formulation of the charge of "protest" in "Many Thousands Gone."

The protest writer, according to Baldwin, is less a creator of cultural texts than a victim. He lacks the informed *individuality* (a term to which we shall return shortly) that would allow him to escape the effects of cultural imperialism. He never, in Baldwin's view, transcends the peculiar status of

Caliban, whose response to language's largesse is always either passive compliance in the restrictive, linguistic terms meted out for his existence or a bitter curse. In "Everybody's Protest Novel," this prospect on protest is illustrated by the following homology: Richard Wright is to the agit-prop naturalism of protest writing as the pagan African is to the crude salvifics of missionary Christianity.

> Thus, the African, exile, pagan, hurried off the auction block and into the fields, fell on his knees before that God in Whom he must now believe; who had made him, but not in His image. This tableau, this impossibility, is the heritage of the Negro in America: *Wash me,* cried the slave to his Maker, *and I shall be whiter, whiter than snow!* . . . [and] Bigger's tragedy [Wright's failure in his protest writing in *Native Son*] is not that he is cold or black or hungry, nor even that he is American, black; but that he [Wright] has accepted a theology [linguistic code of social protest] that denies him life, that he admits the possibility of his being sub-human and feels constrained, therefore, to battle for his humanity according to those brutal criteria bequeathed him at his birth.

The metaphor's terms imply—in the case of both Wright and the analogical African—a primitive, artisanal consciousness incapable of avoiding the constraints and codes of cultural oppression. The productive results of such a consciousness—one perennially shaped by the scripted texts of the cultural "other"—are always imitative, flatly rebellious, metaphorically impoverished. Protest writing is, therefore, in Baldwin's view, only a pale shadow of the cultural missionary's (or cultural arbiter's) resonant acts of language. And insofar as men's and women's needs *vis-à-vis* art include intellectually charged and symbolically rich texts, they are destined to frustration if they place a sizable levy on the efforts of Richard Wright.

A reassessment of Wright must begin with a rereading of the traditional discourse's *lack*. This predicate cannot be taken as a mark of "objective" truth about the life and works of an "artisan of protest." Rather, it must be read as a symptom of the traditional discourse's unposed, but nevertheless answered, question.

Analyzing Marx's relationship to the texts of classical economics, Louis Althusser asserts that Marx's comprehension and revision of the classical texts resulted from his ability to "read the illegible," to measure the theoretical framework initially visible in such texts "against the invisible problematic contained in the paradox of *an answer which does not correspond to any question posed.*" I want to suggest, in the interest of (W)right assessment, that the answer *lack* in classical texts of Wright analysis is a response to the "illegible" problematic constituted by bourgeois aesthetic theory. The un-inscribed question is, "What is art?" And the answer proposed by bourgeois aesthetics is a response that necessarily finds Wright *lacking.*

## II

If we recur for a moment to Baldwin's protest writer and African pagan, we find that both metaphorical entities in "Everybody's Protest Novel" recapitulate one pole of a familiar antinomy. The writer and the savage represent helpless *social* victims juxtaposed with resolutely *individualistic* creators. Baldwin elaborates a contradistinction between *individual* and *society* as though the division possesses the force of natural law, when, in fact, it carries only the reinscribed, metaphorical force of an old problematic. The power of the distinction is contingent upon a model of perceiving "reality" that emerges from a peculiar, cultural ordering of existence. And its very delineation, perforce, implies that the person reinscribing its antinomies is superior to all merely *social* determinants.

If Baldwin's essays are paradigm instances, then traditional evaluative discourse assessing Wright assuredly constitutes a theoretical framework in direct opposition to the well-known Marxian dictate that reads: "It is not the consciousness of men that determines their being, but, on the contrary, their social being that determines their consciousness." Bourgeois aesthetics is an axiological extension of a bourgeois society's privileging of "consciousness" in the domain of expressive culture. The theory is coextensive with the emergence of an industrial society that commodified life and reduced value to a cash nexus. Bourgeois aesthetics postulates an artistically transcendent realm of experience, production, and value as a "cultural" preserve, a domain where individual creativity ("consciousness") secures itself against corruptions of industrialism ("social being"). The British Marxist Raymond Williams aptly summarizes the contours of bourgeois aesthetic theory in his study *Marxism and Literature*. He suggests that such a theory produces: "specializing abstractions of 'art' and 'the aesthetic' " which represent "a particular stage of the division of labour." He further asserts:

> "Art" is [defined in bourgeois aesthetic theory as] a kind of production which has to be seen as separate from the dominant bourgeois productive norm: the making of commodities. ["Art"]

has then, in fantasy, to be separated from "production" altogether; described by the new term "creation"; distinguished from
its own material processes; distinguished, finally, from other
products of its own kind or closely related kinds—"art" from
"non-art"; "literature" from "para-literature" or "popular literature"; "culture" from "mass culture." The narrowing abstraction ["Art"] is then so powerful that, in its name, we find
ways of neglecting (or of dismissing as peripheral) that relentless
transformation of art works into commodities, within the dominant forms of capitalist society. *Art and thinking about art have
to separate themselves, by ever more absolute abstraction, from
the social processes within which they are still contained. Aesthetic theory is the main instrument of this evasion.* In its concentration on receptive states, on psychological responses of an
abstractly differentiated kind, it [aesthetic theory] represents the
division of labour in consumption corresponding to the abstraction of art as the division of labour in production. [my emphasis]

In the well-rehearsed evaluative discourse devoted to Wright, certain
features of the author's career are inescapable. He was certainly a writer of
*socially ordained* fictions. His success in the marketplace is a matter of
record. (His income in the year after *Native Son*'s publication was in excess
of $30,000—a not inconsiderable sum in 1941.) Taken together, these fea-
tures of Wright's career identify him—under a bourgeois aesthetic prospect—as an artist *manqué*. In Ellison's account in "The World and the Jug,"
the author of *Native Son* suffers the fullest condemnations of a dichotomiz-
ing, bourgeois aesthetic code. Ellison, as previously mentioned, laments that
"Wright found the facile answers of Marxism before he learned to use
*literature* as a means for discovering the forms of American Negro humanity" (my emphasis). Extending a cautionary aesthetic wisdom, Ellison goes
on to suggest that Wright's artistic failures in a novel like *The Long Dream*
may constitute a form of "artistic immorality" leading to "chaos."

Wright and his productions are consigned by Ellison to a simplistic,
sociological field of *nonart*. The highest "creativity" of symbolic production
and the deepest affectivity of "aesthetic" response that are characteristic of
"art" are held to be always *lacking* in his career. He is defined, therefore, as
inadequately symbolic and metaphorical—that is, as an artistically lacking
artisan of protest. The signal misfortune of such a traditional reading of
Wright is that it prevents access to the ample symbolic content of such
works as "Big Boy Leaves Home" and "The Man Who Lived Underground."

The question, therefore, becomes, *how*, once a "symptomatic" reading has revealed the unposed query and latent problematic of traditional evaluative discourse, does one institute a forcefully reevaluative investigation. My response is that one begins with a signifying device sufficiently unusual in its connotations to shatter familiar conceptual determinations. (W)right reasoning begins in tropological thought.

## III

In suggesting a tropological perspective on Wright, I will appropriate once again the interpretive modes detailed by Hayden White. The introduction of unusual metaphors (or tropes) where objects of traditional knowledge are concerned generates new conceptual images. The trope is equivalent in effect to a symbol, providing neither icon nor description, but suggesting instead how we should both constitute *and* feel about an object of knowledge. In my subsequent discussion, I want to summon what is known to physics as a "black hole" as a useful trope for a reevaluation of Richard Wright. To meditate on the *black hole* is to understand how tropic thought, as a device of reassessment, serves toward a realignment of conceptual economies. First, however, a definition in answer to the question: What is a *black hole?*

A black hole is "an area of space which appears absolutely black because the gravitation there is so intense that not even light can escape into the surrounding areas." Such areas are posited by the General Theory of Relativity as unimaginably dense remains of stars. They may be only a few miles in diameter yet contain the entire mass of a star three times larger than the sun. The area marked by the black hole is dark because an initially luminescent star has, in its burning, coverted energy to mass. (It has become a "massive concentration," one might say, invoking the term *Mascon*, first appropriated to Afro-American literary criticism by Stephen Henderson.)

But while the black hole is darkly invisible, it is detectable by the energy field resulting from its attraction of hydrogen atoms, cosmic particles, and other objects. As these objects move through the black hole's gravitational field they approach the velocity of light, creating an intense field of electromagnetic radiation. The gravitation is so forceful that it not only attracts cosmic particles but also may hold another massive, luminous star in a binary system.

Black holes are not, however, as simply fathomable as the foregoing implies. They are surrounded by an "event horizon," a membrane that prevents the unaltered escape of anything which passes through. Light shone into a black hole disappears. And at the center of the hole—at what is called its "singularity"—all objects are "squeezed" to zero volume. Space and time disappear.

The black hole as a trope presents an invisible, attractive force—a massive concentration of energy that draws all objects to its center. It reduces matter that passes its event horizon to zero sum. Richard Wright and this trope come together in meditation if *Black Boy* is allowed to serve as a mediating textual ground.

## IV

First there is the luminescent star, burning with furious energy, ravenously consuming. It is like a massive, cosmic furnace of desire. The light produced is that which can be dispensed. The mass is sharply concentrated.

Richard Wright in the intense passion of autodidactic illumination is figured in *Black Boy* as a center of ravenous desire. He is like the Red Giant burning toward fulfilled concentration. He seeks to consume:

> I hungered for books, new ways of looking and seeing. It was not a matter of believing or disbelieving what I read, but of feeling something new, of being affected by something that made the look of the world different. . . . Reading grew into a passion. . . . The plots and stories in the novels did not interest me so much as the point of view revealed. . . . Reading was like a drug, a dope.

The fuel consumed by Wright is the work of H. L. Mencken, Sinclair Lewis, Theodore Dreiser, whose relationship to the quotidian, to "everyday reality," is less mediated by beautifying literary conventions than the works of their contemporaries. But it would not have mattered whether Wright fueled his hunger with Flaubert or Frank Norris, because he was not in search of literary *lights*. As with the black hole, so with Wright: the light is that which can be dispensed (with). The mass remains.

The search presented in *Black Boy* is a quest for a correlative, an articulated set of relationships that will make sense of desire. It is not an expedition in discovery of literary, or "artistic," mastery. Hence the narrator's initial reading of Mencken ends, not with a paean to "literary" genius, but with a statement of absence: "I concluded the book with the conviction that I had somehow overlooked something terribly important in life. I had once tried to write, had once reveled in feeling, had let my crude imagination roam, but the impulse to dream *had been slowly beaten out of me by experience*" (my emphasis). The matter consumed by Wright to fuel desire—to secure an "overlooked" *something* that is "terribly important" for the amelioration of absence—is naturalistic and realistic fiction.

Reading *Black Boy* under the trope of the black hole, one might say that Wright "burns" novels to fuel *his own concentration*. He is unconcerned with novels' truth value ("It was not a matter of believing or disbelieving what I read . . ."), and their literary techniques are of no importance ("The plots and stories in the novels did not interest me . . ."). Rather, he consumes them ravenously, voraciously. "I gave myself over to each novel without reserve, without trying to criticize it; it was enough for me to see and feel something different." Wright's quest is ultimately to achieve articulate structures of vision and feeling that constitute a correlative, supplying an equivalent to that "terribly important" *something* found absent. What he seeks, one might say, is a *difference* that will fulfill desire.

Vision and feeling are primary functions of writing for Wright; the malleability of words before *individualistic* "literary artistry" is a matter of indifference. Words are commodities, a necessary fuel in the meaningful structuring of a concentratedly *different* experience.

The experience that is at issue is squeezed to an unimaginably dense point in *Black Boy*. In the autobiography, the mother's suffering absence becomes a figure gathering to itself all lineaments of a black "blues life." In a single instant of recall, it suggests the foundational image in the repertoire of human desire: "Once, in the night, my mother called me to her bed and told me that she could not endure the pain, that she wanted to die. I held her hand and begged her to be quiet. That night I ceased to react to my mother; my feelings were frozen." "Frozen" means *fixed* as in a stop-action photograph which serves as a set point of significant emotional reference.

The mother's suffering—generalized, internalized, "frozen" as framed image—becomes, for Wright: "a symbol . . . gathering to itself all the poverty, the ignorance, the helplessness; the painful, baffling, hunger-ridden days and hours; the restless moving, the futile seeking, the uncertainty, the fear, the dread; the meaningless pain and the endless suffering." From this long chorus emerges the litany of a lean blues life in black America: a life of "poverty . . . baffling . . . hunger-ridden days . . . restless moving . . . meaningless pain and . . . endless suffering." What is coextensive with this litany (providing, as it were, its brilliant symbolic generality) is the primary image of human desire. Roland Barthes delineates the relationship of absence, desire, and language as follows in *A Lover's Discourse*:

Absence persists—I must endure it. Hence I will *manipulate* it: transform the distortion of time into oscillation, produce rhythm, make an entrance onto the stage of language (language is born of absence: the child has made himself a doll out of a spool, throws it away and picks it up again, miming the mother's departure and return: a paradigm is created). . . . This staging of language postpones the other's death: a very short interval, we are told, separates the time during which the child still believes his mother to be absent and the time during which he believes her to be already dead. To manipulate absence is to extend this interval, to delay as long as possible the moment when the other might topple sharply from absence into death. Absence is the figure of privation; simultaneously, I desire and I need. Desire is squashed against need: that is the obsessive phenomenon of all amorous sentiment.

In the autobiographical instant materializing his mother's suffering absence, Wright linguistically structures desire—the vision and feeling of a *black blues life*—as universal symbol. There occurs a striking conflation of motive, event, and goal when the narrator reports (subsequent to the image's presentation) that the quest is "to wring a meaning out of meaningless suffering." The meaning (appearing *for itself*) is, in fact, the mother's image. It is *always already there* in the text of human life *in general,* and has just been *textualized* in writing by Wright's autobiographical voice of desire.

Novels are depicted by *Black Boy* as the fuel that allows the narrator (at age nineteen) to take a first step in the achievement of the kind of significant structure that is represented by the image of the mother's suffering absence itself. Novels' words fuel, that is to say, an internalized, half-beaten-down-by-experience image of the black blues life's desire. And the "literariness" of such words can be dispensed (with).

The conventions that condition literary "artistry," Wright's narrator implies, maintain life's surfaces. By reducing "literariness" to the concentrated image of *my* mother's suffering absence as symbol, the narrator institutes a descent toward the "meaningless suffering" that is, in his view, the very engine of class division and embittering absence in the segregated society of America.

One way of phrasing the implied expressive-productive norms of *Black Boy* is to say that the narrator's presentation of the desire of a black blues life—one almost under erasure by experience's "slow" beatings—is ontogenetic, symbolized by *my* (Wright's) mother's suffering absence. Yet this desire is also concentratedly phylogenetic—signified by the mother's suffering absence as an image of that primitive form of human consciousness (desire) that strives to annul surfaces (objects). In a Hegelian sense, the phylogenetic desire implied by *Black Boy* is a form of consciousness that achieves—through suffering and "unhappiness"—a recognition that genuine self-certainty consists in community. Only through the intersubjectivity of community can consciousness become *self-consciousness*. In *Black Boy*, words are, finally, objects annulled by a desirous consciousness in order to achieve the communality of "point of view." The narrator, in a passage from the autobiography already cited, says: "The plots and stories in the novels did not interest me so much as the point of view revealed." The phylogenetic "trace" of consciousness's journeyings is thus discovered as "point of view" in realistic and naturalistic fiction. "Point of view," one might say, defined not as subjective intention but as trace of human desire, is the subjective correlative required for (W)right self-consciousness.

A beautifying, "literary" language is a restrictive array of conventions preserving class division, maintaining the status quo surfaces of life, *creating desire* rather than elaborating its transcendence. What is required for the *social* (intersubjective) project comprised by desire's existence, expression, and transcendence is an adequate, expressive vehicle.

The trope of the black hole suggests a "squeezing" of matter to zero sum. Wright, as voracious center of desire—seeking desire's trace as "point of view"—reduces literary language to zero sum. *Black Boy*, in fact, is utterly relentless in its representations of what might be termed a "code of desire" that reduces conventional discourse to zero. Inversive language is repeatedly represented as nullifying fixed discursive norms in the autobiography.

The narrator reports, for example, on a day's encounter during his sixth year with "the blues people" of Memphis, Tennessee: "Toward early evening, they let me go. I staggered along the pavements, drunk, repeating obscenities to the horror of the women I passed and to the amusement of the men en route to their homes from work." The quotidian expectations of street exchange are shockingly voided. Expectations encoded by theological fundamentalism fare no better in the face of the narrator's reductive code of desire. When the young man who lives across the street from his grandmother attempts to set scriptures against the narrator's own articulations, the results are described as follows:

> During our talk I made a hypothetical statement that summed up my attitude toward God and the suffering in the world, a statement that stemmed from my knowledge of life as I had lived,

seen, felt, and suffered it in terms of dread, fear, hunger, terror, and loneliness. "If laying down my life could stop the suffering in the world, I'd do it. But I don't belive anything can stop it," I told him. Frightened and baffled, he left me. I felt sorry for him.

And the holy, matriarchal center of the Wilson clan herself finds church norms scandalously reduced in an instant by the narrator's words. Grandmother Wilson is drying the young Wright after a bath:

> "Bend over," she ordered. I stooped and she scrubbed my anus. My mind was in a sort of daze, midway between daydreaming and thinking [the province of desire?]. Then, before I knew it, words—words whose meaning I did not fully know—had slipped out of my mouth. "When you get through, kiss back there," I said, the words rolling softly but unpremeditatedly. . . . Granny rose slowly and lifted the wet towel high above her head and brought it down across my naked body.

The examples can be multiplied: the narrator's reduction of the discourse of black southern education to zero sum in his unshakable determination to deliver his own commencement speech, the reduction of a white woman employer's text of vocational expectations, for the Negro to zero through his assertion that he wants to be a writer, the "unpremeditated" nullification of bourgeois social exchange at the home of Uncle Clark and Aunt Jody, the inversive countermanding of numinous discourse in his crafting of desirous fiction (tales of Indian maidens and "hellish" voodoo) in the moments designated for prayer at his grandmother's house.

The narrator's reported youthful relationship to Christian discourse in *Black Boy* serves as a shorthand for all his zero-sum reductions of conventional discourse:

> Some of the Bible stories were interesting in themselves, but we always twisted them, secularized them to the level of our street life, rejecting all meanings that did not fit into our environment. And we did the same to the beautiful hymns. When the preacher intoned: *Amazing grace, how sweet it sounds,* we would wink at one another and hum under our breath: *A bulldog ran my grandma down.*

Rejecting "all meanings" that do not fit into the environment means, for the narrator, shaping a code that accords with the lean life of a black blues people's intense desire. The "flat" speech and "vague" gestures of convention are incommensurate with a world that has imprinted the narrator with its desire—a world, "a plane of living," marked by "swinging doors of saloons, the railroad yard, the roundhouses, the street gangs, the river levees, an orphan home." This imprinting existence found him "shifted from town to town," mingling with "grownups more than perhaps was good for me." And it is finally the determinate influence of such an existence that motivates the narrator's refusal to "curb . . . [his] habit of cursing"—to restrain his propensity for engaging in reductively inversive and shocking discursive acts conditioned by a blues life's desire. Such inversive discourse is precisely where Richard Wright's attractive singularity resides.

From one analytical perspective, Wright and his autobiographical narrator are forerunners of Roland Barthes's project in *Writing Degree Zero.* Like Barthes's idealized writer, Wright confounds the "literariness" expected of "novelists," of "literary autobiographers," by inversively inscribing desire into what the Russian formalism of Mikhail Bakhtin describes as "carnivalesque" discourse. *Literature,* reduced to "zero degree writing," becomes in Wright's canon a language in which "ambivalent" words such as obscenities, parodic utterances, inversive or ironical phrases function as reductive junctures. The conventional orders of language are reduced to dialogical (two discourses "yoked," sometimes "violently," together), symbolic occasions. The result is language of startling misalliances, sacreligious punnings, scandalous repudiations.

Following the lead of Julia Kristeva in *Desire in Language,* one might say that zero degree, nonliterary language results when desire "adds itself to the linear order of language" through the types of displacement, arch condensation, and festive inversions witnessed in the writing of Richard Wright. A definition of "carnivalesque discourse" provides an apt characterization of Wright's discursive practice: "Carnivalesque discourse breaks through the laws of language censored by grammar and semantics and, at the same time, is a social and political protest. There is no equivalence, but rather, identity between challenging official linguistic codes and challenging official law." Just as matter crossing the black hole's event horizon is compressed to zero, so conventional, literary language indrawn by Wright's blues life's black desire is forced to "bare its devices." The time and space of conventional bourgeois aesthetic theory break down at desire's signal (w)holeness. Within the black (w)hole's force-field, old laws of "literature" no longer operate.

The paradox in Wright assessment is that traditional evaluative accounts bracket the author of *Black Boy* as an artisan of social protest, charging that he failed to transcend the *social* in order to arrive at *art.* Baldwin, for example, writes as follows in "Many Thousands Gone":

> [Wright's] work, from its beginning, is most clearly committed
> to the social struggle. Leaving aside the considerable question of
> what relationship precisely the artist bears to the revolutionary,
> the reality of man as a social being is not his only reality and that
> artist is strangled who is forced to deal with human beings solely
> in social terms.

From the perspective of the black hole as trope, however, one recognizes
what paradoxes can arise from an inadequate theory. For Wright incon-
testably drew all of *art* into his own singularity and employed it to fuel his
project of articulating a black blues life's pressing desire. He thus became an
irreducibly dark, powerful, and invisible core at the very center of the
Afro-American expressive ("artistic"?) universe. The manifest "unevenness"
of his prose, its pastiche, shards of theological, philosophical, and sociological discourse, sparse (sometimes mechanical) stichomythia are fragments of
a "literature" that *was*—a discursive order reduced to zero in the interest of
the black (w)hole's blues desire.

## V

Invisible, massive in its energies, erasing old law, nullifying time and
space in its singularity, the black hole metaphorically suggests the proportions of Wright's achievement—his space, as it were, in the tradition of
Afro-American expressive culture. The implications of the trope's suggestiveness for practical criticism and evaluative reassessment are not far to
seek. To derive the metaphor's productiveness, one need only play on rich
imagistic possibilities that it reveals.

Transliterated in letters of Afro-America, the *black hole* assumes the
subsurface force of the black underground. It graphs, that is to say, the
subterranean *hole* where the trickster has his ludic, deconstructive being.
Further, in the script of Afro-America, the hole is the domain of *Wholeness,*
an achieved rationality of black community in which desire recollects experience and sends it forth as blues. To be *Black* and *(W)hole* is to escape
incarcerating restraints of a white world (i.e., a *black hole*) and to engage
the concentrated, underground singularity of experience that results in a
blues desire's expressive fullness.

The symbolic content of Afro-American expressive culture can thus be
formulated in terms of the *black hole* conceived as a subcultural (underground, marginal, or liminal) region in which a dominant, white culture's
representations are squeezed to zero volume, producing a new expressive
order. As Richard Wright's work brilliantly demonstrates, there is a set

pattern of rites marking this Afro-American underground experience. Wright knew that in any black life, in any white-dominated society, a "life-crisis" of black identity—an event equivalent to such other life crises as birth, social puberty, and death—was an inevitable event. The scholarship of Belgian anthropologist Arnold Van Gennep is suggestive where such life crises are concerned.

Van Gennep insists that a person's departure from one stage of social life in order to enter another marks a time of critical transformation, creating cultural instability and requiring appropriate ceremonies. The purpose of such ceremonies, according to Van Gennep, is to enable the individual to pass "safely" and profitably from one defined social position to another. The circumcision rites that initiate West African males into manhood might be offered as instances of a ceremonial movement from one stage of social life to another.

Van Gennep persuasively demonstrates in his classic work *The Rites of Passage* that ceremonies accompanying social transition share the tripartite form common to *rites of passage*. Such ceremonies are characterized by the following phases: (1) separation from a fixed social position, (2) movement through a "timeless" and "statusless" marginality, and (3) reincorporation into a new, fixed social state with a new status. A diagram of passage rites borrowed from Edmund Leach's work *Culture and Communication* provides a clarifying graphic for Van Gennep's scheme.

The life crisis of black identity in a white society is instituted by the black person's sudden awareness that he or she represents what Carolyn Fowler calls a "zero image" in the perceptual schemes of the white, dominant culture. Zora Neale Hurston's Janie, the protagonist of *Their Eyes Were Watching God*, offers a striking narrative instance of a black person's encounter with the "zero image." Janie is perplexed and dismayed when she surveys the photograph that an itinerant photographer has taken of her and her childhood playmates: "Where is me? Ah don't see me," she says. Recalling the event in later years, a mature Janie says: "Before Ah seen de picture Ah thought Ah wuz like de rest." Once she "gets the picture," however, Hurston's protagonist reflexively understands that her status is that of an alien, a "nigger," a "zero" in the white world's structures of perception.

One might well think of Janie's encounter with the "zero image" as identical to Richard Wright's narrator's sudden realization that his internal (*essential*) self is "under erasure." Such a realization is always followed in black narratives by passage rites—by what might be termed *rites of the black (w)hole*. The first stage in such rites involves the black person's sep-

aration from a dominant, white society. The act of withdrawal is equivalent
to a conflagrational retreat in which the mass of old edicts is reduced to a
light that can be dispensed (with).

Ellison's invisible man making his *underground* retreat, reports as follows: "I tried to find the usual ladder that leads out of such holes, but there
was none. I had to have a light. . . . I started searching for paper to make a
torch, feeling about slowly over the coal pile. . . . I'd have to open by brief
case. In it were the only papers I had. I started with my high school diploma,
applying one precious match with a feeling of remote irony, even smiling as
I saw the swift but feeble light push back the gloom." And in the moment
of autodidactic passion, Wright's narrator in *Black Boy* fuels desire with
naturalistic and realistic novels. The result of such burning separations is a
new, forceful, and dense black mass that signals the second stage of an
underground ritual.

This second stage of the rites of the black (w)hole commences with a
renewal of desire. Mythic images of experiences internalized by active black
culture bearers are brilliantly summoned, expressed, and passed on as an
educational experience. The black initiand in the second or liminal phase
enters a period of instruction that is "betwixt and between" anything ap-
proximating fixed social status. The timelessness and spacelessness of this
period outside history are characterized by receipt of "ancestral" wisdom.
The initiand, in fact, learns to employ the internalized images of a black
blues life's desire in peculiarly Afro-American ways. Through inversion and
deconstructive parody he sets conventional wisdom on its head—that is, at
zero sum. Achieving what might be termed an "ahistorical," "metaphorical" sense of the black self's *historicity* or placement within a diachronic
series of Afro-American events, the initiand, in the liminal phase, effects a
negation of negation. Grasping his own black timely timelessness through
receipt of ancestral wisdom, he negates a dominant society's perceptual
schemes by re(w)riting (and righting) history. What results is his recognition
of the irreversibility of rites of the black (w)hole. He becomes aware that he
can never "reintegrate" into a dominantly white society with a "socially
responsible" status. And here begins the final stage of the ritual.

The third, and final, phase of conventional *rites of passage* is aggregation. The marginal initiand is reintegrated, with a new status, into the
society from which he has separated. It is at this stage of conventional rites
that the suggestiveness of the black hole trope becomes fully manifest. In the
rites of the black underground, there is *no return* to a renewed plentitude of
"origins." The rites are irreversible. Having passed the event horizon into

the singularity of *(W)holeness,* the initiand and his experience are irretrievably transformed.

Another way of phrasing this irreversibility is to say that once liminality has been accomplished in the rites of the black (w)hole, an enduring *Black Difference* is the only world available to the initiand. For the historicization of the black self in liminal regions of desire—the constitution, as it were, of a concentrated, *mass* Afro-American identity—renders reintegration into "white" society impossible. The achievement of *Black (W)holeness* means that accepted and acceptable roles meted out for blacks by a dominantly white society are no longer feasible.

What is possible is *entry* into the singularity at the black (W)hole's center. This *singularity* consists of an initiated, expressive black *community* that has "gotten the [white world's] picture," used it to fuel retreat, found the center of its own singular desire, and given expressive form to a new and meaningful *Black (W)holeness.* If one were to invoke René Girard's *Deceit, Desire, and the Novel,* one might say that what ultimately occurs in black (w)hole rites is the installation of a black expressive community at the tip of the triangle of desire as a substitute for the perceptual schemes and modes of discourse of white society in a premarginal phase of black existence.

The expressive community at the center of the black hole is always conceived as "marginal" because its members never "return" to the affective and perceptual structures of an old, white dispensation. In actuality, the expressive community of the black (w)hole, as Richard Wright understood so well, is the center of a new order of existence. Invisible, charged with extraordinary attractive force, it draws all events and objects into its horizon; (w)rites a new order of discourse. A graphic presentation like the figure that follows provides some notion of the structure of black (w)hole rites and indicates (in its contrast with Leach's previously adduced illustration) the way in which such rites comprise a re(w)rite.

The black center in rites of the black (w)hole transforms old matter into new light. It "gives birth," in Sherley Anne Williams's apt phrase, "to brightness." For a black hole's intense attraction is responsible for the incredibly brilliant energy sources that physicists call "quasars"—quasi-stellar radio sources—which may be several times the diameter of our own solar system, emitting more energy than a galaxy of a hundred and fifty billion stars. The incredible light of the black underground's "invisible" space (say, 1,369 bulbs multiplied by wattage) finds its expressive fullness in liminality, in the margins. Questions of inside and outside, central ("centered") and marginal become extraordinarily complex in the tropic province of the black hole—the domain of the outside/elsewhere identity of *Black Whole-*

*ness*. Who (including Ellison's Mr. Norton) would not want to be at the blue-black singularity's "center" when experience and desire converge to give birth to light billions of times brighter than the sun?

Examples from Richard Wright's fiction provide an idea of the immensely dense symbolic action that occurs at the center of the black (w)hole. Big Boy, in the short story that bears his name in its title, having slain the white man who murderously seeks to reduce him to a "zero image," tells his parents: "Theres some holes big enough fer me to git in n stay till Will comes erlong." "Will," of course, is simply a proper name in the fiction, but its conjunction with the protagonist's strategy of retreat is significant in a delineation of the rites of the black (w)hole. In successive acts of "will," Big Boy escapes a white world's murderous conception of blackness. The hole into which he enters to avoid a lynch mob in hot pursuit is—in any blue/black reading of Afro-American experience—clearly a *singularly* black route of escape.

Several days prior to their disastrous encounter with the white world's "zero image," Big Boy and his youthful companions have turned a southern hillside into a highballing train, a blues-whistle locomotive of liberation. By digging kiln holes into southern earth and setting tin cans of water in the holes to boiling, the black boys have turned dirt, the earth itself, into an instrument of freedom's desire:

> The train [heard by Big Boy secure in one of the kiln holes] made him remember how they had dug these kilns on long, hot summer days, how they had made boilers out of big tin cans, filled them with water, fixed stoppers for steam, cemented them in holes with wet clay, and built fires under them. He recalled how they had danced and yelled when a stopper blew out of a boiler, letting out a big spout of steam and a shrill whistle. There were times when they had the whole hillside blazing and smoking. Yeah, yuh see, Big Boy wuz Casey Jones n wuz speedin down the gleamin rails of the Southern Pacific.

Indeed, Big Boy in the marginal black hole of escape not only assumes figurative dimensions of the railroad hero Casey Jones, but also metaphorical resonances of Afro-America's arch trickster—Brer Rabbit himself. The agon of "Big Boy Leaves Home" is, finally, that of the wily hare Big Boy against the ferocious white hounds seeking to drive him out of existence— to "beat" his desire down to zero. "Gawddam them white folks!" the protagonist reflects bitterly, "Thas all they wuz good fer, t run a nigger down like a rabbit. Yeah, they git yuh in a corner n then they let yuh have it." But oppression's traditional scenario is thwarted in Big Boy's case. No one lets *him* have it. He violently confronts the green-eyed hound that threatens his (w)hole. Strangling the dog to death, he escapes to the universe of the North when "Will comes erlong" in the morning. The rabbit hole, black hole, train-whistle-heroic domain of Afro-American underground expressive *Will* results in self-defense and escape.

## VI

But a black boy violently initiated into manhood is not, according to Wright's short fiction, presented with substantially altered prospects in the North. "The Man Who Lived Underground," a novella published in 1944, is set in the North and signals what might be termed a "black-hole intentionality" in its very title. When the work's protagonist "gets the picture," he discovers that he—like many thousands before—is always/already "guilty." Escaping from a trumped-up murder charge down a city sewer system manhole, he proceeds to construct an inversively expressive text with the shattered instrumentalities of the white-owned aboveground world.

The story of "The Man Who Lived Underground" is one of Wright's more striking presentations of the crime-magazine plot in a form designed for an implied audience of symbolically aware readers. It presents a system of actions familiar to readers of detective fiction and traces, at this interpretive level, events in the life of Fred Daniels, who is arrested, charged with the murder of Mrs. Peabody, and forced by three white policemen to sign a confession. Daniels escapes the police station and takes refuge in a dry place in an old sewer beneath the city. In this underground world, he comes to a new and authentic consciousness of his own and society's essential condition and eventually ascends to share his new knowledge.

The conjunctions between this sequence of actions and Feodor Dostoyevski's *Notes from Underground* have been remarked by past critics. A descent to a new level of comprehension followed by an emergent desire for dialogue with one's judges brings Wright's work into archetypal accord with that of his Slavic predecessor. Daniels's acts of fleeing the police station and establishing a voluntary underground exile, moreover, seem to imply a central proposition articulated by Dostoyevski. The narrator of *Notes from Underground* says to the judges:

> You see, you gentlemen have, to the best of my knowledge, taken your whole register of human advantages from the averages of statistical figures and politico-economical formulas. Your advantages are prosperity, wealth, freedom, peace—and so on, and so

on. So that the man who should, for instance, go openly and knowingly in opposition to all that list would, to your thinking, and indeed mine too, of couse, be an obscurantist or an absolute madman: would not he? But, you know, this is what is surprising: why does it so happen that all these statisticians, sages and lovers of humanity, when they reckon up human advantages invariably leave one out? They don't even take it into their reckoning in the form in which it should be taken and the whole reckoning depends upon that. . . . One's own free unfettered choice, one's own caprice—however wild it may be, one's own fancy worked up at times to a frenzy—is that very "most advantageous advantage" which we have overlooked, which comes under no classification and against which all systems and theories are continually being shattered to atoms.

Fred Daniels's "anti-system" acts and the point of view that motivates them, however, do not find a responsive audience aboveground. When he is again in the custody of Johnson, Murphy, and Lawson—the three policemen who first extract his confession—he is taken back to the manhole where he first descended. As he summons the officers to his underground cave, promising them the reward of enlightenment, Lawson shoots him in the chest. The novella concludes as the black man's eyes close and he becomes "a whirling object rushing alone in the darkness, veering, tossing, lost in the heart of the earth."

From the perspective of rites of the black (w)hole, Wright's simply described plot becomes an occasion for an exceedingly rich representation of the encounter with a zero image. Like Kafka's Joseph K, Wright's protagonist finds himself under arrest and charged with crime by the authorities for no apparent reason. Daniels, an employee of Mrs. Wooten (Mrs. Peabody's next-door neighbor) and a contentedly married man, is suddenly subjected to brutal and arbitrary constraints of the state. To end his pain he signs a confession he has not even read. His condition is one of uncomprehending guilt. His intitial status in the eyes of white society, therefore, is that of a "branded" man. Separation from this status begins when he leaps from the police station's window. Through an act of will, he moves decisively away from a passive and guilty subjugation.

The sirens (an ironical word given the role of Sirens in Western mythology) that mark the opening of "The Man Who Lived Underground" serve as an audible boundary separating Daniels from the aboveground: "A police car swished by through the rain, its siren rising sharply. They're looking for me all over. . . . He crept to the door and squinted through the fogged plate glass. He stiffened as the siren rose and died in the distance. Yes, he had to hide, but where?" The answer to his query comes when tiny columns of water "snake into the air from the perforations of a manhole cover." The columns are a sign of underground currents, and they draw Daniels to the manhole from which they arise. The audible boundary of the sirens and a spatial boundary marked by the manhole's cover converge as Daniels descends into darkness: "He heard a prolonged scream of brakes and the siren broke off. Oh, God! They had found him. Looming above his head in the rain a white face hovered over the hole." The policeman peering into the underground, however, is only interested in replacing the cover: "The cover clanged into place, muffling the sights and sounds of the upper world."

The rite of separation is complete; the opposition between "aboveground" and "underground" is firmly established. Daniels becomes a liminal figure hovering "between two worlds." His isolation from prevailing classifications aboveground is reflected by the disappearance of time and the loss of social designation that occur in his new existence: "In this darkness the only notion he had of time was when a match flared and measured time by its fleeting light." After stealing a typewriter on one of his excursions through the underground, he "inserted a piece of paper and poised his fingers to write. But what was his name? He stared, trying to remember. He stood and glared about the dirt cave, his name on the tip of his lips. But it would not come to him." Later when he ascends from underground a policeman inquires: "What is your name?" Daniels opens his lips to respond, and "no words came. He had forgotten. But what did it matter if he had? It was not important."

As a nameless figure in a realm of social timelessness, Wright's protagonist is a quintessentially liminal being. His actions include negation, trespass, parody, burlesque, theft, and mockery. He is the agent of dream-visions that are radically inversive in their symbology. And his ironically imaginative creative acts lead ultimately to a transvaluation of value in which guilt is figured as the founding condition of a new order of existence.

The Christian import of Daniels's paradoxical transvaluation of aboveground values is implied by the relationship between the narrative pattern of the novella and the passion and resurrection of Christ. Daniels descends into darkness and the cover is placed on his "tomb" on Friday at dusk. He emerges the following Sunday to the "spirited singing" of a black congregation:

The Lamb, the Lamb, the Lamb
I hear thy voice a-calling
The Lamb, the Lamb, the Lamb
I feel thy grace a-falling.

These messianic lyrics of a second coming are represented as the backdrop for ascent. The aboveground world, however, rejects its new "Savior" by hurling epithets such as "filthy," "rowdy," "drunk," and "crazy." The worshipers forcefully (and with an inversive vehemence worthy of the medieval "feast of fools") eject Daniels.

The conflict between aboveground Christianity and the radical christology represented by an ascendant Daniels begins almost immediately on the protagonist's descent. One of his first subsurface acts is to say an ambivalent no to the proceedings of traditional Christian worshipers whose singing he overhears. When he listens to the religious community enjoining: "Jesus, take me to your home above/And fold me in the bosom of Thy love," Daniels is suddenly aware that he has experienced feelings of guilt like those which prompt the community to enjoin its song. Yet, peering through a small slit in the wall that separates him from the singers in a subbasement, he sees the white robes and shabbily tattered song books and responds as follows: "he shook his head, disagreeing in spite of himself. They oughtn't do that he thought. . . . He felt that he was gazing upon something abysmally obscene."

The singing has first seemed to Daniels like a "siren" or "a baby crying"—hence, it is marked as both a sign of guilt and infantilism. In effect, its subbasement ceremonial context gives it the character of a basic, or primordial, social action in the mediation of guilt. It is, in effect, "primitive" religion designed to "socialize" guilt. Daniels's hesitant negation is directed toward religion conceived in such terms. He thinks of the worshipers' actions as "grovelling" and "begging," reflecting that "those people should stand unrepentant and yield no quarter in singing and praying, yet *he* had run away from the police, had pleaded with them to believe *his* innocence. He shook his head, bewildered."

Thus begins a visual, emotional, and reflective underground encounter with images perceived from what can be called a "threshold perspective." Wily and resourceful, like the trickster of black folklore, Daniels tunnels his way through the earth, transgressing all boundaries in order to secure a distinctive outsider's point of view. He is the unseen seer, the tabula rasa, in fact, for an illicitly gained and radically revisionist comprehension of aboveground existence.

Daniels's perspective is far from a comforting one. The relief provided by a primitive church's "socializing" of guilt is immediately counteracted in the novella by the emotional effects that derive from a "strangely familiar image" which both attracts and repels the protagonist. The vague light of a manhole cover reveals:

> a tiny nude body of a baby snagged by debris and half-submerged in water. Thinking that the baby was alive, he moved impulsively to save it, but his aroused feelings told him that it was dead, cold, nothing, the same nothingness he had felt while watching the men and women singing in the church. Water blossomed about the tiny legs, the tiny arms, the tiny head, and rushed onward. The eyes were closed, as though in sleep; the fists were clenched, as though in protest; and the mouth gaped black in a soundless cry.

The emotional effect of this percept is a sense of "nothingness." The implicit connection between the percept and religious acts of men and women occurs for Daniels at the level of "feeling."

The distinguishing qualities of the baby are its nudity, its "soundless" (and hence *vain*) protest, and its mortality. An array of images complementing this initial representation in the novella allows one (as I shall demonstrate shortly) to infer that the "strangely familiar" image signals the human condition in general. Life is a vast, uncharted sea onto which man is cast naked remaining half-submerged for a breathing instant before sinking to death.

Finitude and nudity (an absence of inherent, or "natural," shelters against an indifferent world) are existentially perceived as distinctive features of man's fate. Philosophies of existence summarize this perspective in the dictum: "Man is nothing special." The defining human act according to such philosophies is to die. The manifest absence of divine, supreme, or holy "essence" that such a determinant mortality signals leads to human feelings of condemnation, imperfection, and guilt. On encountering the dead baby, Daniels feels as "condemned as when the policemen had accused him." The desire for human atonement implied by religious singing such as that he overheard before seeing the baby is a function of men's and women's sense of *nothingness*—of a separation from grace and supreme essence that results from naked mortality.

The protagonist does not comprehend the full significance of the baby's image until a later stage in his underground sojourn, after his consciousness has been shaped by a series of variations of the initial image. When he has

tunneled through a brick wall and ascended basement stairs of a building
beyond the church, for example, he peeps through a keyhole and sees "the
nude waxen figure of a man stretched out upon a white table." He has
surfaced at an undertaking establishment, and the image of naked finitude
that he encounters is rendered additionally haunting by the presence of a
chuckling "invisible voice" in the room where the corpse is lying. The voice
seems to imply an unseen, cosmic joker hovering above man's hapless morality. Only an "empty sky" and "sea," however, mark the scene when
Daniels dreams that "his body was washed by cold water . . . and swept out
to sea." As he dreams of miraculously walking upon the cold seawater of
human existence, he sees himself encountering

> a nude woman holding a nude baby in her arms and the woman
> was sinking into the water holding the baby above her head and
> screaming *help* and he ran over the water to the woman and he
> reached her just before she went down and took the baby from
> her hands and stood watching the breaking bubbles where the
> woman sank and he called *lady*.

Receiving no answer, he lays the baby on the water (where it miraculously
floats) and dives below to rescue the woman. His attempt fails, and on
surfacing he finds the baby gone. He searches the surface and then "he
began to doubt that he could stand upon the water and then he was sinking
and as he struggled the water rushed him downward spinning dizzily."

The dream recapitulates the images of the dead baby and the waxen
figure at the undertaking establishment. Man is born for death; after a brief
attempt at altruistic interaction he submerges in the "gloomy volume" of an
impassive sea. The fact of man's condemnation to death as the condition of
his existence leads to a sense of imperfection. This sense translates as chronic
anxiety that one has fallen from (or been abandoned by) a more perfect
Other.

The "Other" (what Kierkegaard calls the "Wholly Other") is envisaged
by a man as an authority unlimited by death and capable of providing
happiness on the far side of human atonement. Forgiveness and eternal life
are guarantees for such a religious point of view. Daniels achieves his own
perspective on guilt through the power of underground images of mortality.
When he again views black worshipers near the conclusion of the novella,
he understands that their songs express—at an emotional level—a primal
human drive to shed the burden of guilt that seems "innate" to men and
women. Thoughts of transcendent authority (some "Wholly Other" such as
Jesus) lead the religious community to "search for a happiness they [the

black congregation] could never find." And the community's sacred medi-
tations lead, in turn, to its feelings that it "had committed some dreadful
offense." From a newly achieved perspective on guilt and mortality, however, Daniels is able to postulate that the sole "offense" committed by man
is being born: "it seemed that one was always trying to remember [he
thought] a gigantic shock that had left a haunting impression upon one's
body which one could not forget or shake off, but which had been forgotten
by the conscious mind, creating in one's life a state of eternal anxiety."

Daniels's reflection here suggests the Freudian notion of a birth
trauma—a "gigantic shock" that occurs on leaving behind the warm instinctual world in utero. The notion of such a trauma serves to synthesize
and bring to the level of coherent thought the implicit meanings of images
the protagonist has encountered. His experiences with the dead have taught
him, as it were, at least one consoling and liberating interpretation of guilt's
functioning in the life of man. The images of the dead and dying in his
subsurface world provide him with a fruitfully altered conception of the
animate regions aboveground. The interpretive homology resulting from his
revised view reads as follows: religious worshipers seek to make known
their guilt to God, just as accused black men confess their guilt to white
policemen. The irreducible fact of human mortality prompts human sub-
servience—its groveling and begging before an authority from which man
hopes to gain enduring reprieve. Daniels both generalizes his own guilt and,
by the novella's conclusion, contemplates his own *death* as transcendence.
He dreams that he stands

> in a room watching over his own nude body lying stiff and cold
> upon a white table. At the far end of the room he saw a crowd
> of people huddled in a corner, afraid of his body. Though lying
> dead upon the table, he was standing in some mysterious way at
> his side, warding off the people, guarding his body, and laughing
> to himself as he observed the situation. They're scared of me, he
> thought.

Guardianship over his own death is the signal of Daniels's acceptance of the
condition of human finitude. This acceptance forecloses the possibilities of
fear and obviates the necessity to plead innocence before authority. Penitent
confession becomes a needless act.

The dream revery of guardianship over his own death follows immediately on another dream in which Daniels "saw himself rising, wading
again in the sweeping water of the sewer; he came to a manhole and climbed
out and was amazed to discover that he had hoisted himself into a room

filled with armed policemen who were watching him intently." There is no
need for, nor fear of, the authority figures in this dream. *Authority* only has
power over those whose instinctual fear of death and resultant feelings of
guilt make them incapable of transcending aboveground institutions established to socialize their anxieties. By abandoning the confessional structure
of the police station and descending to an emotional level where guilt's
earliest traces are embedded, Daniels therapeutically transcends aboveground arrangements. His readings of images of mortality return him to
himself as a limited—but responsible—agent of his own destiny.

The implicit message of the protagonist's progress is not: "If God is
dead, then all things are possible." Rather, his underground encounters lead
him to infer: If mankind is mortal and born without inherent sheltering
norms, then existential freedom is the founding condition of human existence. Jean-Paul Sartre's realization that "Man is condemned to be free" is
identical to the discovery of Wright's progatonist.

In order to arrive at the view of man's fate attained by Daniels, "The
Man Who Lived Underground" implies that one must tunnel through walls,
trespass sacred religious precincts, peep through keyholes of the unsuspect-
ing, and secure to oneself the boundless and mythical freedom of dreams.
One must move in the unsocial ways of the ludic trickster in order to effect
the type of transvaluation of values represented by Daniels's actions during
one of his forays aboveground. As he prepares to leave the aboveground, he

> [scrubs and rinses] his hands meticulously, then . . . [hunts] for a
> towel; there was none. He shut off the water, pulled off his shirt,
> dried his hands on it . . . he turned on the faucet again . . . drank
> in long slow swallows. His bladder grew tight; he . . . faced the
> wall, bent his head, and watched a stream strike the floor. His
> nostrils wrinkled against acrid wisps of vapor; though he had
> tramped in the waters of the sewer, he stepped back from the
> wall so that his shoes, wet with sewer slime, would not touch his
> urine.

Daniels's actions imply a striking transvaluation. He washes *before* descending into the sewer. He protects slimy shoes from the touch of urine.
The scene suggests that what might be defined as a "polluted" world underground has become a sacred territory.

The employment of the word "polluted" here is meant to extend my
earlier definitions of the "zero image" to include striking insights on pollution beliefs and social categories represented by Mary Douglas's study
*Purity and Danger.* Douglas, in a stunning account of "The Abominations

of Leviticus," demonstrates that the "unclean" items abhorred by the culinary code of Leviticus are, in fact, anomalies. They are not unclean *in themselves*, but merely as the negative and anomalous side of what are defined as *pure* items. Douglas summarizes her conclusions as follows: "a rule of avoiding anomalous things affirms and strengthens the definitions to which they do not conform. So where Leviticus abhors crawling things, we should see the abomination as the negative side of the pattern of things approved." The proposition might be introduced that the abhorrent is that which does not *fit*; "dirt" is matter out of place (or unplaceable matter). Ironically, the very negative, anomalous, and ambiguous character of the "polluted" gives it suprarational efficacy in cultural rituals. The "tainted" (such as twins in some traditional societies) may bespeak the intervention of the divine. "Dirt" and "danger" may thus exist in the same matrix with the sacred and the divine.

We can speak of holy anomalies that mark a boundary between the sacred and the secular—the world of man and the intervention of the gods. The uncategorical nature of the polluted, however, makes it a cause of grave cultural anxiety which society always attempts to ameliorate through the manipulation of verbal categories. In a suggestive essay entitled "Anthropological Aspects of Language: Animal Categories and Verbal Abuse," Edmund Leach persuasively argues that "our world is a representation of our language categories and not vice versa." *Between* such categories, however—in the interstices, as it were, between $p$ and $\sim p$—lies an ambiguous region subject to taboo. In a conventional, white American field of cultural perception, the Afro-American falls between categories into a suppressed, "unnameable," taboo. He is thus a *tertium quid,* a "third thing" giving forth neither human nor animal image. From the perspective of Douglas's analysis of pollution beliefs, the Afro-American—in the white American perceptual scheme—is a threat to order. The physiological avoidances of blacks reflected by "color bars" and "caste barriers" are "symbolic expressions of other undesirable contacts which would have repercussions on the structure of [American] social or cosmological ideas."

The extensions to language categories and social boundaries implied here suggest that a "zero image" is a deeply embedded taboo of white American cultural life, a symbolic mode of processing reality that forestalls even physical proximity with blacks in its attempt to preserve and promote a distinctively white ordering of reality. The black speaking subject who attempts to invert the negative ontology that whites promote as a "natural" entry in American discourse becomes a heroic figure. By separating himself from the white, perceptual void, the inversive black subject achieves new status. His actions contribute to the institution of a new "interstitial" cultural discourse and both substantiate and materialize a distinctively black mode of constituting "reality."

Immediately before washing his hands at the sink, Daniels views with compassion a sea of laughing faces watching the "jerking shadows" of the screen in a moviehouse. The notion of art as illusion, as a means of socializing the instinctual life of man, implied by this encounter leads the protagonist to conclude: "these people [the theater audience] were children sleeping in their living, awake in their dying." He envisions stepping out "upon thin air" and walking "on down to the audience; and, hovering in the air just above them" to awaken them to consciousness. But he judges that such a course would be of little avail. Like the messianic dream journey on the sea previously discussed, Daniels's moviehouse reverie suggests that even a miraculous and saving walk by an altruistic messiah cannot rescue man from his fate. Only by transmuting normative values—by manipulating the boundaries between purity and danger—can man engage emotional experiences that enable him to cast off illusion. Hence the protagonist washes his hands of aboveground experience, descending once more to a sacred, subsurface domain of intense emotional existence.

The emotional, socially uncategorized constructs that Wright's liminal and seemingly inarticulate hero encounters suggest the possibility of a productive phenomenological consideration of "The Man Who Lived Underground." According to Edmund Husserl, the human sense of identity is the result of human consciousness acting in a straightforward manner. A person's sense of himself is formed, therefore, without his being actively aware of its formation. Hence, our identity, or our sense of precisely who we are, is never, as a matter of course, genuine, or "authentic" (to employ Husserl's term) because the origins of identity remain unclear.

The phenomenological act par excellence is to reflectively meditate on the development of the sense of identity as a "specific theme." The mental operations represented by Wright's "The Man Who Lived Underground" constitute such a meditation. Daniels moves beyond an always/already formed sense of identity as a *guilty* social being to a comprehension of the constitutive activities of human consciousness itself. His trespassing of social boundaries and his subverting of social norms enable him, one might say, to grasp the phylogeny of human culture. In effect, he recapitulates in his own discrete meditation the experience of the entire species. The generative images of this recapitulation are ones of economic exploitation and war. The protagonist's formative actions are those of thief and clown.

The most forceful symbolic structure in Daniels's reflections on the constitution of human consciousness is Peer's—Manufacturing Jewelers, the factory that he robs. This factory is an icon of human transformation of the world into commodities with cultural value. Manufacturing cultural value involves such processes as the conversion of *stones* into "diamonds" and the conversion of minerals into watches to serve as instruments of cultural time. An anthropological reading of man's development to a stage of cultural manufacture suggests that he moves from a status as a simple tool user to an industrial order of society in which valuables and values are factory produced. It is not the *labor* of tradesmen who work at factory benches and machines, however, that Daniels discovers in his liminal observations of Peer's. Rather, he gazes in fascination at a disembodied white hand twirling the dial of the factory safe:

> He [Daniels] held his breath; an eerie white hand, seemingly detached from its arm, touched the metal knob and whirled it, first to the left, then to the right. It's a safe! . . . Suddenly he could see the dial no more; a huge metal door swung slowly toward him and he was looking into a safe filled with green wads of paper money, rows of coins wrapped in brown paper, and glass jars and boxes of various sizes.

This image eventually comes to signal the absolute absurdity of aboveground values.

The safe, in fact, is a repository of surplus value. This Marxian concept, which I discussed at length [elsewhere], seems an apt description of the safe's contents. It holds the profitable residue resulting from a discrepancy between subsistence wages paid to the worker for labor power and the increase in store derived from actual labor by managers of the factory. The surplus achieved is *of value,* however, only because an aboveground community has entered into patterns of evaluation that give rise to the factory in the first instance.

The upper world's *estimate* and *use* of products viewed in the safe gives these products value. From an underground, or "primitive" apprehension, such items are no more than toys. And in the most daringly inversive act of his liminal existence, Daniels—who has climbed up a rain pipe (thus reversing the downward path of dirt and debris into the sewer) to oversee the acts of the "white hand"—*steals* the combination to the factory safe.

The sound of a typewriter is the audible sign of the factory world—the world of business—and it is opposed by the crude petroglyph which Daniels scratches into the brick wall of Peer's—Manufacturing Jewelers. With a stolen screwdriver he etches the safe's combination in order to rob the factory. At the time of his robbery, his scratchings on the wall have been transferred to memory as a lesson learned—if not yet fully understood: "He turned the dial to the figures he saw on the blackboard of his memory; it was so easy that he felt that the safe had not been locked at all."

Before effecting his bold theft, Daniels had undergone an experience that brings together in his mind the processes of slaughter—the butchery of the living by the living—and economic change. Attempting to tunnel into Peer's, he finds himself instead in an icebox where "halves and quarters of hogs and lambs and steers [hang from] metal hooks on the low ceiling, red meat encased in folds of cold white fat." A butcher enters the freezer, and Daniels watches as he uses a cleaver to cut away a portion of meat. The man's actions are described in sanguinary terms:

> Each time he lifted the cleaver and brought it down upon the meat, he let out a short, deep-chested grunt. After he had cut the meat, he wiped the blood off the wooden block with a sticky wad of gunny sack and hung the cleaver on a hook. His face was proud as he placed the chunk of meat in the crook of his elbow and left.

A moment later, the man says, "Forty-eight cents a pound, ma'am," as the cash register rings with a "vibrating, musical tingle." Daniels's mind is fixed all the while on the meat cleaver's "sharp edge smeared with cold blood." The associative union between butchery and economics as distinctive features of aboveground existence is not fully realized until later in the narrative when the cleaver merges with images of war broadcast by Daniels's stolen radio.

From his situation inside Nick's Fruits and Meats (an establishment that also converts items of the natural world into cultural commodities), Daniels is driven to a burlesque parody of aboveground's mercantile enterprise. Prying open the door of the delicatessen with his screwdriver, he becomes a clown of commerce. He is the gluttonous trickster who consumes the owner's fruits and then sells grapes to a white woman who has come into the store. Finally, he rejects the economics of the upper world by flinging a coin the woman has paid him "to the pavement with a gesture of contempt." His actions are only the first in a series of inversive gestures in the protagonist's spiraling imagistic meditation on economic and aggressive dimensions of the development of human consciousness.

During his robbery of the factory, he straps on a gun and cartridge belt and clowns at the role of lawman. And when he returns to his underground cave with stolen bounty, he mockingly imitates a businessman and clowns before a typewriter. "Yes," he parodically says to empty walls of his cave, "I'll have the contracts ready to go tomorrow." He then burlesques the role of "a rich man who lived aboveground in the obscene sunshine." Strolling past the mound of stolen diamonds in his cave, he only casually touches them with his foot until the moment when "his right foot smashed into the heap and diamonds lay scattered in all directions."

The fullest realization of such mockeries of aboveground values and evaluation comes when Daniels begins a radical and scandalous act of deconstruction. At the moment of his theft, he has meditatively reduced paper money to essential qualities: "He rubbed the money with his fingers, as though expecting it to reveal hidden qualities. He lifted the wad to his nose and smelled the fresh odor of ink. Just like any other paper, he mumbled." Back in his underground cave, he proceeds to reduce all the items stolen from Peer's to a primitive state in order to reveal their implicit qualities and to subvert their aboveground meanings. The stolen items seem to promise—if they can be properly decoded—an *authentic* understanding of human culture and consciousness. That is, they seem to offer keys to a coherent interpretation of the myriad images that have marked his underground journeyings:

> He saw these items hovering before his eyes and felt that some dim meaning linked them together, that some magical relationship made them kin. He stared with vacant eyes, convinced that all of these images, with their tongueless reality, were striving to tell him something.

In order to seize a meaningful "something" and transform a "tongueless reality" into an articulate message, Daniels converts stolen coins into "a glowing mound of shimmering copper and silver." Hundred-dollar bills become wallpaper for his cave. Watches are textually reduced to "metal . . . casing," then "golden disks," and finally "blobs of liquid yellow." Diamond rings are decomposed into "golden bands," "blue and white sparks," and finally "brittle laughter." Diamonds are pressed back as *stones*, into elemental earth. And after he has driven nails into the wall and hung rings, watches, a stolen meat cleaver and a gun, the protagonist has, in fact, effectively produced a *countertext* to the cultural discourse of the upper world.

His willful creation is a striking and ironic inversion of Plato's classical epistemology. The cave dweller of *The Republic* must leave the underground and ascend to a world of "higher intelligence" before he can attain true knowledge. Daniels, by contrast, makes the walls of his underground cave into a knowledgeable statement of essential forms of reality.

His text invokes an image of conflict between "natural" harmony and "cultural" acts of economic production and global warfare: "Brooding over the diamonds on the floor was like looking up into a sky full of stars; the illusion turned into its opposite: he was high up in the air looking down at the twinkling lights of a sprawling city." The reflexive, natural order of phenomena stands opposed to cities of man. The voice of a radio broadcast tells of "cities . . . razed," "planes scattering death," and "troops with fixed bayonets charging in waves against other troops who held fixed bayonets and men groaned as steel ripped into their bodies and they went down to die." The bloody meat cleaver and industrial processes that convert natural phenomena into surplus value merge, receiving a coherent, interpretive description in graphic visions of war. Sky, sea, and earth are polluted by mankind's acts of butchery: "steel tanks" rumble "across fields of ripe wheat," and warships draw "near each other over wastes of water." The machine has come crashing indisputably into the garden; cultural mechanics have disrupted nature's fundamental harmony. Supporting the senseless arrival and perpetration is a man-made arsenal of commercial values symbolized by items that Daniels has stolen from Nick's and Peer's—Manufacturing Jewelers.

The aboveground world appears as a "wild forest filled with death." And if the aboveground is, in fact, an untamed wilderness, then the underground text created by Daniels as a counterstatement to norms of the social world can serve as a revised logos—a new "Word" transforming chaos and death into a humane order of existence. A life of responsible human freedom can be predicated, that is to say, on the achieved and authentic consciousness implied by Daniels's text.

The fundamental narrative pattern of "The Man Who Lived Underground" suggests a conversion of "instrumental value" of aboveground objects into expressive, underground, textual value. Stolen goods become expressive signs when the protagonist "reads" their implicit message of false values and cultural bloodshed. The understanding that Daniels derives from his emotional transactions, however, is, in actuality, a wordless phenomenon. His new consciousness, in fact, seems far less "discursive" than *ludic*. It has the expressive character of play or a game.

Both during and immediately after his acts of theft, he plays "games." Further, he refers to his bounty as "serious toys" of the upper world. The watchman's gun is like "a momento from a county fair." And the typewriter is not used to compose serious messages, but to manipulate words "merely for the ritual of performing" an *act* of composition. The victory obtained in his phenomenological *meditation on consciousness,* therefore is a ludic triumph. It writes itself at the level of emotions and serves as an idealistic palimpsest covering old cultural tracings. While his new consciousness and the text that it makes available alter irrovacably his definitions of guilt and prompt him to act, they still comprise, in their initial instance, an "inarticulate" victory.

After he has contemplated his own death (in the scene discussed earlier), Daniels arrives at what Heidegger calls a stage of "resolute decision." He decides to ascend and share his liminally attained understanding with aboveground society. Upon his emergence, he has the burlesque appearance of a seedy clown. In a men's clothing store (a cultural establishment designed to cloak man's fundamental nudity) he regards himself in a long mirror and sees "his cheekbones protruded from a hairy black face; his greasy cap . . . perched askew upon his head and his eyes . . . were red and glassy. His shirt and trousers were caked with mud and hung loosely. His hands were gummed with a black stickiness."

Daniels is "dirt" appearing in a world that seeks "purity," a world that conceals nakedness through commercial manufacture and sale of social "clothes." As he moves across the threshold of a black church in the messianic scene referred to earlier, he is summarily rejected. And when he appears, in all of his polluted glory, at the police station where he tendered his earlier confession, the entire establishment is thrown into confusion. For he is not only "polluted" but also culturally inarticulate, a citizen from an underground *mundus inversus*—a world upside down.

The aboveground seeks to contain Daniels with negative verbal epithets—"nut," "psycho," "Fifth Columnist, "fool." But he is existentially beyond words: "he could not longer think with his mind; he thought with his feelings and no words came." His inversion of cultural norms has left him wordless. And his possible reentry into society with a new and responsible role is blocked by the revised rules that constitute his own new "game." Officer Lawson (son of cultural laws) says in response to the protagonist's assertion that he stole valuables from Peer's in order to "play" with them: "What's your game, boy?" And after a further exchange between the two, Lawson proclaims: "He's playing a game and I wish to God I knew what it was."

Daniels is a ludic clown; he is representative of a revised human emotional and expressive understanding of guilt and innocence, the natually harmonious and the culturally disruptive, the inherently free-and-limited condition of man and his social grovelings before authority. The protagonist has returned, like the Messiah, from underground, compelled by a sense of compassion and love: "Mister, when I looked through all those holes and saw how people were living, I loved em." But his drive toward community is thwarted by an uncomprehending and conventional aggressiveness of aboveground society. He cannot effect dialogue, *communitas,* or change because the social world fears and rejects an authentic consciousness that he represents.

Like the textualized wall of his cave, therefore, Daniels is only comprehensible at an expressive level that aboveground citizens are unwilling to survey. Finally, his very confession of guilt—the documentary signal of his initial *social* status—is burned by Lawson in an attempt to drive away this parodic representation of man in an untrammeled condition of expressive freedom.

Daniels is "thunderstruck" by the destruction of his confession. For his underground message is significant only insofar as it marks the conclusive phase of rites of transition that began in an initial, confessional relationship. Still optimistic about reentry, however, he allows himself to be manipulated by the white policemen as they feign a desire to share his underground wisdom. Daniels leads the officers to the manhole. He descends the steps as a willing guide. But at this hopeful juncture, which portends a new order of existence for the world, Lawson fires a bullet into his chest. Aggregation is violently denied.

The protagonist's decoding—indeed, his destruction—of instrumentalities of aboveground life leads to a comprehension of an essential humanness (an intersubjectivity) in which all men and women are not only guilty but also condemned to die. Mortality makes a mockery of the acquisitively brutal existence of aboveground life. This text with its implicit antinomian and egalitarian underground norms is violently repudiated by aboveground authority. Daniels's murder transforms immediate revisional textual possibility into "a whirling object rushing along in the darkness" of the sewer's currents.

It is necessary, however, to regard the demise of Wright's protagonist within its black (w)hole ceremonial context, as a *ritual act.* As Daniels whirls into underground darkness, he returns to the singularity of the black (w)hole's expressive cluster. He rejoins, that is, his radically deconstructive text—the "words" through which he became incarnate in the first instance: the signs by which he came to *live* underground. As a primal, expressive Logos, or Word, he is no more dead at the conclusion of the novella than his Judeo-Christian archetype.

## VII

Freed from limiting terms of a traditional evaluative discourse, guided by the trope of the black (w)hole, and aware of the densely attractive symbolic action at the core of his fiction, a literary critic should be prepared to acknowledge the singular expressive achievement of Richard Wright. With such enabling conditions in force, the critic should be fully equipped to transcend outmoded terms of an old problematic and to appreciate carnivalesque transformations worked by Wright on the devices of traditional literary discourse. Finally, from a symbolic reading of characteristic fictions such as "Big Boy Leaves Home" and "The Man Who Lived Underground," a critic should feel compelled to designate Wright as the very center of that dark (and powerfully invisible) area of Afro-American life that constitutes its underground expressive (w)holeness.

Richard Wright's translation of the desire of a black blues life into an irresistible *difference* makes him undisputed master of Black Wholeness. If a tradition of modern Afro-American narrative exists, it is only possible because Wright achieved the concentrated power of a Black Whole that attracts all nearby stars and gives birth to the quasi-stellar brightness of successors. Wright is the Black Symbolist par excellence. His "entrance onto the stage of language" marked a daring conversion of a uniquely black blues desire into Afro-American fictions—into expressive (w)holes—that present a culture's social being for itself. In the final analysis, Wright's singular force makes all of us his "assessors" in a key sense of that term. Ultimately, we have no choice but to situate ourselves and our expressive traditions *beside* him.

MICHAEL G. COOKE

# The Beginnings of Self-Realization

Richard Wright's *Native Son* evinces a remarkable number of likenesses to *Their Eyes Were Watching God,* including coming to a conclusion with a formal murder trial and a personal scene of human reconciliation that yet leaves the protagonist in a state of solitude. Bigger Thomas, moreover, begins under a threat of self-cancellation and is seduced by materialism and then by images, in the pattern held up before Janie. But where Janie naively begins in a corner of the white world and contracts from there into the black enclave of Eatonville and further into "De Muck," Bigger expands out from the ghetto into the white world and beyond that into the levels where social philosophy and political power are struggled over. The difference in scale is significant, not least because *Native Son* puts the figure of solitude—saved however traumatically from self-cancellation and materialism and its sequel, image-worship—into a public position, whence the kind of representative encounter is possible that the domestic concentration of *Their Eyes Were Watching God* in itself precludes.

Bigger Thomas's experience represents a series of violent swings between self-cancellation and self-assertion, with the urgency of his moods of self-cancellation gradually diminishing while the lucidity and control of his self-assertion correspondingly grows. The opening scene of the novel cryptically blends self-cancellation and self-assertion. The context is oddly Hamletic. The "light tapping in the thinly plastered wall," the presence of a creature that is shifting and invisible ("I don't see 'im") and the pervasive

From *Afro-American Literature in the Twentieth Century: The Achievement of Intimacy.* © 1984 by Michael G. Cooke. Yale University Press, 1984.

sense of dread all suggest the visit of the ghost with the message that some-thing is rotten in the state. At this juncture the rot seems all domestic, symbolized as much by the rat that invades and haunts the Thomas family's one-room life as by the mother's telling her first son she wonders why she had ever "birthed" him. The son, Bigger Thomas, clearly dreads and abom-inates the rat as much as any of them, but once he kills it his hysterical cursing turns into a mixture of vicious play and macho display—he holds the fearful creature toward his sister, and she faints.

The fear Bigger shows toward the rat is involuntary; his attack on his sister is quite voluntary and represents an effort to recover and reestablish himself. But in actuality he has been the one the family has turned to and depended on for protective action. Far from being hostile, they are implicitly complimentary (his younger brother looks up to him with feelings next to idolatry, and his mother cries him down in proportion to her obvious high hopes for him). Why then is Bigger so hostile and self-assertive? The episode with the rat seems less a symbol than a catalyst for feelings of helplessness and worthlessness that Bigger has carried unexpressed for some time. It is a sort of uprising against such feelings that causes him to disappoint his mother and distress his sister:

> Vera [his sister] went behind the curtain and Bigger heard her trying to comfort his mother. He shut their voices out of his mind. He hated his family because he knew that they were suf-fering and that he was powerless to help them. He knew that the moment he allowed himself to feel to its fullness how they lived, the shame and misery of their lives, he would be swept out of himself with fear and despair. So he held toward them an atti-tude of iron reserve. . . . And toward himself he was even more exacting. He knew that the moment he allowed what his life meant to enter fully into his consciousness, he would either kill himself or someone else. So he denied himself.

It is striking that Bigger, who here suspends all reactions in order to keep from killing, goes into "a deep physiological resolution not to react to anything" *after he kills and is captured*. The apparent identification of not feeling and not killing does not stand up under scrutiny. Killing does not release feeling in any basic way, but merely rebounds into not feeling, into not daring to feel. This result has in it less paradox than meets the eye, in that the killings are not undertaken out of an uncontrollable upsurge of feeling, but as a way of stifling feeling. When Bigger identifies himself with the act of killing, then, we need to take close account of two facts: (1) to acknowledge the killing is to go past the mere act and the ensuing "physi-ological resolution not to react," into a stage of open awareness and re-sponsibility; and (2) to accept this stage is to defeat the numbing depression that kept him from himself, his family, and his society, and thus it entails the beginning of his active humanity. It is his ability to *face* the killing, not merely to *perform* it, that counts most in the end. The performance is in itself a reflex of the self-cancellation that marks Bigger at the outset.

Wright sets forth without mercy the state, and the cause, of self-cancellation. He brings home in a radical philosophical way what may have looked like a physical reflex in Janie, or an animal impulse in the cornered rat, namely, the siamese continuity between self-cancellation and a drive to undo others, or murderousness. "Naw; it ain't like something going to happen to me. It's . . . like I was going to do something I can't help." A passive-aggressive seesaw is manifest even in the approach to the holdup; Bigger feels "like a man about to shoot himself." In relation to the job interview he has with Mr. Dalton, Bigger's sister chides him: "you know how you can forget," but it is his very ability to forget that keeps him at the minimum level of stability he exhibits. "Forgetting" essentially means that he suspends "the way he lived; he passed his days trying to defeat or gratify powerful impulses in a world he feared."

The foundation of such a response in the self-protective realities of the human psyche is easy enough to recognize. We may also note that Wright records identical feelings in his own family, in his own life. The situation, with his mother on her deathbed, is admittedly extreme, by contrast with the "normal" signs of weakness and inadequacy in the Thomas household. But the weight of repetition would seem to aggravate the "normal" into the intensity and finality of dying. Here is the pertinent passage from *Black Boy:*

> Once, in the night, my mother called me to her bed and told me
> that she could not endure the pain, that she wanted to die. I held
> her hand and begged her to be quiet. That night I ceased to react
> to my mother; *my feelings were frozen.* (italics added)

Clearly Wright in the emotional realm matches his mother's position in the physical: he cannot endure the pain. She dies, according to the dictates of nature. He makes himself as good as dead, according to the demands of his spirit. Seeing the same reaction in Bigger gives us important if paradoxical evidence of his sensitivity and makes plausible his eventual emergence, or rebirth, from the extreme of self-protection that causes him to kill Mary Dalton and Bessie Mears, as he has earlier metaphorically killed himself.

It is clear that Bigger's response to self-cancellation early in the novel portends his homicidal behavior with Mary Dalton and Bessie Mears (we must remember that Bigger dreads Mary from the start—"*Goddamn that woman!* She spoiled everything!" so that his near-discovery by Mrs. Dalton in Mary's room aggravates an already hostile attitude). But this gives the novel, and Bigger's life, an unduly dark fatalistic cast and favors the view of the attorney Boris Max, which Bigger himself rejects. The novel in fact urges us from the outset to see Bigger as more than a defiant and negative character just spoiling for a chance to do harm. The powerful impulses he wishes to gratify must also be taken into account, for though these do not necessarily exclude killing (himself or others), they go far beyond that.

Bigger's notions of positive gratification are not spontaneous and, as it were, age-old, like the nubile Janie's hankering after sunup and pear-tree blossoms and the kisses of the first youth strolling by. They are in their way sophisticated, secondary notions, stemming from sociocultural observation and from the media ("he tried to decide if he wanted to buy a ten-cent magazine, or go to a movie"). The advertising plane that banners USE SPEED GASOLINE brings out Bigger's response to what he sees in actuality and what the media inspire him to conceive: "[White boys] get a chance to do everything"; "I *could* fly a plane if I had a chance"; "Send your men over the river at dawn and attack the enemy's left flank." It soon becomes clear, in the first encounter with the Daltons, that Bigger is as much governed by *images* as by desire for material comfort; materialism and image-worship, which occur discretely in *Their Eyes Were Watching God*, overlap here, and complicate Bigger's responses. In the Daltons' neighborhood, for example, where he comes in search of a job, he cannot square his inner feelings of "fear and emptiness" and his outward sense of something reduced in power: "he did not feel the pull and mystery of the thing [the wealthy neighborhood] as strongly as he had in the movie." We should recall that *Native Son* was published five years before the passage of the Ives-Quinn Act (1945), the first law forbidding discrimination in employment. Besides the personal conviction of helplessness that he has formed at home, there is a social stamp of hopelessness and uselessness for Bigger to bear. When in actuality he finds that the very neighborhood of the Daltons does not simply overpower him with the compounded weight of magical association and practice exaltation, that is to say, when he finds that he can keep walking, his mind makes a curious compensatory turn. He will be dangerous to "the white man" if the white man is not after all overwhelmingly dangerous to him. Bigger reacts to the loss of movie magic by investing himself with magical propensities: "he wanted to wave his hand and blot out the white man who

was making him feel like this [afraid and worthless]. If not that, he wanted
to blot himself out."

The fact is that Bigger blindly cultivates solitude at this point, desiring
to be away from others or desiring others to be absent from him. This is the
solitude of incapacity, which he must outgrow. The contrast with his final
poised and poignant solitude in his jail cell is a measure of his growth in the
novel. At that point, Bigger will exhibit a great but ineffectual capacity for
communication, in the ambiguous condition of solitude that Wright enun-
ciates in *The God That Failed:*

> Perhaps, I thought, out of my tortured feelings I could fling a
> spark into this darkness. I would try, not because I wanted to,
> but because I felt that I had to if I were to live at all.
>
> I would hurl words into this darkness and wait for an echo;
> and if an echo sounded, no matter how faintly, I would send
> other words to tell, to march, to fight, to create a sense of the
> hunger for life that gnaws in us all, to keep alive in our hearts a
> sense of the inexpressibly human.

In the early stages of *Native Son* Bigger Thomas needs as much to
recover from a philosophical sense of magic as from a social and physical
sense of terror and destruction. The further he goes into the latter, the more
the former takes hold of his mind. He alternates between two complemen-
tary states. First, he feels blithely secure, credulously falling asleep after the
first killing, for example, and experiencing a "sense of fulness [that] he had
so often but inadequately felt in magazines and movies." Second, he takes
to feeling omnipotent, a condition expressed by various modulations of the
following paradigm: "he wanted to wave his hand and blot them out." This
magical gesture is addressed to his family, black people, Bessie, the world,
his visitors in prison, the people at the inquest, "the sun's rising and setting." It is in the grip of this magic that he can be aggressively jubilant about
having "killed a rich white girl and . . . burned her body . . . and . . . lied to
throw the blame on someone else and . . . written a kidnap note demanding
ten thousand dollars." We see a more realistic reaction when he is "afraid
to touch food on the table, food which undoubtedly was his own." Tacitly,
of course, the food-reluctance is related to an older magical belief that one
fell into the power of those who gave one food. But in Bigger the fear of
eating reveals a personal visceral distress and an unfocused, guilty feeling
that others are secretly concocting harm for him.

The desire to sleep that overcomes Bigger when Mary's body is found
and again after he takes Bessie's life represents the exhaustion of his sense

of magic. His sense of reality will develop slowly, because it must be based on relationship and he is little versed in that. But the very idea of sleep grows complex for Bigger; rather than oblivion, it comes to mean peaceful courage and confidence and a religious sense "that all life was a sorrow that had to be accepted."

At this stage, the threat of annihilation no longer leads Bigger to homicidal defiance and magical self-inflation. In the novel's final section, "Fate," it is as though sleep has become metaphysical, and to rise from it a sort of resurrection. The language of resting "eternally" gives way to that of the rotted hull of a seed "forming the soil in which it should grow again." The dream of "a vast configuration of images and symbols whose magic and power could lift him up and make him live so intensely that the dread of being black . . . would be forgotten" gives way to a sense that "maybe the confused promptings, . . . the elation . . . were false lights that led nowhere." He can still resent being made a spectacle and a "sport" for others, especially white people, but he is now open to Jan Erlone in a way inconceivable before; and he is open to himself.

It is probably from Jan, with his comment that Bigger "believed [in himself] enough to kill," that Bigger takes the elements of his metaphysical self-proclamation; we may recall his anxious effort "to remember where he had heard words that would help him." His outcry flabbergasts his attorney, Boris Max: "I didn't want to kill! . . . But what I killed for, *I am!* It must've been pretty deep in me." But this is after all a retrospective posture. More current is his desire for reconciliation, and the fact that "the impulsion to tell" the truth on which reconciliation must be based "was as deep as had been the urge to kill." The same kind of reversal of spirit appears in his desire to console and soothe his family, instead of defying and blotting them out.

And yet the last thing we see of Bigger precludes reconciliation; he is alone in his cell, smiling "a faint, wry, bitter smile," and hearing "the ring of steel against steel as a *far* door clanged shut" (italics added). In effect the novel has brought him to personal, say even spiritual readiness for reconciliation, while removing him from the social context that makes reconciliation possible.

This paradox is lightened if we consider the question of Bigger's solitude. It is striking how often, throughout the story, Bigger finds or feels himself alone. Again and again we see him in the middle of a room or surrounded by others, in a state of presence without connection. From the outset, when his "gang" appears so prominent in his life, he is unconnected, and deliberately so, in that he cannot stand connection; it reminds him of his cowardice in the case of Gus and of his powerlessness in the case of his family. Bigger has thoughts of escaping the sense of solitude, but the escape takes the form of magic on the one hand and self-cancellation on the other:

> It was when he read the newspapers or magazines, or went to the movies, or walked along the streets with crowds, that he felt what he wanted: to merge himself with others and be a part of this world, to lose himself in it so he could find himself, to be allowed a chance to live like others, even though he was black.

But magical identification (magazines and movies) and social identification with others in the world stand in contrast in no more than superficial ways. Each entails a relapse into self-cancellation. Each is a desire for life as "a beautiful dream," for illusion, for unconsciousness. When the "cold white world" forces in on him, Bigger seeks another form of escape, by substitution: "If only someone had gone before and lived or suffered and died— made it so that it could be understood!" (He rejects Christianity, of course, though his language here conjures up Christ.) Again, he shuns his existential situation to join himself with another, in a passive, cheating unison—he wants it done and made easy for him, he wants to get out of going through it for himself.

It is striking that following his capture Bigger becomes his own Christological figure, coming back to himself after "three days" and "feeling . . . like the rotted hull of a seed forming the soil in which it should grow again." The text is replete with (a) suggestions of original *and individual* creation ("some spirit had breathed and created him . . . in the image of a man with a man's obscure need and urge"); (b) images of individual growth ("a seed"); and (c) the language of singularity tempered but also confirmed by the force of the category ("he had to go forward and meet his end like any other living thing upon the earth"). To merge is impossible, but to belong ineluctable. Bigger has striven not to belong, adopting a melange of materialism (note his retroactive effort to make money off Mary Dalton's killing), magical images, and self-cancelling postures. When he can face the mystery and the misery of being black and, more largely, of being human, he has shut himself off from its benefits by murder. The cry "what I killed for, *I am!*" causes Boris Max to flinch away, but that is not the cause of Bigger's being alone. The cause is in the act, and in the result of the act: "*I am!*" From self-cancellation Bigger has come to self-avowal, but through a passage with a cell at the end.

Bigger Thomas takes a place among the multitude of black protagonists who end up hiding away or running away or held away from some vital consummation. Needless to say, the line does not end with him; given that it is an expression of a cultural evolution, we should not expect it to. Earlier stages persist where new ones arise, and even interpenetrate with them. Captain Christian Laurent, in Ernest Gaines's "Bloodline," voluntarily isolates himself from a context in which *he has both purpose and power,* so that he represents an advanced capacity without an enlarged opportunity for black people. In the same vein, Nell finds herself "alone" at the end of Toni Morrison's *Sula,* alone and *looking back* at a lost opportunity for kinship with Sula and participation in the vision of freedom that Sula sought to embody. Bigger, as a preeminent figure in this line of grievous frustration, stands in the condition C. J. Rawson sees as the role adopted by Jean Genet, "homme et captif . . . , affirming his own solitude." But even in his solitude Bigger has something compelling and resonant for the future of black literature, the quality that frightens the same Boris Max who could take mere murder in stride, the ability to say to himself and to the echoing corridors of the society: *"I am!"*

Some difficulty may arise from the fact that Bigger Thomas remains essentially without connections, without amplitude. Ralph Ellison puts it tellingly in *Shadow and Act:*

> I . . . found it disturbing that Bigger Thomas had none of the finer qualities of Richard Wright, none of the imagination, none of the sense of poetry, none of the gaiety. And I preferred Richard Wright to Bigger Thomas. Do you see? [This] . . . directs you back to the difference between what Wright was himself and . . . his conception of the quality of Negro humanity.

In Ellison's view, Wright took an overly "ideological" and deterministic position on the black condition. But it is worthwhile to ask what the essential tenet of Wright's ideology was, and whether at bottom, at least as regards Bigger Thomas, that ideology was sociopolitical or *metaphysical.* For Bigger goes through the naturalistic "fatalism" of the killings and the analytical "fatalism" of Boris Max's courtroom performance (to say nothing of the prosecutor's) into the self-discovery and implicit independence of his basic cry, "I am." In other words, while it would have been attractive to have a more autobiographical figure as protagonist, and a more cultivated personality in the manner of, say, Chester Himes's *The Primitive,* Wright would have paid a price for that. And the price would have had nothing to do with sociopolitical ideology. It would have fallen entirely in the metaphysical sphere, since Wright would have forgone any chance of showing a Bigger Thomas coming out of determinism into determination, out of rigid action into mobile being. The victim of "images" that we see in the early chapters emerges as a participant in a life of the spirit: "some spirit had breathed and created him . . . in the image of a man." Here image and identity fuse, so that he is free of illusion, even while the freedom of giving a certain substance to the image comes vainly into his hands.

KWAME ANTHONY APPIAH

# A Long Way from Home: Wright in the Gold Coast

*One does not react to Africa as Africa is, and this is because so few can react to life as life is. One reacts to Africa as one is, as one lives; one's reaction to Africa is one's life, one's ultimate sense of things. Africa is a vast, dingy mirror.*

*Africa is dangerous, evoking in one a total attitude toward life, calling into question the basic assumptions of existence. Africa is the world of man; if you are wild, Africa's wild; if you are empty, so's Africa. . . .*

—RICHARD WRIGHT, *Black Power*

Africa has played its various roles in Western symbolic geography with an astonishing versatility. Its early role as homeland of the pious Ethiopians is unjustly less well-remembered than its more recent triumph as the heart of darkness; but after twenty-five centuries of continuous performances, this is, perhaps, understandable.

But the story of Africa has its less familiar episodes, and among the most intriguing, I think, is a curious byway in the history of Afro-America's African dream. From the earliest days of the African resettlement schemes that produced Liberia and Sierra Leone, New World blacks have reversed the Middle Passage. Those whose literacy and education allowed them to record their response—priests and scholars like Alexander Crummell and Edward Wilmot Blyden—produced works bearing impressive testimony to the powerful image of Africa that dominated the culture they sought to escape.

Driven by a love of Africa that was rooted in the romantic racism of the

173

nineteenth century, these proto-nationalists were still unable to see her for what she was—even when they no longer saw her darkly through the glass of distance; even when they had stared her in the face. Alexander Crummell and Edward Blyden begin the record of Afro-Americans who have taken the dream to Africa with them, and have travelled there without awakening.

Crummell, though born and raised in New York, was Liberian by adoption. On July 26, 1860—the thirteenth anniversary, by Crummell's reckoning, of Liberian Independence—he addressed the citizens of Maryland county, Cape Palmas, on the subject of "The English Language in Liberia." He claimed that the Africans "exiled" in slavery to the New World had been given by divine providence "at least this one item of compensation, namely, the possession of the Anglo-Saxon tongue." Crummell, who loved Africa enough to give the best years of his life to it, believed that English was a superior language to the "various tongues and dialects" of the indigenous African populations; superior in its euphony, its conceptual resources, and its capacity to express the "supernal truths" of Christianity.

Blyden, with Africanus Horton and Martin Robinson Delany, was one of three contemporaries of Crummell's who could also lay claim to the title of "Father of Pan-Africanism." Like Crummell, Blyden was a native of the New World, Liberian by adoption, and a priest; and, for a while, they were friends and fellow workers in the beginning of Liberia's modern system of education.

These men shared a conception of the destiny of their race, a conception that lay at the heart of their Pan-Africanist convictions: Africa was the proper home of the Negro and the Afro-American was an exile, who should, in Blyden's words, "return to the land of his fathers . . . AND BE AT PEACE." Yet they also shared a distaste for Africa's indigenous culture and traditions. Not only did they scorn Africa's languages—Blyden believed that "English is undoubtedly, the most suitable of the European languages for bridging the numerous gulfs between the tribes caused by the great diversity of languages or dialects among them"—but they each had little faith in African customs and, most especially, traditional—or, as they would have said, "pagan"—religions.

Outside the areas where Islam had brought some measure of exogenous civilization, Blyden's Africa is a place of "noisy terpsichorean performances," "Fetichism," and polygamy; it is, in short, in "a state of barbarism." Crummell's Africa

> is the victim of her heterogeneous idolatries. . . . Darkness covers
> the land and gross darkness the people. . . . Licentiousness

abounds everywhere. Moloch rules and reigns throughout the whole continent, and by the ordeal of Sassywood, Fetiches, human sacrifices and devil-worship, is devouring men, women, and little children.

For Crummell and Blyden, Africa was not so much a *tabula rasa* as a slate to be erased.

It is surprising that even those Afro-Americans like Crummell and Blyden, who initiated the nationalist discourse on Africa in Africa, inherited a set of conceptual blinders that made them unable to see virtue in Africa, despite their need for Africa, above all else, as a source of validation. Since they conceived of the African in racial terms, their low opinion of Africa was not easily distinguishable from a low opinion of the Negro; and, through the linking of race and Pan-Africanism, they left contemporary African cultures with a burdensome legacy.

The centrality of race in the history of African nationalism, both widely assumed and often ignored, is derived from the typical experience of those who led the post-war independence movements. A great many colonial students from British Africa were gathered in London in the years after the Second World War, united in their common search for political independence from a single metropolitan state. They were brought together too by the fact that the British—those who helped as well as those who hindered—saw them first as Africans. But they were able to articulate a common vision of post-colonial Africa through a discourse inherited from pre-war Pan-Africanism, and that discourse was the product, largely, of black citizens of the New World.

Since what bound those Afro-American and Afro-Caribbean Pan-Africanists together was the partially African ancestry they shared, and since that ancestry existed in the New World through its various folk theories of race, a racial understanding of their solidarity was, perhaps, an inevitable development. This was reinforced by the fact that a few crucial figures—Kwame Nkrumah among them—had travelled in the opposite direction to Crummell, seeking education in the black colleges of the United States.

It was the Pan-Africanism gained from his American experience that made Nkrumah open to the small army of New World blacks who beat a path to his door in the early 1950s, when, as first prime minister of the Gold Coast, he began the process that led, in fewer years than most Europeans expected—and than many Africans had hoped—to the decolonization of Africa. In July 1953, he rose in the Gold Coast parliament to argue for "self-government now"; and in proposing what he called the "motion of destiny," he drew attention explicitly to the connection between the Afro-American situation and the African one:

> Honourable Members . . . The eyes and ears of the world are upon you; yea, our oppressed brothers throughout this vast continent of Africa and the New World are looking to you with desperate hope, as an inspiration to continue their grim fight against cruelties which we in this corner of Africa have never known—cruelties which are a disgrace to humanity, and to the civilisation which the white man has set himself to teach us.

Nkrumah knew that despite what decolonization meant to Africans, to Afro-Americans it was a beacon of hope. He would not have been surprised to hear James Baldwin say to Robert Penn Warren a decade later:

> For the first time in American Negro history, the American black man is not at the mercy of the American white man's image of him. This is because of Africa. For the first time in the memory of anybody now living, African states mean Africa. It's still, you know, very romantic for an American Negro to think of himself as an African, but it's a necessary step in the recreation of his morale.

## I

Sitting in the gallery on the July day when Nkrumah tabled his motion was one of those Afro-Americans who found their way to Nkrumah's Gold Coast. He was there at the prime minister's invitation, and he listened with rapt attention. His name was Richard Wright, and *Black Power,* the book that records his visit, holds a special place in the literature of "return" that begins with Crummell and Blyden.

It also holds a special place in its author's career. As John M. Reilly, one of the book's more devoted readers, has argued, *Black Power* was written at a crucial moment in Wright's literary development, the result of "an intellectual crisis manifest in the implicitly nihilistic philosophy" espoused by Cross Damon, the protagonist of his novel *The Outsider.* What Wright needed in order to resolve this crisis was a "newly compelling subject that would permit him to reaffirm his writer's identity." In *Black Power,* Reilly claims,

> Richard Wright wished to build a bridge of words between his self and the world. He succeeded, and we acknowledge the ac-

complishment by discovering within the constructions of
langauge the prerequisite endeavor to create his expressive self.

Reilly correctly describes the project of self-fashioning that haunts this book,
but he misrecognizes its shape: for the *failure* of that "bridge of words
between his self and the world" is precisely what the success of that "prerequisite endeavor to create his expressive self" demands.

   Although self-expression is the book's latent objective, this is hardly the
impression left by the book's preface, "Apropos Prepossession," which opens
with these words:

> In today's intellectual climate—a climate charged with ideolog-
> ical currents in the service, paid or voluntary, of some nation,
> party, movement or interest—it behooves a writer reporting in
> nonfictional terms on vital material to lay before the reader his
> working frame of reference, his assumptions and preoccupa-
> tions.

Generically, the stilted diction signals a work of "scientific" ethnography, a
transparent conduit answering only to the facts. As he says a little later:

> In presenting this picture of Africa, I openly use, to a limited
> degree, Marxist analyses of historic events . . . If anyone should
> object to my employment of Marxist methods to make mean-
> ingful the ebb and flow of commodities, human and otherwise,
> in the modern state, to make comprehensible the alignment of
> social classes in modern society, I have to say that I'll willingly
> accept any other method of interpreting the facts; but I insist that
> any other method *must not exclude the facts*. (his emphasis)

In striking contrast to the preface, the opening of the first chapter marks an
abrupt generic shift. Here, where he is concerned to explain the circumstances of his trip to Africa, his dissertative style is promptly abandoned as
inadequate to the task.

   The chapter begins with a moment after luncheon on Easter Sunday in
the Wrights' home in Paris, when "we were stirring the sugar in our cups."
"We" are Richard and Ellen Wright and their guests, among whom is
Dorothy Padmore, "wife of George Padmore, the West Indian author and
journalist." The Padmores were friends of Nkrumah's, influential actors in
the culture of Pan-Africanism that spanned the three continents of the triangular trade that had created the black diaspora. Out of the silence, Mrs.
Padmore turned to me and asked:

"Now that your desk is clear, why don't you go to Africa?"

The idea was so remote to my mind and mood that I gaped at her a moment before answering.

"Africa?" I echoed.

"Yes. The Gold Coast," she said stoutly.

"But that's four thousand miles away!" I protested.

"There are planes and ships," she said.

My eyes glanced unseeingly about the room. I felt cornered, uneasy. I glanced at my wife.

"Why not?" she said.

A moment ago I had been collected, composed; now I was on the defensive, feeling poised on the verge of the unknown.

"Africa!" I repeated the word to myself, then paused as something strange and disturbing stirred slowly in the depths of me. I am an African! I'm of African descent.

It is a scene, one is bound to observe, that evokes nothing so much as Conradian dread; a dread intensified, no doubt, by the thought that Wright, the Afro-American, already has the horror stirring "in the depths" of him, even in the tranquillity of Paris. The melodramatic language of this opening passage—the langauge, dare I say, of a bad Edwardian novel—is, as I suggested, oddly in conflict with the high purpose announced in Wright's preface and the "scientific" language of the informational discourse that he has promised. The relation between the book and this vignette echoes strangely the relation between *Native Son* and the famous essay which precedes it (since the second edition), the preface which tells us "How Bigger Was Born." Just as that preface prepares one for a sociological reading of the novel, this initial scene-setting prepares one for a novelistic reading of the sociology. At the start, *Black Power* is a book that doesn't seem to know where it's going.

## II

Wright chose a stanza from Countee Cullen's famous poem "What Is Africa to Me?" as the first epigraph of his book:

What is Africa to me?
Copper sun or scarlet sea
Jungle star or jungle track,
Strong bronzed men, or regal black

Women from whose loins I sprang
When the birds of Eden sang?
> *One three centuries removed*
> *From the scenes his fathers loved*
> *Spicy grove, cinnamon tree*
> *What is Africa to me?*

At one level, the whole book is an intensely personal answer to this oldest of Afro-American questions. But Wright's invocation of descent on the first page does not serve to introduce the straightforward racialism of Blyden or Crummell. For he asks immediately "But am I African?"; and goes on to wonder how he will feel in the presence of someone whose ancestors might have sold his ancestors into slavery—to wonder, we might say, if he can feel African—and then to ask how "the Africans" will think of him. From his first response—"Africa?"—the scattered question marks of the next few pages largely indicate rephrasings of a central mystery, the puzzle that is the insistent theme of the book: what can Africa mean to an Afro-American who does not share—at least, officially—what Blyden called "the poetry of politics" that is "the feeling of race"?

> Had three hundred years imposed a psychological distance be-
> tween me and the "racial stock" from which I had sprung? . . .
> But am I African? . . . What would my feelings be when I looked
> into the black face of an African, feeling that maybe his great-
> great-grandfather had sold my great-great-grandfather into slav-
> ery? Was there something in Africa that my feelings could latch
> onto to make all of this dark past clear and meaningful? Would
> the Africans regard me as a lost brother who had returned? . . .
> and I wondered, "What does being *African* mean . . . . ?"

> Was Africa "primitive"? But what did being "primitive" mean?
> . . . How much of me was African?

Wright arrived in Africa apparently unencumbered with the Victorian views of his distinguished predecessors: he was a rationalist, with no time for Christianity; an ex-Marxist, who still retained a predilection for materialist analyses; and a foe of the sentimental racism that gave meaning to Crummell's and Blyden's African adventures. But, deprived of this intellectual baggage, he also lacked answers to the one question they could always answer, namely, what am I doing here?

Without Christianity he could not see his visit as the work of providence; he could not say, with Crummell, that the demands that Africa makes on black people everywhere are "a natural call," a "grand and noble work laid out in the Divine Providence." His materialist analyses could offer him the shared experience of racial exploitation as an answer, but that could give him no special reason to be in Africa rather than anywhere else in the non-white colonized world. And his consistent resistance to racial explanations, rooted in "blood," deprived him of the answer that runs through the more than a century of Afro-American thought about Africa, from Crummell to Du Bois and on into the Black Nationalism of the sixties.

Because he has no reason for "being there," Wright's reactions seem to oscillate between condescension and paranoia. "Lock your car and come with me," he orders a taxi driver

> expecting him to demur. But he didn't. I found that that was the only way to get any consideration out of a native.

When he is not in this condescending mood, Wright often meets gestures of friendship with suspicion: the first day in the Gold Coast a salesman in a store unwisely asks Wright whether he knows where his African ancestors came from:

> "Well," I said softly, "you know, you fellows who sold us and the white men who bought us didn't keep any records."

Even laughter and smiles recurrently produce distrust. At his first meeting with Nkrumah:

> The Prime Minister threw back his head and laughed. I got used, in time, to that African laughter. It was not caused by mirth, it was a way of indicating that, though they were not going to take you into their confidence, their attitude was not based on anything hostile.

And when Wright met my late great-uncle Otumfuo Sir Osei Agyeman Prempeh II, then king of Ashanti, my distinguished affine obviously made the mistake of smiling once too often:

> He was poised, at ease; yet like other men of the Akan race, he smiled *too* quickly; at times I felt his smile was artificial, that he smiled because it was required of him.

Somehow, one feels that in Paris, or Chicago or back home in Mississippi, even Wright might have grasped that a poised old man in a position of power, who smiled his way through dinner, could just be a fellow with good manners.

The prime minister and the king are merely inscrutable; but everywhere he goes, people are trying to cheat him out of his money, or lie to him about their customs.

> I found that the African almost invariably underestimated the person with whom he was dealing; he always placed too much confidence in an evasive reply, thinking that if he denied something, then that something ceased to exist. It was childlike.

There are no doubt some who would read this as a parody of colonial discourse, but, as Saunders Redding has observed, Wright lacked "the ironic cast of mind and heart . . . he took all men and the world as he took himself: with grim seriousness."

Wright's failure of sympathy mars even the three passages Michael Cooke has recently commended as "brilliant scenes" from a novelistic perspective: the episode set in a Las Palmas whorehouse—amusingly absent from the bowdlerized British edition that presumably went to the colonies; Wright's "feminizing" attempt to purchase a cooking pan from a woman in the street; and the tale of the stolen purse, recounted by his British host in Koforidua. Each evokes from Wright a signal moment of condescension: to a judge of the Nigerian Supreme Court; to African women (all of them, one fears); to the colonizing British who cannot "live side by side with the Africans without becoming infected with the African's religious beliefs."

Wright finally reveals explicitly the structure of assumptions that governs his interpretation of African behavior.

> Most of the Africans I've met have been, despite their ready laughter, highly reserved and suspicious men. It would be easy to say that this chronic distrust arose from their centuries-long exploitation by Europeans, but the explanation would not elucidate the total African attitude. They never seem to feel that they have judged a man rightly unless they project some ulterior motive behind his most straightforward conduct. . . . I submit that the African's doubt of strangers, his panic in the face of reality has but peripheral relations to objective reality.

Every word here reads easily as a projection of Wright's own failings. Face to face with Africa, Wright retreated from reason; and his book is the record of a mind closed to the world through which he travelled.

This paranoid hermeneutic reaches its extraordinary climax in Kumasi, my hometown, capital of the "brooding Ashanti," when Wright is discussing the "human sacrifice" which, he has been assured, follows the death of an Ashanti chief. This passage of attempted anthropology invites serious attention, precisely because of the book's analytical pretensions. Subtly, the tale he has been told is transmuted so that, by the end, the killing of *local* people to accompany the king to the "other world" has become a "homicidal attitude toward the stranger." Finally, there passes very close to the surface the thought—reinforced by the fact that Wright had considered entitling the book *Stranger in a Strange Land*—that our author fears that these smiling, inscrutable black men are, in fact, out to kill him.

This interpretation is achieved through an anthropological fantasy, a fantasy incredible by the standards of ethnological speculation on ritual murder.

> If the human sacrifice—and that of animals: bulls, sheep, goats, and chickens—does not represent displaced hate of the living, why then is blood the gift that will appease the dead ancestor? The staunch conviction that the dead ancestor wants blood is their inverted confession of their own lust for blood. So that they feel that by killing a stranger and bathing the bones of an ancestor in the blood of that stranger, the ancestor will, for the time being, hold off haunting them, will leave them in peace.

"Distrust," Wright says of the Ashanti, "is the essence of such a life" and we no longer know if he is speaking of them or of himself.

### III

References to the traditional religion of the Gold Coast pervade *Black Power;* religion was obviously central to Wright's reactions. Indeed, as John Reilly has discovered, Wright went along with a request from the readers at Harper and Brothers that he excise from the original manuscript "repeated references to his incredulity at aspects of religious practice." But the references that remain are multitudinous enough; and they have the effect of establishing a massive distance between Wright (and his readers in the West) and the people of the Gold Coast.

Of course, the religious practices of the people Wright meets are certainly strange to him, as they are to most Western readers. But Wright's preface tells us that "the book seeks to provide Western readers with some insight into what is going to happen in Africa," and to do this he must seek to render Africa intelligible. To see Wright's account of traditional religion as governed by his rhetoric of distance is to draw attention to the ways in which he seems studiously to avoid any opportunities to render these admittedly alien habits of thought more familiar.

I was raised in the Ghana that Nkrumah's Gold Coast became. I spent my youth in the landscape and among the people Wright seeks to anatomize; and what strikes me repeatedly is the way that *Black Power* defamiliarizes a world I know. And because, like every African intellectual nowadays, I know my way around the thought-world of the West, I am constantly struck, too, by the missed opportunities for understanding; the points at which a route for the Westerner into the traditional world is barred by Wright's desire not to understand. In *Black Power* there is never any real attempt to render familiar the traditional modes of thought whose unfamiliarity inevitably strike the Western stranger; instead we are constantly deluged with indecipherable signs of "African religion."

Wright's desire for distance is highlighted in an anecdote he retells of his first encounter with a Gold Coast funeral. Early on in his visit Wright hears "sounds of drums, of shouting, of shooting" outside his hotel. He rushes out into the noisy procession and watches a brass coffin borne aloft by a group of men:

> they'd run to a corner, stop, twirl the coffin, then, amidst shouting, singing, chanting, they'd turn and race with the coffin spinning above their heads in another direction.

Unable to keep up with the spinning coffin, Wright gives up trying to follow.

> I . . . stood feeling foolish and helpless in the hot sun, sensing sweat streaming down my face.
> I had understood nothing, nothing. . . . [his ellipsis] . . . My mind reeled at the newness and strangeness of it. Had my ancestors acted like that? And why?

Wright seeks enlightenment from an "African dressed in Western clothes"; and the African offers an elaborate explanation of the beliefs underlying many elements of the scene that has just transpired, asking Wright finally whether he understands.

Wright never answers his informant; at the very moment when he is offered entry to this hermetic world, he turns his back on the guide. "Yes;" he tells *us* (as his informant disappears into the crowd forever), "if you accepted the assumptions all the rest was easy, logical. The African's belief in the other world was concrete, definite."

Wright's narrative draws our attention to the sudden breaking off of dialogue, precisely at the point where he is offered the opportunity to find out whether he has understood. But he goes on to account for his estrangement in these extraordinary words:

> If there was another world, the African was about the only man
> really believing in it; . . .

You wonder what has happened to the "haints" of his native Mississippi, to the *lares* and *penates* of the European classical world, to Christian Europe's belief in an afterlife. To establish distance, it seems, Wright is willing to address "the Western reader" with a travesty of his own world.

Wright reports that he inserted an advertisement "in a local newspaper asking to buy an out-of-print book, R. S. Rattray's *Ashanti*," the classical ethnography of the region; and he has an extended discussion of J. B. Danquah's *Akan Doctrine of God*. Captain Rattray, a British Colonial Office anthropologist, had written that the Ashanti would

> become better and finer men and women by remaining true
> Ashanti and retaining a certain pride in their past, and that their
> greatest hope lies in the future, if they will build upon lines with
> which the national *sunsum* or soul has been familiar since first
> they were a people.

And his account renders intelligible much of what Wright seeks to render mysterious.

But Wright will have none of this. His account of Danquah begins with the question how "these strange notions came about" and ends with the remark that the Akan belief in life after death makes their lives "as charged and exciting as the moving tables and floating trumpets in a seance in a dreary London flat." The rhetorical sleight-of-hand here is breathtaking: if these "strange notions" operate in dreary London flats, why is their presence in *Africa* something that needs explaining? The human mystery of religious belief is dressed up as an African mystery: once more the sense of alterity is enforced.

At the end of Wright's exposition of Danquah's *Akan Doctrine of God* we read this one-sentence paragraph:

> I come up for air, to take a deep breath. . . . (his ellipsis)

The ellipsis, here as elsewhere, marks a moment when Wright seems literally to be at a loss for words. The figure implies that he is drowning, sucked down, perhaps, into the primal squalor of Africa. For Wright, as he admits, "the religion of the Akan is not primitive; it is simply terrifying."

Despite his exposure to Rattray's humane anthropological account of the "logic" of Akan traditional religion, Africa is still for Wright, as Crummell put it, "the victim of her heterogeneous idolatries." *Juju*, Gold Coast magic, is as offensive to Wright's rationalism as "Fetishes . . . and devil-worship" were to Crummell's Victorian Christianity. And each is equally a projection of the alientated stranger. The truth is that, though Wright's anthropological reading had prepared his mind for the religions of the Gold Coast, he was unable, when faced with the raw experience, to keep that intellectual apprehension. When he came to write about it, he found himself able to report "African religion" only as yet another mark of his own distance from Africa: "the religion of the Akan" becomes just another device to establish his alienation.

## IV

Mary Louise Pratt has recently discussed some of the mechanisms by which a discourse—and, in particular, nineteenth-century travel writing about Africa—renders people alien. In her essay "Scratches on the Face of the Country; or, What Mr. Barrow Saw in the Land of the Bushmen," she observes, for example, that "the people to be othered are homogenized into a collective 'they,' which is distilled even further into an iconic 'he' (the standardized adult male specimen)." Pratt also remarks on the role of certain rhetorical strategies in this process of textual distancing: crucially the "temporal distancing" achieved by what Johannes Fabian has called the "denial of coevalness."

Wright's text is quite overt in the use it makes of just these devices of distancing. There are, for example, regular references to "the African." Even an old-style Ashanti imperialist, convinced that all the worthwhile culture of the region originated with the Akan, would be puzzled by Wright's assumption that learning about Ga villages, or the burial customs of the Northern Territories entitled one to generalize about the Gold Coast, let alone about the continent. Wright displays ignorance again and again of the significance of terms, like "Twi" or "Akan," which he uses to characterize languages or "tribes"; and yet this does not seem to matter for his purposes precisely because, in the end, he only recognizes the people he meets as "Africans." Subtler distinctions may be mentioned, but only to add authority to his voice—here is a fellow who knows his Fanti from his Ashanti—not to illuminate the specificities of different human cultures.

There is even a passage where Wright reports "an intuitive impression that these people were old, old, maybe the oldest people on earth," thus securing a remarkably explicit temporal distancing; remarkable, because, if this is not a device of distance, this sentence hardly seems to tell us anything at all.

But the central devices of distance in this text are provided, I believe, not so much by rhetoric as by two *themes:* one of them, as I have suggested, is religion; the other, as Pratt would perhaps have predicted, is the African body.

We have been in the Gold Coast only a few hours, travelling along the coast in a government bus, when Wright looks out of the window to see "a crowd of naked man, women and children, bathing." This scene is absorbed into "the kaleidoscope of sea jungle, nudity, mud huts and crowded market places" which "induced in me a conflict deeper than I was aware of"; and these unfamiliar scenes fill him with "a mild sense of anxiety." At the first stop,

> I stared down at a bare-breasted young girl who held a huge pan of oranges perched atop her head. She saw me studying her and she smiled shyly, obviously accepting her semi-nudity as being normal. My eyes went over the crowd and I noticed that most of the older women had breasts that were flat and remarkably elongated, some reaching twelve or eighteen inches (length, I was later told, was regarded as a symbol of fertility!), hanging loosely and flapping as the women moved about . . .

Still, "bit by bit," Wright assures us in an attempt to reestablish narrative poise, "my eyes became accustomed to the naked bodies."

Yet, next day, Wright's second day in the colony, on his first morning in Accra, he goes into the city and finds himself the physical anthropologist once more:

> I reached a street corner and paused; coming towards me was a woman nursing a baby that was still strapped to her back; the baby's head was thrust under the woman's arm and the woman had given the child the long, fleshy, tubelike teat and it was suckling. (There are women with breasts so long that they do not bother to give the baby the teat in front of them, but simply toss it over the shoulder to the child on their back . . . (his ellipsis)

It is not just breasts that draw Wright's sideways glance: there are "monstrous umbilical hernias"; girls are "skinny, their black shoulder blades stuck out at sharp angles"; beggars have "monstrously swollen legs, running sores, limbs broken so that jagged ends of the healed bones jutted out like blackened sticks"; blind men have "empty eye sockets [that] yawned wetly, palsied palms extended"; "once or twice" he sees "women who had induced strange swellings on their skins in order to beautify themselves."

What is striking in these passages is the way that these bodies alienate by evoking disgust. The umbilical hernias, though monstrous, evoke no pity; the beggars' wounds "moved me not to compassion, but to revulsion"; the strange swellings conspicuously fail in their object, which is to beautify. Even where the bodies are graceful they are strange: "they walked as straight as ramrods, with a slow, slinging motion"; the men who bring the goods to shore in their tiny canoes are "wet glistening black robots."

How are we to read these significant bodies? Each record is of an encounter with a body, an encounter that Wright could not have had in Paris and Chicago. We understand how these bodies have caught his traveller's eye. But in a narrative that shifts erratically between an informational and a subjective register, it is striking how these bodies, even those young breasts, whose openness offers the Western imagination erotic possibilities, remain almost always in the information register. When they do not, the subjective register records them as objects of revulsion.

Indeed, so unerotic is Wright's encounter with the African body that he projects his own de-sexualization:

> Undoubtedly these people had, through experiences that had constituted a kind of trial and error, and in response to needs that were alien and obscure to me, chosen some aspect of their lives other than sex upon which to concentrate their passions . . .

It takes a moment to grasp that Wright is here suggesting: that sexual desire means nothing to "the African." We can only wonder where all those filthy children with their "monstrous umbilical hernias" came from.

There is one final, oppressive regularity in Wright's encounter with the African bodyscape: again and again, these African bodies are, above all else, *black*.

We can assume, with Wright, that his readers know that most Africans have black skins. If he is constantly drawing attention to that fact, it is in order to sharpen the central paradox of the book:

> I was black and they were black, and my blackness did not help me.

This is a paradox in the root sense: it goes against received opinion. And it is, I think the fact that he cannot understand the minds behind these black faces—these minds that his culture (though not his official theory) had prepared him to find immediately accessible precisely because of the blackness of the faces—that generates first the defensive condescension and then, in the end, the frank paranoia.

> I'm of African descent and I'm in the midst of Africans, yet I
> cannot tell what they are thinking and feeling.

Saunders Redding, one of Wright's astutest readers, has written of Wright's travels to Africa—and to Paris—as a failed search for a home. Despite his repeated resistance, in this book, as in his other writings, to the view of Africa as the homeland of the Negro—"I stoutly denied the mystic influence of 'race'—it is hard to resist Redding's claim that Wright's trip to Africa was yet another quest for a place of his own. When, in the final pages of the book, he tells Nkrumah that "our people must be made to walk, forced draft, into the twentieth century," we do not need to ask *whose* people. Scratch the native son and you'll find the native.

Even Wright's reaction to the pidgin English of the servants in the bungalow Nkrumah had arranged for him reveals an uneasiness about his identity:

> But the pidgin English! I shuddered. I resented it and vowed that
> I'd never speak it.

This resentment can only mean that this "frightful kind of baby talk" reflects badly on *him*. There is here a palpable anxiety about redescending into the ancestral mire.

Wright had arrived in Africa convinced, so he says, that a shared race gave him no basis for understanding the people he would meet, convinced that he had no basis for identifying with them: and *Black Power* is the record of his resentment that they proved him right. *Black Power*'s desire for distance is Wright's revenge for Africa's rebuff: his exaggeration of the gap between Africa and his Western experience is a response to the gap between his African experience and his African dream.

V

What energy and purpose there is in this book derives from Wright's sense of the importance of what Kwame Nkrumah was doing: in a splendid inversion of the strategy of authentication that Robert Stepto, among others, had identified in the affixed letter of the Afro-American slave narrative, Wright prefaced his book with an authenticating letter from Nkrumah. On the prime minister's letterhead and over his signature we read:

> This is to certify that I have known Mr. Richard Wright for
> many years, having met him in the United States.

For the first time an Afro-American can seek legitimation from a black man, a black head of government: the gesture underscores the truth in Baldwin's claim that the Afro-American is no longer "at the mercy of the American white man's image of him."

But the text not only begins with a letter *from* Nkrumah, but ends with a letter *to* him. The "response" to the African Prime Minister's note "to whom it may concern" is a long letter to "Dear Kwame." Wright's open letter is not drawn in the cold impersonal language of Nkrumah's *pro forma* note, but forged in the red heat of passion. The rhetorical distance, the disproportion between stimulus and response, between Nkrumah's impassive authorizing pre-text and Wright's final hysterical message to "the unknown African," is a measure of the asymmetry of feeling. Wright needs Nkrumah, needs him as his symbol of hope for black humanity; but all Nkrumah has to offer is a brusque acknowledgment that Wright is a suitable visitor, "to the best of my knowledge and belief."

Wright's letter proposes that the heart of "Africa's" problem is that "the African" has no sharply defined ego, no real individuality:

> there is too much cloudiness in the African mentality, a kind of
> sodden vagueness that makes for lack of confidence, an absence
> of focus that renders that mentality incapable of grasping the
> workaday world. And until confidence is established at the cen-
> ter of African personality, until there is an inner reorganization
> of that personality, there can be no question of marching from
> the tribal order to the twentieth century. . . . (his ellipsis)

If Wright cannot penetrate "the African personality," perhaps there is no personality to be penetrated.

And what is Wright's solution to Africa's problems; to the problems of these cloudy and unfocused personalities? "AFRICAN LIFE MUST BE MILITARIZED." Crummell's nineteenth-century vision of an Africa civilized by Christianity is replaced by the twentieth-century's desperate alternative: the protestant soldiers of God have become a rationalist army of progress. There is something simply mad in proposing from Paris, less than a decade after the Second World War, that Nkrumah—like Hitler and Mussolini?—needs the instruments of fascism if the trains of the Gold Coast are to run on time. And in proposing what is, despite his explicit denials, the introduction of the fascist state (uncomfortably suggestive of the totalitarian states that we deplore in Africa thirty years on), in proposing a solution that he acknowledges will appear "hard, cruel," the overwhelming impression Wright leaves is that he needs to punish Africa for failing him: and that its failure is, ironically, that it did just what he had asked of it. Blyden or Crummell may have hated much that they found in Africa, but they knew it was theirs. Deprived of the right, which Crummell or Blyden could have claimed, to take pride and pleasure in Nkrumah's achievement by virtue of race; convinced, against his hopes, that this is a place he does not understand, Wright responds with the fury of the lover spurned.

ABDUL JanMOHAMED

# Rehistoricizing Wright:
# The Psychopolitical Function of Death
# in Uncle Tom's Children

> But her fear was a quiet one; it was more like an intense brood-
> ing than a fear; it was a sort of hugging of hated facts so closely
> that she could feel their grain, like letting cold water run over her
> hand from a faucet on a winter morning.

This brief sentence from "Bright and Morning Star," the last story in
Richard Wright's first anthology, describing the protagonist's anxiety about
her son's involvement in a local political and racial struggle in the South,
reflects the development of Wright's early fiction, from the first story in
*Uncle Tom's Children* to the problematic ending of *Native Son*. The syn-
tactic structure—a series of short clauses moving from abstract definitions
of emotions to increasingly concrete representations and finally ending with
a concrete and apt, if paradoxical, simile—not only accurately maps the
relation between emotions and their underlying sociopolitical causes and
effects but also traces the trajectory of the thematic development of his short
stories. The fear, aroused by racist oppression and by the need to struggle
with racism, to both of which Wright testifies so often in his fiction and
autobiographical statements, is one of the most significant emotions in the
very construction of the black psyche; and Wright's fictional investigation
of the emotional and intellectual structures of that psyche, an investigation
which can be characterized in its tone precisely as an "intense brooding," a
"hugging" and nurturing, eventually reveals the structures, the "grain," of
the subjective "facts" of racism as experienced by a black person and of the
objective "facts" responsible for the existence of racism as a political and
cultural phenomenon, both of which he hated in different ways.

---

By doggedly and unflinchingly exposing himself to the cold facts of his own racial experiences, Wright gradually begins to understand and reveal the essence of the dual structure of black racial experience in the United States. On the one hand, he gradually articulates the important role of what Orlando Patterson has called the "social death" of the slave's condition, and its corollary, the liminal incorporation of the slave in the interstices of society. On the other hand, Wright incrementally maps through his short stories the only viable, but highly paradoxical, route of escape from radical liminality: the voluntary acceptance of actual death (albeit in the symbolic realm of fiction), which turns out to be the only possible way of negating the negation of a full life that is entailed in the condition of "social death."

Wright's own discovery of the dialectical relation between "social death" and actual death, of the fact that the slave's "social death" is predicated on the postponement of his actual execution and that liberation from the former can be achieved only by his willingness to accept the latter, is gradual and incremental. He intuitively begins his anthology with a story depicting the rapid and gruesome death of three black boys who have committed relatively minor infractions of Jim Crow segregation rules and ends with a story wherein the protagonist willfully chooses death as a form of psychopolitical liberation. This last story, with its politically motivated courtship of violence and death is not markedly different from the psychopolitical function of death in *Native Son.* Yet, remarkably, both Wright and his critics have been unable to perceive either the underlying thematic of death in the anthology and the novel or the evolutionary continuity between the two works. Wright felt that he had portrayed the protagonists in *Uncle Tom's Children* in such a way that they seemed entirely powerless in the face of violent racism and that such depiction only aroused pity in his reader. In the preface to *Native Son,* Wright confesses that when the reviews of *Uncle Tom's Children* appeared, he realized that he had made "an awfully naive mistake":

> I found that I had written a book which even bankers' daughters
> could read and weep over and feel good about. I swore to myself
> that if I ever wrote another book, no one would weep over it;
> that it would be so hard and deep that they would have to face
> it without the consolation of tears.

Thus he proceeds to create a more deliberately angry, violent, and horrifying hero in *Native Son,* a hero who is not amenable to sentimentalization and who could not thus be ideologically appropriated and neutralized.

Similarly, Wright's later critics, partly taking their cue from him, have tended to perceive and analyze *Uncle Tom's Children* in terms tacitly governed by the notions of powerlessness and pity. The critics' failure to read the subtextual function of death and the author's inability to perceive the radical significance of his own short stories are both due, I would suggest, to the powerful perceptual limitations created by the ideological implications of a subgeneric category: "protest literature," which retains, in the realm of literary criticism, the essential structure of the power relation between master and slave. The protagonists of fiction classified under this subgenre are automatically perceived as powerless in relation to the reader, who is assumed to be more powerful and omniscient. The category is ideologically designed more for the reaffirmation of the reader's position than for an illuminating analysis of the text. However, both the ideological blindness imposed by the above category and the psychopolitical function of death in Wright's fiction can be understood better if we first briefly examine Orlando Patterson's modification of Hegel's master-slave dialectic in light of his remarkably thorough historical study of different slave societies. Although Wright was not brought up in an actual slave society, I shall shortly demonstrate that the Jim Crow society that shaped his life (and that of other blacks) was organized around the same fundamental social structures as those defined by Patterson as being universal to slave cultures throughout the world.

Using the Weberian definition of power and the assumption that all human relationships are structured and defined by the relative power of the interacting persons, Patterson demonstrates that slavery is one of the most extreme forms of the relation of domination, approaching the limits of total power from the viewpoint of the master, and of total powerlessness from the viewpoint of the slave. The three facets of power relations that he outlines—first, the use or threat of violence in one individual's attempt to control another; second, the capacity to persuade another person to change the way he perceives his interests and circumstances; and third, the cultural legitimation of the authority that is used to translate force into "right" and obedience into "duty"—can be reformulated more succinctly in terms of Gramsci's distinction between dominant and hegemonic power relations. In dominant relations the "consent" of the powerless individual is passive and indirect, that is, he complies because he is unable to resist; whereas "consent" under hegemonic relations is active and indirect, that is, the oppressed individual has accepted the oppressor's definitions about the constitution of material and cultural reality and the rules that govern normative human relations. Of course, neither dominance based on violence nor hegemony based on discursive control is ever able to subjugate the oppressed entirely and completely; in practice some form of resistance will always remain. And it is precisely in the margins where resistance is possible that Richard Wright's work is located. Also, since in practice given human relations will be governed by complex and varied mixtures of dominance and hegemony, the important theoretical distinction between the two allows us better to appreciate Patterson's insistence that slavery is maintained by the constant and brutal use of violence, that violence is necessary not only to induce work from the slave but also to remind him of his powerless status. Thus, slave societies are never quite able to make a complete transition to hegemonic relations, and the complex relations between master and slave remain a sublated state of war.

Based on such a theory of power and on examinations of specific slave societies, Patterson identifies three constituent elements of slavery: the slave's utter powerlessness; his "natal alienation" and "social death"; and his overwhelming experience of dishonor. While Patterson's analysis of the constitution and dispersal of these three elements (summarized below) considerably illuminates the condition of the slave, it is unable to explore thoroughly the extremely unstable and explosive nature of the contradictions which typify every moment of the slave's life.

According to Patterson, "the most distinctive feature of the slave's powerlessness was that it always originated . . . as a substitute for death, usually violent death." However, in all slave societies, the condition of slavery did not dissolve his prospect of death; rather, death was conditionally commuted and could be revoked at the master's whim. The implication is that in order to live the slave had to acquiesce in his own powerlessness; by asserting any significant power against the master he courted death. Thus in "his powerlessness the slave became an extension of his master's power. He was a human surrogate, recreated by his master with god-like power in his behalf."

Patterson identifies two aspects of the "idiom of power" used in slave societies, the social and the conceptual, and further divides the former into "the personalistic and materialistic idioms." In the personalistic idiom, he argues, "power is direct—or nearly so—and is frequently transparent." Although the use of such a mode is accompanied by an attempt to disguise direct personal control and dependency under various ideological explanations, it never achieves complete opacity. In Patterson's notion of the "materialistic" idiom, which is based on Marx's definition of commodity fetishism, "relations of dependence are 'disguised under the shape of social relations between the products of labor' "; power relationships are no longer viewed as control over persons but as control over commodities. These distinctions allow Patterson to demonstrate the extreme flexibility of slavery, or its ability to exist within a capitalist mode of production in the South in spite of the fact that slavery itself was organized as a precapitalistic mode. (This insight is important because the nature of Richard Wright's experience of racism, based on a personalistic rather than materialistic idiom of power, will allow us to modify significantly what has traditionally been defined as the "naturalistic" style of *Native Son*.) According to Patterson, the relevant "conceptual aspect of the [materialist] idiom of power" is the notion of property, which he ultimately defines not as a mode of ownership but as a "web of social relations" that ultimately define one's relations to objects. I shall return to this notion of property presently since it provides us with the avenue to the most fundamental contradictions in the experience of the slave. Finally, Patterson stresses the fact that slavery is a highly symbolized domain of human experience, the structure of which is determined by the need to reinforce and legitimate, in the discursive realm, the "authority" of the master that is essentially based on a monopoly of violence.

At the ideological level, the slave is incorporated by almost all slave societies as a "socially dead person." Induction into slavery involves several transition phases. In the external phase the slave is violently uprooted from his milieu and often from his culture and is then desocialized and depersonalized. In the next phase, he is inserted into his master's community, but not as a fully fledged member of that society. Rather, he is paradoxically introduced as a non-being. In the new society, he has none of the legal, moral, or cultural rights that his masters enjoy. In fact, slave cultures are organized in such a way that he has no socially organized existence except that which is allowed him by the master, who becomes the sole mediator between his own living community and the living death that his slave experiences. Alienated from rights or claims of birth, he cannot belong of his own right to any legitimate social order. Not only is he cut off from his culture and any legal power, but his immediate community is also destroyed: he is forcefully removed from his ancestors, and his spouse or descendants can be taken from him at any time. Thus the slave becomes a "genealogical isolate," most often castrated in cultural and political terms, but, at times, literally so. Patterson alternately defines the social death of the slave as his "natal alienation," thus stressing his condition as perpetual and inheritable. Unlike other bonded workers, he can never work his way out of his slave status. He is deprived of his past and of any significant control over his future; thus he knows no teleology or direction except that of his master, or rebellion against the latter.

Of the two cultural modes of representing social death that Patterson identifies, the most prevalent, and the one most relevant to the American context, is the intrusive. This mode or representation prevails when the slave is recruited from an external, alien society; he is then ritually incorporated as the permanent enemy on the inside, as the domestic enemy. His "intrusion" in the master's society has a dual ideological function; his presence as an alien becomes a living affront to the local gods, for he is seen as an intruder in the sacred cultural space (or its secular equivalent); however, his presence as a conquered non-being also validates the power of the local gods, the superiority of the master's community and its centrality and humanness—in short, it affirms the community's self-identity. Paradoxically, the social liminality of the slave is used to affirm those aspects of the master's culture considered most important and stable.

Finally, Patterson identifies the constitutive function of honor/dishonor in a slave society. The slave's experience is pervaded by a generalized sense of dishonor for the following interrelated reasons: his condition has originated in defeat; he has to accept all kinds of indignities; he is perpetually indebted; he has no independent social existence; and, most importantly, he has no power except through his master. Patterson convincingly argues that ultimately a sense of honor depends upon an individual's ability to impose himself on or assert himself against another within culturally acceptable terms. Honor in this sense rests on personal autonomy, and the slave has none. Degradation, the fundamental existential aspect of the individual slave's experience, is compounded by its communal proliferation. For to belong to a community is to have a sense of one's place among one's fellows, to feel the need to assert and defend it and to experience satisfaction when one's position, and even that of the whole community, is successfully defended against others. A sense of position and the ability to assert oneself are minimal, at best, in a slave community, which thus is able to provide little sustenance for the individual slave: the community as a whole is "socially dead." In the economy of honor in such a society, the master gains what the slave loses. This economy, Patterson argues, is as important as the material economy of slavery, for in many societies masters retained slaves solely for their honorific value rather than for material gain.

Thus where slavery becomes a structually important part of society, the culture tends to become increasingly honorific and eventually turns into a timocracy as in the antebellum South. Drawing on John Hope Franklin's study, Patterson argues that the antebellum South, the most articulate and highly developed timocracy, manifested a direct link between slavery and the valorization of honor. It is because of this extreme development that any attempt by a black slave in the South, and later by a free black, to assert his "manhood," or to overcome the "Sambo" stereotype, elicited passionate and violent retaliation from whites. The disproportionate nature of this response has to be accounted for not only by the potential threat to the master's material wealth but by the very real challenge that any form of rebellion posed to the psychopolitical benefits of his position as master.

Although, strictly speaking, the black American living in the Jim Crow society at the turn of the century was not a slave, his status was no different in essence. If we examine his condition in terms of the three constitutive elements of slavery defined by Patterson—powerlessness, social death, and lack of honor—the effective continuation of slavery becomes readily apparent.

The black man living in Jim Crow society was as powerless as his slave ancestor. As I. A. Newby points out, the basic premise of social segregation of blacks from 1900 to 1930 in the South "was the conviction that Negroes had a definite place in American society; and the chief object of anti-Negro thought was to define that place in detail. It was, of course, subordinate and its limits were well defined." According to Thomas Pearce Bailey, whom Newby considers the most succinct and articulate ideologue of the Jim Crow ethic, it was the black's "*assertion,* present or possible, of his equal worth" that so outraged the descendants of the master and drove them to violence against the sons of slaves. In essence, the South demanded, by force when necessary, servility, i.e., powerlessness, from the black. The " 'good' Negro, the 'right-thinking' Negro" was the one "who recognized his place and accepted it without complaint." As Lawrence J. Friedman demonstrates so amply, the quest for the servile or docile black has been one of the central motifs of Southern racist ideology and practice. However, it would be erroneous to imply that the Southerner simply fantasized about an "image" of a servile, powerless black. Ideology worked in close conjunction with practice to deprive blacks of any effective political power. As Newby points out:

> In 1890 Mississippi commenced the long, dreary process of constitutional amendments and statutory enactments which disfranchised the Negro and made his segregation virtually complete. Before 1900 South Carolina and Louisiana followed suit, and by 1910 Oklahoma and the remaining states of the old Confederacy had done likewise.

A variety of direct and indirect means—literacy, property qualification, poll taxes (payable months in advance and for several consecutive years), and finally purely subjective criteria like tests of character and reputation—were used to disfranchise blacks from equal participation in the hegemonic field. As with slavery, however, all ideological concepts and hegemonic institutions and practices were ultimately underwritten by violence. "Between 1900 and 1910 an average of more than ninety Negroes were lynched each year in the South, and [white] race riots frequently accompanied disfranchisement." White violence increased with black political assertiveness. Immediately after the return of black soldiers from the First World War the possibility of increase in black power resulted in twenty-five white riots throughout various urban centers between June and December of 1919. In effect, then, during the thirty years after the turn of the century, blacks were virtually as powerless as they were during slavery.

The second structural feature of slavery, the liminality and social death of the slave, is also readily apparent in this period. According to Newby, Southerners in general and their political spokesmen in particular "saw the *presence* of the Negroes [in the South] as a problem in itself." In other words, the presence of blacks as the "enemy within" created the same paradox as the presence of the slave: on the one hand, blacks were caricatured as the antithesis of humanity and as a menace to white society, particularly to the ideal of the virtuous white woman; on the other hand, Southerners believed that blacks were happiest in the South and so should be confined there. The blacks simultaneously affronted and affirmed the humanity of the South. Thus both religious and scientific tracts strove to define blacks as subhuman, as apes with whom whites could have no social intercourse. This kind of "social segregation" was in effect another term for social death. Politically disfranchised from participation in the white culture of the South and from the hegemonic institutions of America, blacks in this period were as dependent on their white contemporaries for access to the legitimate social order as were their "slave" ancestors on their "masters." As one might expect, nowhere is the social death of postbellum blacks more clearly evident than in the practice and justification of lynching. The proliferation of lynching in this period led to some Northern attempts to pass anti-lynching legislation, which in turn produced some Southern justifications that are most revealing.

> The white man's law, said many racists, was unsuited to Negroes, who were adapted by racial experience to the ways of the jungle. *Due process, trial by jury,* even imprisonment, were meaningless to them, for they saw no connection between crime and punishment unless one was *immediately* followed by the other.

> Not only was federal legislation unnecessary, [Southerners] de-
> clared, but it was unwise in the highest degree. Ignorant and
> vicious Negroes would interpret it as a *concession to social
> equality,* and racial problems would be aggravated rather than
> diminished.

These "justifications" perfectly clarify three fundamental features of the
continued efficacy of "social death." First, blacks of the postbellum South
had no more access to legal due process (or to political power) than did their
slave ancestors: they were as firmly relegated to the realm of "social death"
as the latter. Second, and most important, the Southerner's preference of
death rather than imprisonment as an appropriate form of punishment and
his insistence that the punishment instantly follow the crime together verify
the fact that the black, like the slave, "lived" under the conditional commutation of his death and that the commutation could be revoked at the
master's whim (without any recourse to due process) if the black refused to
remain servile and powerless. Third, the Southerner seemed perfectly aware
that any alteration in the "social death" of the black would imply a corresponding change in his liminality, that it would open the doors to social
equality.

Finally, one must point out, though it hardly seems necessary, that the
black had no more "honor" in this period than during slavery. The main
objection to social integration was the personal repulsiveness of blacks.
Racists "considered the Negro's personality and character traits depraved,
immoral, and repugnant to the sensibility and sensitivity of civilized white
men. Especially popular among extremists, this idea was a basic element in
anti-Negro thought." The controlling impulse of the black was an unduly
exaggerated "sexual passion." According to the physician William Lee
Howard, the phylogeny of blacks was such that the "libidinous substances"
that controlled his brain robbed his mind and conscience of food in order to
administer to the strong demands of his genital organs. Even in small black
girls, he felt, lust was present "to an extent scarcely possible of belief." The
consequence of this sexual excess was the lack of control, the personal
moral irresponsibility, and the moral corruption of the black. In fact, the
black mind was entirely overtaken by the animal in him: he "was a creature
of the moment, for whatever feeling, desire, or passion seized him he expressed in immediate action. As a result, he was sexually incontinent and
had a congenital tendency to quarrelsomeness, crime, and violence. He was,
in short, unfit for social equality with the white man." It seems, then, that
the generalized sense of dishonor experienced by the black slave is inherited

by his "free" descendant; the only difference is that now the master's society chooses to focus the degradation through sex.

There are, however, two aspects of this dishonor that need to be stressed. First, according to the Southerner the New Negro was even more degraded than the slave. It would seem that as the timocracy declined the black had to be degraded even further in order for white society to retain the same ratio of honorific difference between the white and the black. Second, the sexualization of racial difference culminated in the myth of the black rapist, according to which the black man had an innate fondness for white women and was predisposed to rape them. According to Newby, this myth was pervasive: "no discussion, diatribe, or treatise was complete without noting it, and every idea, action, and policy was examined in light of it. In bluntest form it said simply that the object of racial policy was to protect pure and undefiled white maidenhood from the nameless and unspeakable crime of brutal black assaulters." For Congressman James F. Byrnes, "rape was 'directly and indirectly [responsible] for most lynchings in America.' " However, as Newby argues, this myth had little substance behind it: according to a study conducted in 1942, only seventeen percent of the blacks lynched between 1889 and 1941 *were even accused of rape.* Whatever the psychopolitical function of this myth, there can be little doubt that it had a profound effect on Wright, who was born in Mississippi in 1908 and whose formative years were spent in the South. Rape and castration figure prominently in Wright's fiction, from *Native Son* to his last novel, *The Long Dream,* and later we shall return to the ideological function of this myth in a racist society and to Wright's use of it.

In order to explore thoroughly the deepest contradictions which define the black psyche within this setting (contradictions which Patterson's work implies but which he does not articulate), we need to begin by reiterating Patterson's succinct and eloquent description of how different master-slave relations are from other human relationships:

> Husbands and wives give and take, sometimes; employers and wage earners, maybe: masters and slaves, never. What masters and slaves do is struggle: sometimes noisily, more often quietly; sometimes violently, more often surreptitiously; infrequently with arms, always with the weapons of the mind and soul.

Paradoxically, our analysis of this perceptual struggle waged in the psychopolitical terrain of individual minds and social relationships, this sublated war between master and slave, must begin with the definition of the slave as property, as object of ownership. In Patterson's schema, the conceptual aspect of the idiom of power that defines slavery is based on the notion of property that, in turn, has two constituent elements: (1) "the object," and (2) " 'the web of social relations, which establishes a limiting and defined relationship between persons' with respect to the object." And the object has far less significance in the definition of property than social relations. The contradiction arises for the slave because he is simultaneously the object of ownership and, as a human subject, part of the social relation that defines him as an object of that very social relation. In Gramscian terms, the slave has to consent, at some level actively and directly, to defining himself as an object, as a "socially dead" person. Of course, the irony is that only as a subject can he consent to anything, even to defining himself as a non-subject; the very process of consenting to his own objecthood "affirms" his subjectivity, but, of course, not in any self-enhancing or constructive sense. To some and perhaps a great extent, his consent is passive and indirect; that is, he accepts his status because he cannot resist the superior material power of the master's society. But as Patterson points out, in practice a complex set of factors—"The viability of the slave system, the solidarity of the ruling class, the absence of revolutionary openings"—often lead slaves to accept their dishonored condition. While this does not necessarily mean that a desire for freedom and for a self-constituting subjectivity are permanently alienated, the "provisional" acceptance of objectness may be so overwhelming in its duration and the daily acquiescence to brutality may be so demoralizing that in effect they produce a virtually complete acceptance of the slave condition.

Patterson also argues that a slave is not a slave only because he is the object of property, but also because he cannot be the subject of property. The implication is that he cannot even own himself as property. That is, his own relation to himself is profoundly mediated by the master. If he comes to accept himself as a "socially dead" person, as an object, then that part of himself that strives for emancipation has to struggle against the part that has accepted his own death. If the slave finds himself in a condition in which he is effectively dead, then he can only liberate himself, in the final analysis, either by killing the master who holds him in the position of conditionally commuted death or by "killing" that part of him which has accepted death. In a schematic sense, then, we can say that murder or suicide are the only effective avenues open to the slave who wants to liberate himself.

The point is that the slave occupies a highly contradictory and explosive subject position. In the realm of dominance, of social relations that are ultimately determined by violence, the slave can either accept his social death or he can willingly accept the risk of actual death by physically and violently struggling with his masters. In the realm of hegemony, of the discursive formation of self, his struggle is far more complex and contradictory. To the extent that a given individual slave's psyche is formed within the hegemony of an existing slave society, his discovery of his own social death will be a gradual and painful process. In order to effect his own liberation, he will first have to recognize his powerlessness, his genealogical isolation, his lack of control over any aspect of his present and future life— in short, his emasculation and death. Then, he will be obliged to confront that part of himself that has collaborated in his own formation as a socially dead person, as an object; he will have to recognize his own agency in his emasculation. And finally, he will have to destroy or effectively overcome his own formation. In short, he will have to annihilate his old self and (re)form another one. However, even the slave's desire to be free and to re-create himself, a desire for which there is abundant evidence, is vulnerable to ideological manipulation. As Patterson points out, manumission was often used by the master as an incentive to keep the slave obedient and to make him work harder. Thus the slave's desire for freedom could become a trap. And this factor adds a further twist to the contradictory position of the slave: the more his desire for freedom is manipulated, the more degraded he feels. Patterson stresses the fact that the slave's desire remains unquenchable. But in order to balance the dialectic of liberation and bondage we need to emphasize equally the depth of the slave's experience of degradation: he must feel the latter profoundly in order for his desire for dignity and freedom to become deep and tenacious. Of course, there is an ever present danger that the deeply felt degradation can break the slave's will and desire for freedom. Thus it is precisely this fine demarcation between utter despair and defeat, on the one hand, and an adamant desire for liberation, on the other (both of which can potentially lead to different kinds of death), that we must appreciate in order to understand how the willing acceptance of death functions as the most viable form of liberation in the fiction of Richard Wright.

The slave's attempt to liberate himself is further complicated by two factors. The first is quite simply the fact that the process of self-recognition and reformation are permeated at every level of different facets of the slave's social death and the violence that lies behind it. Second is the fact that in the American context the black slave or freedman is allowed only marginal entrance into the hegemonic field. For example, as Richard Wright testifies, it was illegal for him as a black to borrow books from the Memphis public libraries. Without adequate access to the hegemonic field of the master's culture, reformation of the self in the discursive field becomes a virtually impossible task. The attempt at reformation, therefore, constantly breaks out into violence, which is the ultimate source of the slave's condition and identity as well as the underlying constitutive principle of a slave society.

Thus Richard Wright's preoccupation with violence and death does not come from some perversely willful or personally idiosyncratic or even aesthetic decision on his part, but rather it is inherently and inseparately a part of the very contradictory subject position of the slave, which Wright chose as his topic. His commitment to the task and his intuitive understanding of this position allow him to thematize in a progressively clearer manner the psychopolitical function of death in the transformation of the ex-slave. However, the power of the prevailing aesthetic categories prevents him from seeing the value of his own thematization of death, and he easily accepts his readers' views of his apparently powerless protagonists, seen not as inert objects but as barely human victims (and in that sense, objects) who elicit only pity.

The critical response to *Uncle Tom's Children,* which still continues implicitly to treat the characters as objects of pity, is best represented by the most extensive and thorough commentary to date, that of Edward Margolies. Margolies, while recognizing the "final irony that once [Wright's protagonists in *Uncle Tom's Children*] have come to a recognition of themselves and a realization of the world that has made them, they are destroyed physically," finally falls back on the rhetoric determined by the category of "protest literature":

> But above all they are stories whose sweep and magnitude are suffused with their author's impassioned convictions about the dignity of man, and a profound pity for the degraded, the poor and oppressed who, in the face of casual brutality, cling obstinately to their humanity.

However, it is the more ambivalent but penetrating criticism of James Baldwin that permits us to understand better the ideological dynamics involved in this aesthetic category and, by extension, in the discursive field which Richard Wright attempted to transform with his intervention. In a sense Baldwin is fully aware of the psychopolitical function of Bigger as a symbol:

> If, as I believe, no American Negro exists who does not have his private Bigger Thomas living in the skull, then what most significantly fails to be illuminated here [i.e., in *Native Son*] is the paradoxical adjustment which is perpetually made, the Negro

being compelled to accept the fact that this dark and dangerous
and unloved stranger is a part of himself forever. Only this recognition sets him in any wise free.

Yet even in this, his most intimate acceptance of Bigger as the rebellious
slave and his understanding that such an acceptance of the Bigger in him is
a necessary step towards his own freedom, Baldwin distances himself from
Bigger by describing him as a "dark and dangerous and unloved *stranger*."
This act of simultaneously accepting and distancing Bigger is a form of
repression, which Baldwin ultimately legitimates by arguing that Bigger is
not an adequately well-rounded, complex character, that he is a flat character typically appropriate to the realm of "protest literature." Earlier in his
essay Baldwin begins by arguing that the representation of the black American and "his history and his progress, his relationship to all other Americans, has been kept in the social arena. He is a social and not a personal or
human problem." Towards the end of the essay, Baldwin returns to this
liberal dichotomy that opposes the personal and human to the social and
political, and he claims that to use Bigger as a warning to white Americans,
as he feels Wright has done,

> is simply to reinforce the American guilt and fear concerning
> him, it is most forcefully to limit him to that previously men-
> tioned *social* arena in which he has no *human* validity, it is
> simply to condemn him to *death*.

Clearly, then, it is this unexamined but rigorous distinction between the
"human" and the "social" realms that forces Baldwin to cast his profound
insight in a negative form. For while accepting the Bigger/slave in himself,
and in all blacks, Baldwin is obliged by the ideological category to "condemn" him to the realm of the "non-human," bereft, like the slave, of all
human dignity and honor: in Baldwin's own terms, Bigger is relegated to the
realm of "social death." Clearly, then, by negatively appropriating Bigger,
Baldwin fails to see that all Biggers have always existed in the liminal state
of "social death." Baldwin's ambivalence, his simultaneous acceptance and
repression of the Bigger in himself, illustrates the depth of the slave's contradictory position and his difficulty in confronting and transforming himself. The complexities inherent in that subject position are also aided by
ideological limitations entailed in the category of "protest fiction," which
prevent Baldwin and other critics (as well as Wright himself to a much lesser
extent) from fully bringing to consciousness the positive and liberating
psychopolitical function of death in *Uncle Tom's Children* and *Native Son*.

Richard Wright's own difficulty in fully recognizing the value and meaning of his project is partly revealed by his intuitive aesthetic decision, repeated in *Uncle Tom's Children* and *Native Son,* to separate the formation and confinement of the black subject in the realm of "social death," on the one hand, from the gradually emerging liberation of that subject through the positive functioning of death, on the other hand. The former is presented through the "autobiographical" (putatively "factual") introductions—"the Ethics of Living Jim Crow" in the case of *Uncle Tom's Children* and "How Bigger Was Born" in the case of *Native Son;* the latter is explored in the purely "fictional" realm of the short stories and the novel. Doubtless, the division is also dictated by the fact that the psychopolitical efficacy of actual death can be explored more fruitfully in the experimental realm of fiction than it can in real life. Nevertheless, the bifurcation of formation and liberation (or re-formation) implies a psychic disjunction that cannot be overcome easily. In fact, it reflects the profound contradiction that engulfs the slave: if liberation is partly predicated on the destruction of the self formed within the hegemony of slavery and if such self-destruction is desperately painful, then clearly a formal bifurcation between formation and liberation avoids some of the pain that a more direct self-confrontation would entail. Or, to put it conversely, a fictional integration of the two is extremely difficult to achieve because the processes of formation and liberation are in direct, mortal conflict—in fact, as we shall see, they are both centered on different forms of death. However, the tension between these two processes is best revealed by a critical examination that adheres to Wright's bifurcation.

The autobiographical preface to *Uncle Tom's Children,* ironically entitled "The Ethics of Living Jim Crow" consists of a series of vignettes that define Wright's developing awareness of the different facets of the racist society in which he grew up. They depict the ways in which the desires and aspirations of a young black individual are restricted by the racist hegemony and the boundaries of the self are limited in such a manner that rarely, if ever, can he succeed in becoming a full member of the civil society. Wright's anecdotes stress the point that the individual is coerced into internalizing the external, social boundaries in such a manner that he will learn to restrict himself "voluntarily." Thus hegemony seeks to inform the very self-conception of the young man and his view of reality, knowledge, possibility of progress, etc. There is no luxury of choice available in this process of self-construction; rather, hegemony forces the developing black individual to accommodate himself to the very absence of choice. The black boy must be taught to reify himself and the world; that is, he must perceive his liminality not as the product of social relations but as a natural, metaphysical fact. The poignancy of these anecdotes lies in the fact that Wright's narration depicts the hegemonic process without analyzing it theoretically. The violence, the persecutions, the daily limitations and frustrations, as well as the astounding discoveries are presented without embellishment, without elaboration of subjective reactions and in such a matter-of-fact tone that the contrast between the outrageous racist behavior and the stylistic understatement is shocking and revealing.

At every turn in the development of young Richard Wright, hegemonic coercion is based on violence, but it is the understated, casual acknowledgments of violence at the beginning and end of the sketch that emphasizes the formation. The first paragraph of the sketch describes the house and yard behind the railroad tracks where Wright lived as a young boy. It is not the absence of the greenery of white suburban lawns that Wright laments; rather, the child delights in the cinders that cover the yard because they make "fine weapons" for the war with the other boys, an activity that the child considered "great fun." In contrast to this opening, where the world is unproblematically perceived as an arsenal, the end represents the world in a latent state of siege. In his speculations regarding how blacks feel about the oppression, Wright offers the answer of one of his acquaintants: "Lawd, Man! Ef it wasn't fer them policies 'n' them ol' lynchmobs, there wouldn't be nothin' but uproar down here!" Thus racist hegemony, the marginalization of blacks, and the hegemonic distortion of their psyches are based on the daily use of the threat of overwhelming violence, which the blacks, in order to survive, eventually have to accept as a pedestrian fact of life.

Yet the acceptance is neither automatic nor unreserved nor permanent. In the first place the hegemonic system and the underlying violence have to be internalized, reluctantly and painfully. Ironically, the process of internalization begins with the black's use of violence against himself. When Wright is badly injured in a fight with white boys, instead of receiving sympathy from his parents he is beaten by his mother:

> She grabbed a barrel stave, dragged me home, stripped me naked, and beat me till I had a fever of one hundred and two. She would smack my rump with the stave, and, while the skin was still smarting, impart to me gems of Jim Crow wisdom. I was never to throw cinders any more. . . . I was never, never, under any conditions, to fight *white* folks again. . . . She finished by telling me that I ought to be thankful to God as long as I lived that they didn't kill me.

By thus linking pain and knowledge in the education of the child and in making him understand the boundaries he cannot cross, the parents "voluntarily" reproduce within the family the structure and dynamics of the dominant order. In stressing that Wright was lucky not to have been killed, they also try to communicate their preconscious awareness that the death of all blacks is only conditionally commuted and that in order to survive they must not violate these conditions.

Thus begins the process of hegemonic formation, and Wright swiftly moves from the external, physical violence to its internal, psychic effects. The beating made him delirious and sleepless, and each time he closed his eyes he "saw monstrous white faces suspended from the ceiling, leering at me." Blurry white faces, embedded in the young boy's mind, recur throughout Wright's fiction as a complex, ambivalent symbol. However, another crystallization that accompanies the faces is even more insidious. The beating destroyed the naive charm of the cinder yard for the boy and replaced it with the fear of "the green trees, the trimmed hedges, the cropped lawns" of the houses in the white suburbs. "Even today when I think of white folks," Wright continues, "the hard, sharp outlines of white houses surrounded by trees, lawns, and hedges are present in the background of my mind." Hegemony thus permeates the core of the mind and forms what we might call subjective ontology: by ensuring that the mind associates deep emotions, in this case fear, with "natural" objects, it structures the very nature of individual and collective perception. The economy of racist hegemony also enacts an exchange analogous to Marx's motion of commodity fetishism. That is, it obliges the individual to perceive the products and results of social relations as those of nature; it masks social relations as ontology. As we shall see, in accordance with this economy Wright's fiction also abounds with impossible "natural" barriers that in fact separate the races.

The racial boundaries continue to be reinforced throughout the child's growth in different facets of his life. When Wright is forced, by white coworkers, who do not want him to learn their trade, to resign his job, his family, rather than being outraged, chides him for being foolish: "They told me that I must never attempt to exceed my boundaries. When you are working for the white folks, they said, you got to 'stay in your place' if you want to keep working." Similarly, when Wright recounts to his fellow porters his experience of helplessly witnessing a black woman being beaten for late payments to a store, their reaction is completely casual: they consider her lucky for not having been raped in addition to being beaten. The point is that blacks in this period are not only restricted by white society but

that they are forced to internalize these restrictions and "voluntarily" trun-
cate their desires, aspirations, and expectations. They are forced, in other
words, to accept without significant protest the drastically diminished world
of social death—a world without prospects, without honor, and without
any substantial security: a world that is entirely dependent on the power of
whites.

This fact becomes clearly evident in Wright's interaction with Southern
white society. His white coworkers force him (without the knowledge or
consent of their more enlightened supervisor) to resign his job in an optical
factory by putting him in an impossible position. Wright is accused by one
of his white colleagues of disrespectfully addressing another coworker. If
Wright accepts the charge, he would be "guilty of having uttered the worst
insult that a Negro can utter to a Southern white man"; if he refutes the
charge, he accuses the other white man of being a liar. In either case he
would receive a severe beating at the very least. Faced with this impossible
double bind, Wright resigns from the job, thus satisfying the underlying
design of his fellow workers and allowing himself to be restricted and
dishonored yet once again. In acceding to this solution Wright is also forced
to recognize racial difference as something other than an epidermal or even
cultural difference.

Nowhere is his hegemonic insistence on the categorical, metaphysical
nature of racial differences more apparent than in sexual relations between
whites and blacks, not surprisingly so since sex is the most intimate area in
which the racial boundary can be violated. And if social death imposes a
kind of impotence on the slave and at times literally castrates him, then
castration, both symbolic and actual, becomes the logical and most effective
means of imposing social/racial difference on the black man. Wright first
describes the symbolic version of castration. While working as a hall boy in
a hotel often used by prostitutes, Wright is asked at times to bring them
liquor and cigarettes. These prostitutes, he says, rarely bothered to clothe
themselves in the presence of black hall boys: "When you went into their
rooms, you were supposed to take their nakedness for granted, as though it
startled you no more than a blue rose or a red rug. Your presence awoke in
them no sense of shame, for you were not regarded as human." To treat
these young men as if they have no sexual desire in front of a naked woman
is to taunt them and in effect to castrate them, for if they manifest even the
slightest curiosity, as Wright did, the prostitute's client immediately threatens them with castration. One of Wright's coworkers is literally castrated
and run out of town for actually sleeping with a white prostitute. Again,
Wright has been rendered powerless and, in a sense, castrated. However, the

economy of this kind of exchange, which recurs frequently in various forms in Wright's fiction, needs to be clarified. The slightest resistance or assertion from a black man is deliberately and instantly (mis)interpreted as if it were a major rebellion that calls forth the use or threat of overwhelming force. The economy of racist exchange, then, is characterized by what we might call synecdochic inflation: in order for complete subordination to be maintained in an absolute manner, the slightest resistance is immediately interpreted as a major rebellion, which in turn makes the commutation of death instantly and whimsically revocable. This kind of inflation also sheds light on a related feature of the economy of racist signification. The actual impotence of blacks, the literal and social castration, is inversely proportional to the insatiability of the libidinal desire that is ascribed to them; it would seem necessary to inflate their sexual powers in order to justify white society's repression of their mythic potency. The sexualization and the animalization of the black are a necessary precondition for defining him as the "enemy within," as an alien being in the midst of an otherwise "homogeneous" society and as a reflection of one's own libidinal desires.

The autobiographical sketch also illustrates the "subtle cruelty" with which racial barriers operate in the more refined cultural areas. While working in Memphis, Wright found that as a black he could not borrow books from the public library. He thus contrived, with the help of a sympathetic Northerner, to borrow books under the pretense that they were for his white master. Thereafter Wright had the use of this man's card yet had to forge notes from him requesting certain books and had to pretend to be illiterate while in the library. In a similar vein, Wright found that even with friendly whites he ought not to discuss "any topic calling for positive knowledge or manly self-assertion on the part of the Negro." Once again, it is obvious that this confines the black to a radically marginal role in society. But it is important to stress that Wright is put in the paradoxical position wherein he can only borrow books on the assumption that he cannot and will not read them. Similarly, in his attempt to possess any form of knowledge, he has to lead a double existence: his subjectivity as a dignified, knowledgeable human being will never be recognized by most whites who surround him. Orlando Patterson argues that the slave can never be the subject of property, only its object. We should add that the black in Jim Crow society, like his enslaved ancestor, can never be the subject of (white) culture, only its object. Having illustrated these forms of "subtle cruelty," Wright abruptly ends the autobiographical sketch by pointing out that in the final analysis only the threat and use of massive violence keep this hegemony in place and confine blacks to the realm of social death.

While the sketch explores the cultural mechanisms employed in the construction of a racist society and in the hegemonic formation of black individuals, the short stories in the anthology take these as givens. As Houston A. Baker, Jr. has accurately observed, Wright's world is one in which "events seemed predetermined by heredity (the simple fact of melanin), and the environment seemed under divine injunction to destroy." The stories are pervaded by a sense of massive social pressure since the protagonists are confined by a racist society to a very narrow range of permissible behavior and since from their viewpoint oppression seems quite arbitrary and irrational. The characters struggle against pressure and confinement, and gradually the stories begin to portray an increasingly aware, deliberate, and organized counterassertion by blacks. Towards the end of the anthology there is a sense of what Baker calls "a fused strength based on black religion and reinforced by the belief that not God but 'the black people' should receive one's sincerest tributes." But to imply that the fully developed assertion pervades the entire anthology or to define it as "a kind of black nationalism," as Margolies does, is to overstate the case and neglect two crucial factors in these stories: first, that a unified assertion develops slowly, painfully, and incompletely; second, that what Baker calls the "affirmation of a positive good" operates in fact only as the negation of social death through the affirmation of actual death.

I shall focus almost entirely on the psychopolitical function of death that constitutes the subtext of *Uncle Tom's Children* since critics have tended to neglect it. Other aspects of the anthology—narrative techniques, the role of religion in the black counterassertion, the connection between this anthology and Wright's developing naturalism and later existentialism, Wright's indebtedness to the blues mode, etc.—have been more than adequately covered. I shall only refer to these matters where they are germane in elucidating the function of death.

The interrelation between the narrative structure of the stories and the theme of death is important and needs to be clarified at the outset. As Edward Margolies has pointed out, "the twist and turns of the plot are essential for an understanding of the characters' feelings and the nuances of their emotions" because, in keeping with their uneducated background, the characters are inarticulate and, in keeping with their harassed lives, they do not have leisure to verbalize their feelings. One must add yet another reason to this. Because their lives are constantly threatened by death, because they are constantly struggling with the racist society's arbitrary use of violence, their lives are highly dramatic and cataclysmic (those who prefer the novel of manners would say melodramatic). However, emphasis on the consciousness of characters gradually increases throughout the anthology. Initially, there is little exploration of interiority, and the narration relies primarily on dramatic turns of events and symbolism, but progressively the characters are endowed with greater reflexivity, and their decisions are more deliberate. It would seem that Wright is obliged to work through the more intense and immediate feelings of frustration, rage, hostility as well as powerlessness in the early short stories before he can begin to explore the deeper reaches of subjectivity and the dynamics of a more deliberate and thorough rebellion. In other words, Wright gradually discovers the complexities of his own theme. The movement from drama to reflexivity is accompanied by and linked with a progressively better understanding of the efficacy of actual death. Initially, death functions in a purely reactive manner, that is, blacks kill only in order to survive; eventually, however, death becomes part of a deliberate strategy, that is, a black woman kills in order to protect a larger political movement and deliberately sacrifices herself in the process. Thus the plots and the function of death are intertwined as closely as in detective stories, but for a very different end: the discovery of a way out of social death.

On the surface level, the first short story simply depicts the irrational confrontation between a white man and four black boys who are harmlessly trespassing on his father's property. In the confrontation the man kills two of the teenagers, and the protagonist in turn kills him in self-defense. The rest of the story depicts the consequences of the conflict and the flight of the hero, in the course of which he sees the fourth teenager being tarred and feathered and then burned at the stake by a white mob. Read at this level, the story can easily evoke the standard response reserved for protest fiction: the obvious innocence of the four boys and irrational overaction and callous brutality of the white mob produce feelings of pity and outrage. However, at a deeper level, the story ironically reveals an awareness of the structure of social death and of the inevitability of actual death, and it begins to explore, in a tentative, subconscious manner, the confluence of race, sex, and violence to which Wright returns repeatedly in his later fiction.

The title of the story, "Big Boy Leaves Home," ironically plays on the rite of passage to maturity, which traditionally involves a break with one's parents as well as sexual awakening. The irony is twofold: given the confinement to the realm of social death, the black man never really matures— he will always remain an emasculated "boy"; and Big Boy's coming of age does not open up for him a world of possibilities wherein he can fulfill himself, but rather a world of increasingly narrow confinement. The themes of liberation and sexual maturity are represented through several symbols that recur at strategic points in the story.

The first of these is the overdetermined symbol of the train. An over-used Freudian symbol, it also represents the freedom train of the black spiritual, which the boys sing while playing in the fields, as well as the underground railroad, which the slaves used to escape to the free states and a version of which is finally used by Big Boy for his flight. The story opens with the boys singing a lewd song about "Yo mama don wear no drawers." This is soon followed by the whistle of a train, which evokes for the boys an image of "north," of liberation from the Jim Crow restrictions. Thereafter the oedipal implications of the song (that is, sexuality) become linked with the symbol of the train and its implications of freedom. Next the boys decide to go swimming in old man Harvey's creek in spite of Big Boy's reluctance and warning that they might get lynched for trespassing on white property. The first section of the story then ends with the affirmation of Big Boy's strength, virility, and intelligence.

At the swimming hole the confrontation, essentially sexual and racial in nature, is preceded by the boys' jokes about old man Harvey's sexual impotence. As they are about to jump in, Wright describes them standing there, "black and naked," the implication being that their *black* nakedness is somehow more threatening than nakedness itself. This is precisely how the white woman who suddenly appears on the bank interprets it. Her arrival, however, is immediately preceded by the boys' discussion of white oppression and the limitation of their lives and then by another whistle from a train and the boys' repetition of their desire to go "North" to freedom someday. The woman reacts simply with shock and paralysis. She can only utter brief exclamations of horror and scream for her fiancé who runs up and simply shoots two of the boys who had been standing around in the confusion. Big Boy lunges at him and shoots him in the ensuing struggle. The manner in which Wright represents the boys playing is markedly different from his depiction of the confrontation. In contrast to the boys' verbal play and relaxed cavorting, the confrontation is condensed into a rapid and tense sequence of events in which there is no rational exchange between the antagonists. This stylistic contrast as well as the sexual symbolism of the train, the black nakedness of the boys, the coincidental retreat of the woman to the point on the bank where the boys have left their clothes (which forces them to remain naked and hence vulnerable or unable to run), and the "affront" of black boys who dip their bodies in a white man's swimming hole—all of these stress the fact that the confrontation is over black sexuality or, to put it differently, over black "manhood," that is, over Big Boy's prospects for normal maturation.

The subtext of the rest of the story, depicting Big Boy's flight, elaborates the conjunction of sexuality and death. Big Boy returns home and leaves to go into hiding via the railroad tracks, and in addition to the further punctuation of the remaining narrative by train whistles, Big Boy's hiding place again symbolically links trains and the swimming hole. He hides in a kiln that he and his friends had dug many years ago in order to play at trains. While he hides in the kiln, the rain fills it, and it becomes reminiscent of the swimming hole. Within this context there is a somewhat different reenactment of violence and death. In order to enter the kiln Big Boy has to kill a snake, and, as Edward Margolies points out, his motions in killing the snake are identical to those in his fantasies of killing members of the white mob. Later one of the white men's dogs discovers him in the kiln and in order to protect himself he has to kill it with his bare hands. The displaced violence towards whites is accompanied by two other representations of death.

The last of the two, a gruesome depiction of the mutilation and murder of Big Boy's remaining companion, Bobo, is helplessly witnessed in its entirety by Big Boy. Bobo, on his way to meet Big Boy and escape with him, is caught by the mob, which tars and feathers him, cuts off his fingers and ears for souvenirs, and then burns him at the stake. Wright contrasts the mob's mood, that of a town picnic at which the burning of Bobo provides the main attraction of the festivities, with Big Boy's reaction to this rite of passage, his horrified paralysis which is soon broken by his own need to survive by killing the dog that has found him. Thus Big Boy's maturation consists of his witnessing the sudden and unexpected death of two of his companions, the slow and torturous murder of the third friend, and his own responsibility for killing a white man in self-defense—all this for the apparently innocuous violation of boundaries, i.e., trespassing at the swimming hole, and the ensuing coincidental sexual confrontation. In other words, maturation, leaving "home," means becoming aware of the constant presence of commuted death and recognizing the rapidity and arbitrariness with which the commutation can be revoked. Big Boy's witnessing of Bobo's death is preceded by his fantasies of killing as many members of the white mob as he can before they can capture or kill him. He imagines the entire flight in detail and then pictures the newspaper headlines: "NIGGER KILLS DOZEN OF MOB BEFO LYNCHED!" or "TRAPPED NIGGER SLAYS TWENTY BEFO KILLED!" In his embattled state, Big Boy is able to derive momentary satisfaction from this fantasy, which thus defines an important moment in the emotional structure of the story. His satisfaction is bracketed by the tension and shock of the initial confrontation and the ensuing anxiety, on the one hand, and the horrifying death of Bobo, on the other. Thus retaliation rather than escape, which does not afford Big Boy great relief, is valorized as the most efficacious avenue out of the realm of social death, and, as we shall see, what remains a fantasy here becomes an actuality in a later story.

"Big Boy Leaves Home" can be appreciated best as an initial, tentative recognition (rather than an investigation) of the realm of social death. The dramatic nature of the plot is dictated by the emotive subtext, by the shocking recognition of the fact that one's continued existence is predicated on accepting the emasculation entailed in social death and its implicit boundaries, by the knowledge that it is virtually impossible to become a mature "man"—either one can try to become a man by facing actual death or one must remain a "boy" forever. However, this recognition is subtextual, for the fantasy of self-assertion through killing members of the mob remains an abstract potentiality, and the entire story is characterized by passivity, coincidence, and reaction. The narrative only allows Big Boy the kind of initiative that is necessary for self-defense: he is only concerned with survival and escape; he neither initiates the confrontations nor does he wish to assert himself. By contrast the later stories are characterized by more deliberate, planned, and committed assertions against the condition of social death.

The progression, however, is gradual and exploratory: before advocating a more committed assertion, before developing a more positive negation, Richard Wright must investigate the condition of the black man more systematically and in greater depth. Thus the next story, "Down by the Riverside," is even more passive, coincidental, and reactive, indeed, excruciatingly so. This is deliberate, for passivity allows him to explore more thoroughly the psychological implications and ramifications of the acceptance of social death. Critics have complained that this story's reliance on coincidence stretches beyond credibility. However, as we shall see, the protagonist's personality and situation—the lack of choices available to him, the paralysis of will, his inordinate capacity to accept his lot—are an inverse, but necessary, complement to the coincidences and the conspiracy of circumstances that work against him. Rather like Thomas Hardy's *Tess of the D'Urbervilles,* Wright's story explores the mind of a character whose capacity to withstand suffering and punishment is as deep as is the relentless cruelty of his fate. The significant difference is that in Wright's story the place of fate is taken by the arbitrary and callous power of a racist hegemony, i.e., Mann's skin color is his fate, and his capacity for suffering exposes the thoroughness with which hegemony has formed his mind. The story is designed to investigate the deep internalization of the condition of social death and the acceptance of powerlessness.

In fact, lack of power is the given condition of the protagonist on which Wright plays ironically through the story's title, and he deliberately dramatizes the setting in order to test the limits of the slave's psyche under intense pressure. The setting and situation are both drastic. The low lying countryside is being flooded, and the levees on the river are about to break. Mann and his family, including his wife who has been in labor for four days, are trapped in a house about to be inundated. Eventually, a friend provides Mann with a stolen boat, which he uses to row his wife to the hospital, only to find that she is dead upon arrival. However, before they begin the journey, the family surrounds the ailing woman in order to pray and sing. Part of the prayer supplicating God to "soften the hard hearts of them white folks" is immediately followed by the song "Down by the Riverside," with its promise of pacificity and acceptance. The irony of this ritualistic acquiescence in powerlessness is heightened by the fact that the flood has risen and now the "river" surrounds the entire society and thus produces the dramatic situation in which Mann is going to be tested. In other words, Wright has created a setting that simply extrapolates the normal condition of blacks in the South so that he can map more thoroughly the psychic implications of their powerlessness.

Mann's emasculation is explored in the context of a series of crucial choices. First, he either has to accept the stolen boat or stand by and watch his wife die; he is caught between his natural desires to be a "man" (that is, to provide for and protect his family) and his fear of violating the laws of a racist hegemony, the boundaries of his social death. As Mann keeps saying, he has no choice; he simply hopes that Heartfield, the owner of the boat, will understand the mitigating circumstances and forgive him. As Mann rows out in the driving rain and pitch-darkness of the night his blindness and directionlessness perfectly symbolizes his lack of control over his life. Then Wright furnishes Mann with the same choice as given to Big Boy: fight or be killed. Recognizing his boat as Mann rows past, Heartfield fires his gun, and in order to protect himself the hero retaliates and kills the white man.

However, this time Wright does not permit his protagonist to escape. Unlike Big Boy, Mann is already "mature," that is to say, he has profoundly internalized the racist hegemony and does not even have the will to escape. After the confrontation, Mann is paralyzed by the thought of having killed a *white* man: "he felt he was lost because he had killed a white man: he felt there was no use in his rowing any longer"; "he was limp, nevertheless; he felt that getting the boat to the hospital now meant nothing." However, he does get to the town, only to discover that he has been rowing a corpse to the hospital and that he has arrived there only to be commandeered to work on the levees. When he is put to work with other blacks, he is relieved from his anxiety about having killed Heartfield, but his sense of security is superficial. He desperately wishes to communicate his plight to his black coworkers and to ask for their assistance in escaping, but he is unable to muster the will to do so. The story depicts in minute detail Mann's excruciating reluctance to help himself. When he is sent with another black man to rescue the Heartfield family from the flood, he has the perfect opportunity to escape. Only he knows that they have to rescue the Heartfields and the location of their house, but he cannot get himself to make a deliberate mistake about the individuals to be rescued or about the location, even though he is aware that such a mistake would go unnoticed in the chaos of the emergency. He also knows that if he persuades his coworker to leave him at some place along the river from where he could run away, nobody would miss him. But, again, he does not have the courage to do so. Mann struggles desperately with himself in an attempt to become the subject of his own life, but in vain. The agony of his struggle is compounded when they arrive at the Heartfield house, which is tilting badly and about to be washed away. Even though it is difficult to enter the house, Mann uses his ingenuity in spite of himself in order to enter the window, and once there he is instantly recognized by the family as the murderer. He thinks of killing them but cannot.

All of this, of course, represents the depths of Mann's self-alienation that has resulted from his complete internalization of the racist hegemony. When he attempts to enter the window, he acts as though "he were outside himself watching himself." And when he is driving off in the boat with the Heartfields, he feels that "it was someone else sitting in the boat; he was beyond it all now; it simply passed in front of his eyes like silent, moving shadows; like dim figures in a sick dream. He felt nothing; he sat, looking and seeing nothing." This paralysis characterizes Mann's emasculation. Having accepted social death and renounced power, Mann has in effect given up control of his own life and stopped choosing between alternatives, except in life-threatening situations that require immediate and instinctive reaction. He has internalized the hegemony so thoroughly that instead of caring for his own welfare he has found contentment in working for his masters. Only when he is working for them does he forget all his problems—his wife's death, the confrontation with Heartfield, and his own current dilemma.

Although unable to assert himself, Mann is aware, at a deep, repressed level, of what the acceptance of social death entails. He knows perfectly well that in killing a white man he has crossed one of the major boundaries that circumscribe his existence. Yet the worst punishment for this, his execution, frightens him more than the idea of suicide, of simply allowing himself to drown. Similarly, instead of asserting himself by trying to escape or by killing the rest of the Heartfield family, he passively but fervently wishes for their death. This linkage of passivity and death defines the essential feature of his psychological makeup, which account for his paralysis throughout the story. Wright captures this condition most poignantly when he describes Mann's feelings just prior to being accused of Heartfield's murder: "His body seemed encased in a tight vise, in a narrow *black coffin* that moved with him as he moved" (emphasis added). This characterization of the black body as a coffin represents Mann's awareness that, as a black man in the Jim Crow South, he is already dead.

Wright ends this painful story with several ironies that reveal the nature of the impossible contradictions surrounding social death and the attempt to transcend it. In response to Mann's abject groveling and begging for mercy (after he has been accused and summarily condemned) one of the soldiers escorting him tells him to get up, adding "you ain't dead yet!" This casual remark helps define the narrow, coffin-like space between social and actual death that is occupied by Mann and other blacks. As we will see, it is a space within which there is no room to maneuver, no alternatives from which to choose. The final irony or paradox is defined by Mann's belated attempt to escape and his view of death that provides the rationale for the attempt. When the soldiers are about to execute Mann, he decides, quite suddenly, to run: "They were going to kill him. Yes, now he would die! He would die before he would let them kill him. Ah'll die for they kill me! Ah'll *die*." As he runs, a soldier shoots him and then vehemently cries over Mann's dead body: "You shouldn't've run, nigger! . . . You shouldn't've run, Goddammit! You shouldn't've run." Mann, of course, never ran when he had the chance. His final decision to bolt, then, is not really an attempt to escape. Rather it constitutes a belated and positive, if paradoxical, self-assertion. That is to say, in choosing to die rather than being killed, Mann defines death in a positive rather than a negative manner. The story implies that the only significant avenue of escape from the restrictions of social death and the prolonged agony of commuted death is the voluntary choice of actual death.

"Down by the Riverside," thus maps Wright's investigation of the lack of choices in the narrow realm of social death. Mann is repeatedly faced with a series of impossible choices, most of which are crucially concerned with life and death and oblige him to violate fundamental ethical imperatives. First, he is forced either to use a stolen boat or allow his wife to die, then either to shoot Heartfield or allow himself to be killed. Finally, he must escape or allow himself to be conscripted and used by the white masters; he must choose between self-mastery and bondage, between freedom and hegemonic coercion. Normally, the latitude in this area is enormous: living within the hegemony or rebelling against it is a complex choice rendered murky by the subtle ideological manipulation of the psyche. However, for Mann the choice is virtually non-existent; either he must accept the realm of social death or he must fight back and risk actual death. After struggling with his own hegemonic formation Mann finally realizes that the only choice available to him is between voluntary and involuntary death. Having explored the death of internalized hegemony, Wright seems to conclude that the only luxury available for the slave is the ability to choose his mode of death.

The next story in the anthology, "Long Black Song," though relatively brief and straightforward, masks a significant turn in Wright's conception and use of death. Unlike the previous two stories, where the protagonists are reactive and preoccupied by survival, here the hero deliberately courts death in an emotional, though not yet political, gesture that is a compound of frustration, anger, and pride. The story also differs in that the awareness of social death is no longer subconscious or subtextual. The limitation of social death and the imperative to espouse actual death finally rise to consciousness. For the first time, the story also distinguishes sharply, through characterization, between an amorphous, apolitical consciousness, entirely unaware of the problem of social boundaries, and a focused consciousness, which, though not yet politically sophisticated, is perfectly cognizant of the modes of the hegemonic system and the sublated nature of the war between blacks and whites.

In a sexually stereotyped manner, Wright represents the amorphous mind through the woman, Sarah, and the focused view of the world through her husband, Silas. Sarah glides easily from one object to another, from one desire to another, uniting everything in a mystical manner. When she reminisces about her past affairs, it becomes clear that Silas is a substitute for an absent true lover. And when a white salesman attempts to seduce her, she succumbs with token resistance that is based more on the man's color than on any notions of fidelity. Her poetic mind easily links her child, the graphaphone brought by the salesman, the salesman himself, and her sexual climax into one all encompassing experience. Later, while witnessing the confrontation between Silas and the salesman, Sarah feels that these racial divisions and conflicts are childish and petty.

In contrast to her, Silas is a hard, practical, worldly man, who understands that in order to get ahead in the world he has to learn the rules of white hegemony and imitate white business practices. He already owns his farm and plans to buy more land and to hire helpers with the current year's profits. However, he is entirely undone by Sarah's infidelity, which hurts particularly since it involves a white man. Initially, when he suspects that Sarah might have slept with the salesman he is outraged that a white man has violated his privacy. However when he finds incontrovertible evidence that Sarah has betrayed him, he throws her out of his house. Thus the story gradually weaves the conflict around Silas's most cherished possession—his house. He is determined to become the subject rather than simply the object of property. When the salesman returns the following day, Silas whips him and eventually shoots him because he has violated his property (his wife and his house). After this point, he breaks down momentarily; all the pent-up frustration and rage aroused by his status as a black man pours forth in gestures of speechless fury. Only when he stands over the dead white man and addresses him does he suddenly begin to articulate the essence of his social death.

> The white folks ain never gimme a chance! They ain never give no black man a chance! There ain nothin in yo whole life yuh kin keep from 'em! They take yo lan! They take yo freedom! They take yo women! N' then they take yo life!

He also succinctly articulates the fact that in the realm of social death he has no choices, thus raising the subtext of the previous story to a conscious, thematic level: "But, Lawd, A don wanna be this way! I don mean nothin! Yuh die ef yuh fight! Yuh die ef you don fight! Either way yuh die n it don mean nothing." Thus he realizes the absolute negation of his life by the Jim Crow society. However, unlike the heroes in previous stories, Silas is determined to take a stand and fight; he sets out to affirm himself by negating the negation. Like Mann, though in a more "productive" manner, he realizes that the only choice available to him is that of his mode of death. So he decides, once again, to imitate white hegemony. "Ah'm gonna be hard like they is! So help me, Gawd, Ah'm gonna be *hard!* When they come fer me Ah'm gonna be *here!*" Thus when the posse arrives he kills as many of them as he can before they burn him alive in his house. As Sarah, who watches the entire episode from a nearby hill, realizes, he stays in his house and burns to death without a murmur.

Silas's "hardness" is reproduced on a different register by Wright's style. The description of the final battle and the burning of the house is detailed, graphic, and unflinching. The emotional reaction, on the other hand, is registered by Sarah, who watches the entire episode from a safe distance and then runs "blindly across the fields." Wright thus divorces the inevitable blindness of emotions, of sentimentality, from the necessity of developing a hard, clear-headed understanding of the structure of social death. The story is also "affirmative" in a different sense. Not only does it articulate Mann's belated awareness, but it also fulfills Big Boy's fantasy of killing as many members of the mob as possible before they murder him. Unlike the situations in the previous stories, here, Silas is not obliged to kill in order to survive: he easily could have avoided the confrontation if he chose to swallow his pride—after all, he would have had the consolation of his financial success. However, the point is that he fights not for survival or some abstact notion of power, but for his honor. Thus, voluntary death has a more complex ideological function in this story, although, in comparison to the next two stories, this notion of honor seems luxurious in that it is purely personal. It is not yet yoked to a more conscious and deliberate political purpose. Nevertheless, the ability to die for personal honor and pride is an important and necessary step in the development of Wright's fictive exploration of social death.

Wright's next story, "Fire and Cloud," is also a significant departure from the preceding narratives, most obviously because it does not involve mortal conflict. Yet Wright has not abandoned his investigation of social death and the ways to transcend it; rather, it has entered a new phase. While honorific death of an individual may be meaningful in its own terms, by itself it does little for the political emancipation of a group condemned to social death. Thus for the first time Wright explores the role of social death in the relation between an individual and his community. In this story many characters are lucidly aware of their entrapment between social and actual death, and they are quite willing to face the latter. The Reverend Taylor eventually rebels against white society even though he is aware of his dilemma from the beginning: if he does rebel, he will be branded a "bad nigger stirrin up trouble" and will possibly court death, but if he acquiesces, then his community, caught between the Depression and a white injunction on their agricultural activity, will starve. His young and impetuous son feels that someone has to die in the struggle between the two communities and that it is just as well to "git killed fightin as t git killed doing nothing." Even an old, peaceable deacon declares in final exasperation, "Ah ain got but *one* time t die." While this willingness to die forms the implicit foundation of the black communal and individual assertion in this story, Wright refuses to romanticize death by further valorizing the impulsive, honor-obsessed inclination.

Wright's interest in death has become more sophisticated in several respects. First, the efficacy of death is now measured in terms of its ability to liberate others. Taylor is willing to give his life if it will feed the hungry, but he knows that such a simple exchange will not work and that he must strive towards developing a political organization that might be able to regain some power for his community. Second, and more important, is the implicit realization that the literal death of the biological individual accomplishes little; in the long run it is the total eradication of the slave mentality—of the subject position based on the acceptance of social death—that is politically efficacious. "Fire and Cloud" is designed to explore this kind of transformation in Taylor—the death of the enslaved subject position that has controlled his behavior until the crisis of communal hunger (and the potential of collective death) and the birth of a new—more liberated, more powerful, and prouder—subject position. This story therefore maps the complex, less heroic psychopolitical changes necessary for the realistic transcendence of social death, and in keeping with this greater intricacy Wright introduces two new elements: the question of the appropriate relations between a prominent individual and his community and the function of religion in Southern Black society. As we will see, the individual's burden of responsibility for others compounds the experience of oppression, deprivation, and powerlessness, but the community can also provide him with support in the struggle against hegemonic forces. Similarly, religion functions in a dual manner: it can be used equally well to justify either one's acquiescence in powerlessness or rebellion against enslavement. In this story the "death" and rebirth of Taylor involve a restructuring of his psyche and his own reassessment of his role in the struggle between hegemonic and counterhegemonic and between religious and secular forces.

From the beginning of the story, Taylor is aware of the relative distribution of power. Whites, he feels,"jus erbout own this whole worl! Looks like they done conquered *everything*. We black folks is jus los in one big white fog." He has the inclination to resist this power, and he even realizes that he has access to the potential power of about six thousand blacks and poor whites who are all on the verge of starvation and could be organized to assert themselves. Yet this awareness is emotionally overwhelmed by his habitual knowledge of the historical powerlessness of black Americans. In response to communal pressure on him to do something about their hunger, he feels deeply ashamed of their powerlessness. Caught between these two impulses, he struggles with them and eventually realizes that the relations between the black and white communities have been a sublated form of war and that he is now being pressured to bring the battle out into the open. Naturally, he is horrified at the prospect, for he sees himself as a peaceful man of God.

Yet in accommodating himself to his powerlessness, he has transferred all secular power to God. Thus he has a tendency to alleviate frustration and postpone present gratification through his firm belief in a future religious utopia: God, he feels, will eventually mete out justice and empower the powerless. While this postponement of gratification makes him more amenable to secular manipulation, his adamant belief in God's power and justice eventually works against the hegemonic forces. One of the prayers in the story ends with a supplication for greater secular power and guidance:

> The white folks say we can raise nothing on Yo earth! They done put the lans of the worl in their pocket! They done fences em off n nailed em down! *Theys a-trying t take Yo place, Lawd!*

> Yu puts us in this worl n said we could live in it! Yu said this worl wuz Yo own! Now show us the sign like Yuh showed to Saul! Show us the sign n well ack! (emphasis added).

By defining racist hegemony as the secular usurpation of divine power and by asking God to empower his people against that hegemony, Taylor puts himself in a position to rationalize and justify his intervention. Whenever he is faced with a dilemma, Taylor returns to this source of power by putting his trust in God; whenever he is challenged, he trusts in his "duty as Gawd lets me see it." Thus religion becomes the potential source of rebellion, but the final transformation of Taylor does not occur until that source of power is ridiculed and seems to have failed.

Wright situates Taylor at the center of a series of contending groups and influences, all of which contribute in their different ways to his transformation. The hegemonic forces, including the mayor, the police chief, and several business leaders, have been using him to pacify the black community, and during the crisis they pressure him to diffuse the tension and call off a march on the city. Motivated by their direct and indirect ambitions, several members of the black group also collude with the racists. Deacon Smith, who wishes to replace Taylor as the black leader, constantly tries to depict the latter as a dangerous radical in the black community, while

Taylor's wife, afraid that his rash actions will jeopardize their son's future standing in white society, is constantly urging him to be more conservative. Arrayed against these hegemonic pressures are the white and black members of the communist party, who are urging Taylor to lead the march against the city government. Young blacks, including Taylor's son, are also impatiently advocating drastic action against the repressive authorities. A large portion of the black community, verging on starvation, looks to him to solve its problems. Finally, Taylor feels trapped between secular demands and his notion of religious duty. He is expected and pressured by all of these groups to mediate between them. There is little doubt that his ultimate allegiance will belong to the black community, for it is an integral part of his mind and personality, and he, in turn, has become its expression: "Those huts were as familiar to his eyes as a nest is to the eye of the bird, for he had lived among them all his life. He knew by sight or sound every black man, woman, and child living within those huddled walls." As we will see later, Taylor's rediscovery of this bond becomes the final ingredient in his transformation and rebirth.

Taylor's transformation begins under these varied pressures and develops gradually, but it takes a violent physical confrontation to catalyze it, after which point the old subject position is discarded for a new one. The Mayor and Police Chief flatter, cajole, bribe, and threaten him to diffuse the crisis by persuading his people not to march on the town. Since Taylor owes his leadership to these officials he is unable to confront them directly, but at the same time he cannot ignore the plight of his people. Unable at this point to side with either group, Taylor can only repeat the facts of the situation, which are so awful that repetition functions as persuasion for Taylor. The facts become clear enough for him, but he is unable to decide on a course of action because he is not accustomed to exercising power in his role as a leader. Not until he is kidnapped and beaten mercilessly by some white thugs for not cooperating with the mayor does the old subject position, characterized to some extent by paralysis, begin to disintegrate. As they whip him, the thugs make him pray, presumably in order to mock his reliance on God's power and justice, and as he screams out the Lord's Prayer he simultaneously affirms and denies the value of his religion. As he realizes later, God will not answer his call. But the void left by God's absence also reveals that without some form of power he is useless and helpless. In his agony and desperation he verbally lashes out at his tormentors and defies their ability to kill him. However, he is only whipped until unconscious, and this state functions as the equivalent of literal death in this story. His rebirth begins when he regains consciousness.

Initially, the reborn Taylor is entirely negative, and only gradually does he convert his feelings into a positive negation. He begins by invoking God again, not in order to affirm His kingdom or will but in order to ask for the strength that He gave Samson to destroy his enemies. However, this militant posture is short-lived, and upon returning to his house Taylor breaks down. The fire of the whipping is echoed in the fire of shame felt at the dishonor and powerlessness of blacks. In this mood he plumbs the nadir of his negative existence. He feels that God has abandoned him, and in the same breath he affirms his willingness to "die fer mah people ef Ah only knowed how." Having acknowledged his powerlessness, which is absolute without the support of God, and having faced the commuted death that is the foundation of that powerlessness, Taylor now commences the positive part of his re-formation.

Taylor pours out his feelings and his understanding of the situation to his son who is impatient to confront death. His articulation, Wright implies, is the most important aspect of his attempt to create a new subject position, for the struggle must be carried on as much in the discursive/hegemonic realm of cultural contestation as in the dominant realm of violent physical confrontation. Taylor finds that the new position is "elusive and hard to formulate": "And when the words came they seemed to be tearing themselves from him, as though they were being pushed upward like hot lava out of a mountain from deep down." Thus out of the fire of humiliation and shame comes a rearticulation, and he is anxious that his son should comprehend thoroughly, "for it seemed that in making him understand, in telling him, he, too, would understand." Articulation, then, is not only a form of self-creation but also of persuading others; it is a way of creating a universe of discourse, a community: he hopes that in listening to him his son would be "fashioning his words into images, into life." The discovery that he wants to articulate is the efficacy of communal solidarity and power. Clichéd as it may seem, Taylor is profoundly committed to this idea. He had defined prayer as a continuous daily activity; it amounted to allowing God to be so real in one's life that one did everything because of Him. Now the function of God as the sacred center of secular life is replaced by his people, whom Taylor will serve with unflinching dedication. He would be willing to die for their liberation, the story implies, as Jesus had. Finally, when he decides to lead the march and faces his people to address them, the fusion of individual and community is completed: "He felt neither fear nor joy, just a humble confidence in himself, as though he were standing before the mirror in his room." Just as he had tried to form a community of self and other when he talks to his son, so he attempts to fuse himself together with his people. And in the process of articulating a new subject position he publicly discards the old one, which, he realizes, had been used by the racists to control blacks. When he marches with the community, in their midst rather than at the head, he feels invulnerable: " . . . whatever would or could happen could not hurt this many-limbed, many-handed crowd that was he." Finally, when the Mayor comes to him and promises food, Taylor is filled with a "baptism of clean joy." His rebirth is complete.

The story ends with Taylor mumbling "out loud, exultingly: 'Freedom belongs t the strong.' " As many critics have pointed out, the story seems to be organized around clichéd communist notions of solidarity, struggle, and so forth, that are so aptly represented by the awkward slogan at the end. This impression is correct in many respects, but it is created by an exclusive reading of the surface structure of the story. The subtext returns in a more complex manner, as we have seen, to a new articulation of the method for transcending social death. If the previous stories imply that the slave only has the luxury of choosing his mode of death, "Fire and Cloud" takes that understanding further. To affirm his liberation the slave must choose literal death, but then his victory is short-lived. Here, Wright decides that a more prolonged and socially meaningful victory is possible only if one learns to sublate one's willingness to die for honor, freedom, and the power inherent in a viable social position. Taylor constantly tries to persuade his son that rushing into action will only get him killed. Political organization now seems to be the better part of valor.

The thoroughly developed imagery of fire in "Fire and Cloud" is accompanied by a "pregnant cloud," which it seems, will be the soothing product of a hot, fiery day. However, this image remains perfunctory. It is perhaps appropriate, then, that the single day covered by the last story, "Bright and Morning Star," is drenched with rain. In many ways this story bears the fruits of the entire anthology. As the passage quoted at the beginning of this chapter implies, the story is quite reflexive. It reveals the narrative strategy of the anthology; that is, it shows us that like the protagonist, Sue, Wright has been bitterly nurturing the "grain" of black experience, the fundamental experience of social death, in each short story. "Bright and Morning Star" is also reflexive to the extent that Wright now openly criticizes the impulsive desire to affirm oneself through a confrontation that leads to actual death, though, as we will see, he still values such a death when it becomes politically necessary. Finally, it is reflexive in that Wright moves away from a purely racial conflict and replaces it with a multiracial struggle against a hegemony that is still racist. For the first time in Wright's fiction some of the substantive personal relations between members of different races are represented positively.

At the same time, "Bright and Morning Star" represents personal relationships as being ephemeral in comparison to the value of political relations. The story in effect examines the strength of the political resolve that Wright feels is necessary to carry on a successful struggle against oppression. It depicts a major crisis in the life of a woman who has committed herself firmly to the stoicism of a long and bitter political struggle, even though she does not quite know how to resolve the dilemmas produced by her commitment. In the face of racial oppression she has turned to religion and found a calm and steady strength in it: "The days crowded with trouble had enhanced her faith and she had grown to love hardship with a bitter pride; she had obeyed the laws of white folks with a soft smile of secret knowledge." Her faith changes as her two sons grow and become members of the Communist Party. Out of love for them she too changes allegiance and finds that her new beliefs are even more adamant. In fact, she is so sure of her strength that she fantasizes about her ability to prove her toughness if someone ever tried to force her to divulge the names of party members. Just as this fantasy is later disastrously realized, so she too gets to resolve her dilemma as a result of her wish fulfillment. Her dilemma concerns her son Jonny-Boy and his clandestine party activities. Her elder son has already been captured and jailed, and she fears that the same fate awaits Jonny-Boy. She feels that if she loves him, she must allow him to continue his activities and risk being jailed sooner or later; however, if she tries to stop him, as she would like to, she would negate both of their lives. She is torn between the two alternatives and cannot find a solution.

The opportunity to test her strength and to find the answer to her dilemma presents itself when the sheriff comes looking for her son, who is out contacting party members because the infiltration of their organization by an informant has obliged them to cancel a meeting. She relishes the opportunity: "There was nothing on this earth, she felt then, that they could not do to her but that she could take. She stood on a narrow plot of ground from which she would *die* before she was pushed" (emphasis added). Once again Wright returns to the psychopolitical function of literal death in Sue's desire to prove her willingness to die. Her desire is so urgent that she deliberately and repeatedly taunts the sheriff until out of exasperation he beats her unconscious. When she regains consciousness, a new, white member of their party, Booker, persuades her to tell him the names of the party members so that he can warn them. In spite of her reluctance she does so because she is confused and weakened and because somebody has to undertake Jonny-Boy's mission since he has been captured. Only too late does she deduce that Booker must have been the informant and that she has inadvertently betrayed the party because of her anxiety to test her strength.

After much deliberation she formulates a plan to undo the damage. She takes a gun, hidden under a sheet that serves as a shroud, and goes to the place in the woods where the sheriff is torturing Jonny-Boy in order to extract the names of the party members. She has correctly surmised that, because she knows the terrain better than Booker, she would arrive there before him. While she stalls for time and pretends that she has come to collect her son, she is obliged to muster all her strength, stoicism, and discipline as she watches them break Jonny-Boy's legs at the knees and smash both his ear drums. When Booker finally arrives, Sue shoots him before he can reveal the names she has confided to him. After they have recovered from their surprise, the sheriff and his men shoot Jonny-Boy and then Sue.

Thus, even though Sue redeems herself, Wright remains critical of her hubris that precipitates the unnecessary crisis in her life. His criticism is never overt; rather, it manifests itself through Sue's own realization of her mistake. But the mistake allows her to prove an even greater strength: not only is she unwilling to reveal the names in the first encounter, but she refuses to do so even while she watches her son being tortured. This text also answers her dilemma: her desire to protect the party turns out to be stronger than her desire for Jonny-Boy's welfare. Wright finally seems to value political relations and commitments more than personal relations. Yet, to oppose the personal and the political aspects of life is to misread the thrust of Wright's work, for "Bright and Morning Star" ends with a valorization of Sue's voluntary death. After she has shot Booker she retreats into herself and waits, "giving up her life before they took it from her." And after Jonny-Boy is killed Wright returns to Sue's willingness to die. Finally, after they shoot her, she musters the last vestiges of her strength to yell at them: "Yuj didn't get what yuh wanted? N yuh ain gonna neveh git it! Yuh didnt kill me; Ah come here by mahsef." Thus like Mann, Sue finds enough room in that narrow space between social and actual death to be able to affirm the latter. Her self-sacrifice is simultaneously personal and political. Wright also affirms her death and the theme of death throughout the anthology by describing Sue's body as lying in the rain "growing cold, cold as the rain that fell from the invisible sky upon the doomed living and the dead that never dies." Thus in a sense he memorializes all his heroes whose voluntary deaths permit the author to find a way out of the realm of social death and toward the realm of a fuller life. Yet the deep penetration of the psyche by the effects of social death cannot be easily eradicated by fictive or discursive exorcism: the compulsion to rework the problem is powerful enough to force Wright to return to it in his major work, *Native Son*.

# Chronology

| | |
|---|---|
| 1908 | Richard Wright born to Ella and Nathan Wright on a farm outside Natchez, Mississippi. |
| 1914 | Nathan Wright deserts the family. |
| 1916–25 | Attends, with interruptions, public and Seventh-Day Adventist schools. |
| 1924 | Publishes "The Voodoo of Hell's Half-Acre" in the black *Southern Register*. |
| 1925 | Graduates as valedictorian from Smith-Robinson Public School; moves to Memphis. |
| 1927–36 | Works as a postal clerk in Chicago, where he becomes an active writer for leftist publications. He joins the John Reed Club and the Communist Party USA. |
| 1937 | Becomes Harlem editor of the *Daily Worker*. |
| 1938 | *Uncle Tom's Children,* a collection of short stories, published. |
| 1939 | Receives Guggenheim Fellowship. Marries Dhimah Rose Meadman. |
| 1940 | Publishes *Native Son:* Wright and Dhima are divorced. |
| 1941 | Marries Ellen Poplar. Works with Paul Green towards a stage version of *Native Son. Twelve Million Black Voices* published. |
| 1942 | Julia Wright born. |
| 1945 | Publishes *Black Boy*. Meets James Baldwin. |
| 1946 | Visits France. |

1947      Moves to France, his home for the rest of his life.

1949      Rachel Wright born.

1949–50   Stays in Argentina, filming *Native Son*. Wright himself appears as Bigger.

1953      *The Outsider* published. Visits the Gold Coast (now Ghana).

1954      *Black Power* and *Savage Holiday* published. Visits Spain.

1955      Attends the Bandung Conference in Indonesia.

1956      *The Color Curtain: A Report on the Bandung Conference* and *Pagan Spain* published.

1957      *White Man, Listen!* published.

1958      *The Long Dream,* to be the first of a trilogy, published.

1959      Dies suddenly of heart failure during a hospital stay for an unrelated complaint. At the time of his death Wright was selecting the best of some thousands of his haiku for publication.

# Contributors

HAROLD BLOOM, Sterling Professor of the Humanities at Yale University, is the author of *The Anxiety of Influence, Poetry and Repression,* and many other volumes of literary criticism. His forthcoming study, *Freud: Transference and Authority,* attempts a full-scale reading of all of Freud's major writings. A MacArthur Prize Fellow, he is general editor of five series of literary criticism published by Chelsea House.

EDWARD MARGOLIES is Professor of English at the College of Staten Island, City University of New York. He is the author of *The Art of Richard Wright* and *Native Sons: A Critical Study of Twentieth-Century Negro American Authors.*

GEORGE E. KENT has written on contemporary black American fiction and poetry and is the author of *Blackness and the Adventure of Western Culture.*

MICHEL FABRE is Professor of American and Afro-American Studies at the Université de la Sorbonne Nouvelle. His books include *Les Noirs Americains, Planteurs et esclaves,* and *The Unfinished Quest of Richard Wright.*

ROBERT B. STEPTO is Professor of English, African and Afro-American Studies, and American Studies at Yale University and the author of *Beyond the Veil.*

A. ROBERT LEE teaches American literature at the University of Kent. He has edited collections of essays on black fiction, Hawthorne, and Hemingway.

HOUSTON A. BAKER, JR., is the Albert M. Greenfield Professor of Human Relations at the University of Pennsylvania. His books include *The*

*Journey Back: Issues in Black Literature and Criticism* and *Blues, Ideology, and Afro-American Literature: A Vernacular Theory* as well as two volumes of poetry.

MICHAEL G. COOKE is Professor of English at Yale University. His books include *Afro-American Literature in the Twentieth Century: The Achievement of Intimacy* and *Acts of Inclusion: Studies Bearing on an Elemental Theory of Romanticism.*

KWAME ANTHONY APPIAH teaches philosophy at Cornell University. He is the author of *Assertion and Conditionals, For Truth in Semantics,* and *African Reflections: Essays in the Philosophy of Culture;* and coeditor of the forthcoming *Encyclopedia of African and Afro-American Literature* and of *Bu me bé: Proverbs of the Akan.*

ABDUL R. JANMOHAMED teaches English at the University of California at Berkeley. He is the author of *Manichean Aesthetics: The Politics of Literature in Colonial Africa* and is completing a full-length study of Richard Wright.

# Bibliography

Aaron, Daniel. "Richard Wright and the Communist Party." *New Letters* 38, no. 2 (1971): 170–81.

Agosta, Lucien L. "Millennial Embroidery: The Artistry of Conclusion in Richard Wright's 'Fire and Cloud.'" *Studies in Short Fiction* 18 (1981): 121–29.

Alexander, Margaret W. "Richard Wright." *New Letters* 38, no. 2 (1971): 182–202.

Avery, Evelyn Gross. *Rebels and Victims: The Fiction of Richard Wright and Bernard Malamud.* Port Washington, N.Y.: Kennikat, 1979.

Baker, Houston A. *Blues, Ideology, and Afro-American Literature: A Vernacular Theory.* Chicago: University of Chicago Press, 1984.

———. *Long Black Song: Essays in Black American Literature and Culture.* Charlottesville: University Press of Virginia, 1972.

———. *Reading Black: Essays in the Criticism of African, Caribbean, and Black American Literature.* Ithaca: Africana Studies and Research Center, Cornell University, 1976.

———. *Singers at Daybreak: Studies in Black American Literature.* Washington, D.C.: Howard University Press, 1974.

———. *The Journey Back: Issues in Black Literature and Criticism.* Chicago: University of Chicago Press, 1980.

Bakish, David. "Underground in an Ambiguous Dreamworld." *Studies in Black Literature* 2, no. 3 (1971): 18–23.

Bakish, David. *Richard Wright.* New York: Frederick Ungar, 1973.

Bolton, H. Philip. "The Role of Paranoia in Richard Wright's *Native Son.*" *Kansas Quarterly* 7, no. 3 (1975): 11–124.

Bone, Robert A. *Richard Wright.* Minneapolis: University of Minnesota Press, 1969.

Brignano, Russell C. *Richard Wright: An Introduction to the Man and His Works.* Pittsburgh: University of Pittsburgh Press, 1970.

———. "Richard Wright: A Bibliography of Secondary Sources." *Studies in Black Literature* 2, no. 2 (1971): 19–25.

Bryant, Earle V. "Sexual Initiation and Survival in Richard Wright's *The Long Dream.*" *Southern Quarterly* 21, no. 3 (1983): 57–66.

Bryant, Jerry H. "Wright, Ellison, Baldwin: Exorcising the Demon." *Phylon* 37 (1976): 174–88.

Butler, Robert James. "Wright's *Native Son* and Two Novels by Zola: A Comparative Study." *Black American Literature Forum* 18, no. 3 (1984): 100–105.

Campbell, Finley C. "Prophet of the Storm: Richard Wright and the Radical Tradition." *Phylon* 38 (1977): 9–23.

Cobb, Nina Kressner. "Richard Wright: Exile and Existentialism." *Phylon* 40 (1979): 362–74.

College Language Association. *Richard Wright Special Number. College Language Association Journal* 12, no. 4 (1969).

Cooke, Michael G. *Afro-American Literature in the Twentieth Century: The Achievement of Intimacy.* New Haven: Yale University Press, 1984.

———. *Modern Black Novelists: A Collection of Critical Essays.* Englewood Cliffs, N.J.: Prentice-Hall, 1971.

Cripps, Thomas. "Native Son." *New Letters* 38, no. 2 (1971): 49–63.

Davis, Charles T. "From Experience to Eloquence: Richard Wright's *Black Boy* as Art." In *Chant of Saints: A Gathering of Afro-American Literature, Art, and Scholarship,* 425–39. Urbana: University of Illinois Press, 1979.

Davis, Charles Till. *Richard Wright: A Primary Bibliography.*

Demarest, David P., Jr. "Richard Wright: The Meaning of Violence." *Black American Literature Forum* 8 (1974): 236–39.

Dickstein, Morris. "Wright, Baldwin, Cleaver." *New Letters* 38, no. 2 (1971): 117–124.

Dixon, Melvin. "Richard Wright: Native Father and Long Dream." *Black World* 23, no. 5 (1974): 91–95.

Fabre, Michel. "Fantasies and Style in Richard Wright's Fiction." *New Letters* 46, no. 3 (1980): 55–81.

———. *The World of Richard Wright.* Jackson: University of Mississippi Press, 1985.

——— and Edward Margolies. "Richard Wright (1908–1960): A Bibliography." *Bonner Beitrage* 24 (1965): 131–33, 37.

Felgar, Robert. *Richard Wright.* Boston: Twayne, 1980.

Feuser, Willfried F. "The Men Who Lived Underground: Richard Wright and Ralph Ellison." In *A Celebration of Black and African Writing,* edited by Bruce King and Kolowole Ogungbesan, 87–101. Oxford: Oxford University Press, 1975.

Fishbur, Katherine. *Richard Wright's Hero: The Faces of a Rebel-Victim.* Metuchen N.J.: Scarecrow, 1977.

Gaffney, Kathleen. "Bigger Thomas in Richard Wright's *Native Son.*" *Roots* 1, no. 1 (1970): 81–95.

Gayle, Addison. *Richard Wright: Ordeal of a Native Son.* Garden City, New York: Anchor Press, Doubleday, 1980.

Green, Gerald. "Back to Bigger." In *Proletarian Writers of the Thirties,* edited by David Madden. Carbondale: Southern Illinois University Press, 1968.

Gross, Barry. "Art to Act: The Example of Richard Wright." *Obsidian* 2, no. 2 (1976): 5–19.

Gross, Seymour. *"Native Son* and 'The Murders in the Rue Morgue': An Addendum." *Poe Studies* 8 (1975): 23.

Gysin, Fritz. *The Grotesque in American Fiction: Jean Toomer, Richard Wright, and Ralph Ellison.* Bern: Francke, 1975.

Hakutani, Yoshinobu. *"Native Son* and *An American Tragedy:* Two Different Interpretations of Crime and Guilt." *Centennial Review* 23 (1978): 208–26.

———, ed. *Critical Essays on Richard Wright.* Boston: G. K. Hall, 1982.

Hoeveler, Diane Long. "Oedipus Agonistes: Mothers and Sons in Richard Wright's Fiction." *Black American Literature Forum* 12 (1978): 65–68.

Jordan, June. "On Richard Wright and Zora Neale Hurston: Notes toward a Balancing of Love and Hatred." *Black World* 23, no. 10 (1974): 4–8.

Kent, George E. *A Dark and Sudden Beauty.* Philadelphia: Afro-American Studies Program, University of Pennsylvania, 1977.

Kinnamon, Keneth. *The Emergence of Richard Wright: A Study in Literature and Society.* Urbana: University of Illinois Press, 1972.

———. *"Lawd Today:* Richard Wright's Apprentice Novel." *Studies in Black Literature* 2, no. 2 (1971): 16–18.

———. "The Pastoral Impulse in Richard Wright." *Midcontinent American Studies Journal* 10, no. 1 (1969): 41–7.

———. "Richard Wright: Proletarian Poet." *Concerning Poetry* 2, no. 1 (1969): 39–50.

Kostelanetz, Richard. "The Politics of Unresolved Quests in the Novels of Richard Wright." *Xavier University Studies* 8 (1969): 31–64.

Lenz, Gunther H. "Southern Exposure: The Urban Experience and the Re-Construction of Black Folk Culture and Community in the Works of Richard Wright and Zora Neale Hurston." *New York Folk Quarterly* 7, no. 1–2 (1981): 2–39.

Margolies, Edward. "The Letters of Richard Wright." In *The Black Writer in Africa and the Americas,* edited by Lloyd W. Brown, 101–18. Los Angeles: University of Southern California Studies in Comparative Literature 6, Hennessey & Ingalls, 1973.

———. *The Art of Richard Wright.* Carbondale: Southern Illinois University Press, 1969.

McCall, Dan. *The Example of Richard Wright.* New York: Harcourt, Brace, & World, 1969.

McCluskey, John, Jr. "Two Steppin': Richard Wright's Encounter With Blues-Jazz." *American Literature* 55 (1983): 332–44.

Miller, Eugene E. "Richard Wright and Gertrude Stein." *Black American Literature Forum* 16 (1982): 107–12.

———. "Voodoo Parallels in *Native Son." College Language Association Journal* 16 (1972): 81–95.

Moore, Jack B. "The View from the Broom Closet of the Regency Hyatt: Richard Wright as a Southern Writer." In *Literature at the Barricades: The American Writer in the 1930s,* edited by Ralph F. Bogardus and Fred Hobson, 126–43. Tuscaloosa: University of Alabama Press, 1982.

Nagel, James. "Images of 'Vision' in *Native Son." University Review* 35 (1969): 109–15.

*Negro Digest.* (Richard Wright: His Life and Works.) 18, no. 2 (1968).

Primeau, Ronald. "Imagination as Moral Bulwark and Creative Energy in Richard Wright's *Black Boy* and LeRoi Jones's *Home." Studies in Black Literature* 3, no. 2 (1972): 12–18.

Ray, David, and Robert M. Farnsworth, eds. *Richard Wright: Impressions and Perspectives*. Ann Arbor: University of Michigan Press, 1973.

Reilly, John M. "Richard Wright's Experiment in Naturalism." *Studies in Black Literature* 2, no. 3 (1971): 14–17.

———. "Self-Portraits by Richard Wright." *Colorado Quarterly* 20 (1971): 31–45.

Roache, Joel. "What Had Made Him and What He Meant: The Politics of Wholeness in 'How "Bigger" was Born.' " *Sub-Stance* 15 (1976): 133–45.

Rubin, Steven J. "The Early Short Fiction of Richard Wright Reconsidered." *Studies in Short Fiction* 15 (1978): 405–10.

Savory, Jerold J. "Bigger Thomas and the Book of Job: The Epigraph to *Native Son*." *Black American Literature Forum* 9 (1975): 55–56.

Singh, Raman K. "Marxism in Richard Wright's Fiction." *Indian Journal of American Studies* 4, no. 112 (1974): 21–35.

———. "Some Basic Ideas and Ideals in Richard Wright's Fiction." *College Language Association Journal* 13 (1969): 78–84.

Skerrett, Joseph T. "Richard Wright, Writing and Identity." *Callaloo* 2 (1979): 84–94.

Stephens, Martha. "Richard Wright's Fiction: A Reassessment." *Georgia Review* 25 (1971): 450–70.

Stepto, Robert B., and Michael S. Harper, eds. *Chant of Saints: A Gathering of Afro-American Literature, Art, and Scholarship*. Urbana: University of Illinois Press, 1979.

*Studies in Black Literature*. (Special Number on Richard Wright.) 1, no. 3 (1970).

Walker, Ian. "Black Nightmare: The Fiction of Richard Wright." In *Black Fiction: New Studies in the Afro-American Novel since 1945*, edited by Robert A. Lee, 11–28. New York: Barnes & Noble, 1980.

Webb, Constance. *Richard Wright: A Biography*. New York: G. P. Putnam's, 1968.

Williams, John A. *The Most Native of Sons: A Biography of Richard Wright*. Garden City, N.Y.: Doubleday, 1970.

Williams, Sherley Anne. "Papa Dick and Sister-Woman: Reflections on Women in the Fiction of Richard Wright." In *American Novelists Revisited: Essays in Feminist Criticism*, edited by Fritz Fleischmann. Boston: Hall, 1982.

# Acknowledgments

"Foreshadowing: *Lawd Today*" by Edward Margolies from *The Art of Richard Wright* by Edward Margolies, © 1969 by Southern Illinois University Press. Reprinted by permission.

"Richard Wright: Blackness and the Adventure of Western Culture" by George E. Kent from *Blackness and the Adventure of Western Culture*, © 1972 by George E. Kent. Reprinted by permission of the author and Third World Press.

"Richard Wright: Beyond Naturalism?" by Michel Fabre from *American Literary Naturalism: A Reassessment*, edited by Yoshinobu Hakutani, © 1979 by Michel Fabre. Reprinted by permission of the author.

"I Thought I Knew These People: Wright and the Afro-American Literary Tradition" (originally entitled "I Thought I Knew These People: Richard Wright and the Afro-American Literary Tradition") by Robert B. Stepto from *Chant of Saints*, edited by Michael S. Harper and Robert B. Stepto, © 1979 by Robert B. Stepto. Reprinted by permission.

"Literacy and Assent: *Black Boy*" (originally entitled "Literacy and Ascent: Richard Wright's *Black Boy*") by Robert B. Stepto from *From Behind the Veil: A Study of Afro-American Narrative* by Robert B. Stepto, © 1979 by the Board of Trustees of the University of Illinois. Reprinted by permission of the University of Illinois Press.

"Inside Narratives" (originally entitled "Richard Wright's Inside Narratives") by A. Robert Lee from *American Fiction: New Readings*, edited by Richard Gray, © 1983 by Vision Press Ltd. Reprinted by permission of Vision Press Ltd., and Barnes & Noble Books, Totowa, New Jersey.

"Reassessing (W)right: A Meditation on the Black (W)hole" by Houston A. Baker, Jr. from *Blues, Ideology, and Afro-American Literature* by Houston

237

A. Baker, Jr., © 1984 by the University of Chicago. Reprinted by permission of the University of Chicago Press.

"The Beginnings of Self-Realization" (originally entitled "Solitude: The Beginnings of Self-Realization in Zora Neale Hurston, Richard Wright, and Ralph Ellison") by Michael G. Cooke from *Afro-American Literature in the Twentieth Century: The Achievement of Intimacy* by Michael G. Cooke, © 1984 by Michael G. Cooke. Reprinted by permission of the author and Yale University Press.

"A Long Way from Home: Wright in the Gold Coast" by Kwame Anthony Appiah, © 1987 by Kwame Anthony Appiah. Published for the first time in this volume. Printed by permission.

"Rehistoricizing Wright: The Psycho-Political Function of Death in *Uncle Tom's Children*" (originally entitled "The Psycho-Political Function of Death in *Uncle Tom's Children*) by Abdul JanMohamed, © 1986 by Abdul JanMohamed. Published for the first time in this volume. Printed by permission.

# Index

239